THE GREAT HARTFORD CIRCUS FIRE

Henry S. Cohn
and David Bollier

THE GREAT
HARTFORD
CIRCUS FIRE

Creative Settlement
of Mass Disasters

YALE UNIVERSITY PRESS

NEW HAVEN AND LONDON

Published with assistance from the Louis Stern Memorial Fund

Set in Garamond No. 3 type by Marathon Typography Service, Inc.,
Durham, North Carolina. Printed in the United States of America
by Vail-Ballou Press, Binghamton, New York.

Library of Congress Cataloging-in-Publication Data

Cohn, Henry S., 1945–
    The great Hartford circus fire : creative settlement of mass
    disasters / Henry S. Cohn and David Bollier.
    p.   cm.
    Includes bibliographical references and index.
    ISBN 0-300-05012-7
    1. Ringling Brothers Barnum and Bailey Combined Shows—
Trials, litigation, etc.   2. Torts—Connecticut—Hartford—History
—20th century.   3. Dispute resolution (Law)—Connecticut—
Hartford—History—20th century.   4. Receivers—Connecticut—
Hartford—History—20th century.   5. Hartford Circus Fire,
Hartford, Conn., 1944.   I. Bollier, David.   II. Title.
KF228.R495 1991
346.746'303—dc20
[347.463063]   91-15361
                        CIP

The paper in this book meets the guidelines for permanence and
durability of the Committee on Production Guidelines for Book
Longevity of the Council on Library Resources.

10   9   8   7   6   5   4   3   2   1

Discourage litigation. Persuade your neighbors to compromise whenever you can. Point out how the nominal winner is often a real loser in fees, expenses and waste of time. As a peacemaker, the lawyer has a superior opportunity of being a good man.

Abraham Lincoln

CONTENTS

List of Illustrations   ix

Foreword by Stephen Joel Trachtenberg   xi

Acknowledgments   xvii

Part One: The Fire

1. Fire at the Circus   3

2. The Rescue of a Circus   19

3. Anatomy of an Arbitration   40

4. The Fight for Control of Big Bertha   49

5. The Receiver's Just Rewards   69

6. Fire Safety Reforms   93

*Part Two: Mass Torts and
the Art of Creative Settlement*

7. The Mass Tort Mess   110

8. The Bankruptcy "Solution"   124

9. Why Arbitration Saved the Circus   138

10. Alternative Dispute Resolution and Mass Torts   148

Notes   169

Source Materials   197

Index   203

ILLUSTRATIONS

Diagram of the Big Top. Reprinted with permission from the *NFPA Quarterly*, © 1944, National Fire Protection Association, Quincy, Massachusetts, 02269

1. Clown Emmet Kelly with crowd. Photo: *Hartford Times*, courtesy of Southern Connecticut State University.
2. Big Top interior (before the fire). Photo: *Hartford Times*, courtesy of Southern Connecticut State University.
3. Interior of tent, with black arrow marking first flames. Photo: *Hartford Times*, courtesy of Southern Connecticut State University.
4. Flames at top of tent. Photo: *Hartford Courant*.
5. Big Top in flames. Photo: *Hartford Courant*.
6. Crowd fleeing tent. Photo: *Hartford Courant*.
7. Firemen with hose. Photo: Connecticut State Library.
8. Flaming bleachers. Photo: Connecticut State Library.
9. Emmet Kelly with bucket of water. Photo: Ralph Emerson.
10. Roustabouts. Photo: *Hartford Courant*.
11. Elephants in field. Photo: Connecticut State Library.
12. Aerial view of circus ruins. Photo: *Hartford Courant*.
13. Makeshift morgue at armory. Photo: Connecticut State Library.
14. Little Miss 1565. Photo: Connecticut State Library.
15. Women check whereabouts of the missing. Photo: *Hartford Times*, courtesy of Southern Connecticut State University.
16. Dale Segee, alleged arsonist. Photo: *Hartford Times*, courtesy of Southern Connecticut State University.
17. Arraignment photo. Photo: *Hartford Courant*.

18. Judge John T. Cullinan. Photo: *Hartford Times*, courtesy of Southern Connecticut State University.
19. Judge John Hamilton King. Photo: *Hartford Times*, courtesy of Southern Connecticut State University.
20. Group picture of attorneys. Photo: Dan Judge, Jr.
21. John Ringling North. Photo: Circus World Museum, Baraboo, Wisconsin.
22. Edith, Aubrey, and Robert Ringling. Photo: UPI/Bettmann Archive.

FOREWORD

Insurance companies located in Greater Hartford, like those located in other parts of the world, make their money by investing in calculated risk. At a deeper level, of course, they make their money from the human race's individual and collective *fear* of risk. And of all the fears that most of us can name, few are deeper or more terrifying than sudden, unanticipated death or mutilation— especially involving those whom we love.

That is one of the reasons that the Hartford circus fire of 1944 continues to fascinate us. This fire confronted the "insurance capital of the world" with the kind of disaster against which it *insured*. That confrontation with an awful human disaster took on mythic proportions when a city still regarded by many Americans as provincial met the challenge in a highly innovative manner that had a long-term impact on American law; that was particularly influential in the creation of modern Chapter 11 bankruptcy proceedings; that crystallized the nation's sense of appropriate fire safety standards for public places; and that speaks to the contemporary handling of mass torts.

The insurance industry has always had to grapple with a paradox between its style and its business. Its business is risk, disaster, and the unexpected. But its style is steady, rational, and thoughtful—as befits the premier industry of a state often characterized as the "land of steady habits." The story of Hartford's response to the circus fire thus resembles a fugue between two contrary attitudes: conservative, moral rationalists grappling with a wildly unexpected, tragic event during the tumult of World War II.

This valuable history by Henry S. Cohn and David Bollier enables us to immerse ourselves in all the human and legal dimensions of the Hartford circus fire. It shows that the workings of law and justice are not blindly mechanical but propelled by the most complex traits of human character. In the aftermath of the fire, a handful of strong-minded, highly ethical attorneys proved that a community beset by a disaster that positively invited mass litigation could cooperate with each other, with the owners of the Ringling Bros. and Barnum & Bailey Circus, and with hundreds of area residents whose losses included family members, bodily integrity, and life functions.

Striking characters emerge from this history: the diplomatic, high-minded receiver for the circus, Edward S. Rogin; his flamboyant associate, Julius Schatz; the creative judge who sanctioned the receivership, John Hamilton King; the grumpy titan of the Hartford bar, Robert Butler; the aggressive state's attorney, Hugh Meade Alcorn, Jr.; and the beleaguered circus attorneys trying to make the best of a bad situation, Dan Gordon Judge and Cyril Coleman. These and other figures emerge from the following narrative as lawyers committed not only to their profession but to their communities. Through their courage and respectful interplay, they reshaped the norms of their profession, often at great personal expense, to alleviate acute human suffering. Their quest to transform and transcend the law succeeded only because they shared a deep commitment to *real* justice, as opposed to paper justice.

That these admirable qualities became less obvious after the tidal wave had passed and the final indemnity payments dispersed is itself a comment on human nature. The peaceful resolution six years after the fire had a destabilizing effect. Though nearly four million dollars had been paid out through an arbitration process virtually without precedent in American law, attorneys on both sides of the case ultimately resorted to litigation to resolve a final, important matter —what "reasonable" fee should be paid to the heroic circus receiver, Edward Rogin?

It is difficult to read Henry Cohn's and David Bollier's narrative without recognizing the extent to which they are describing an insiders' "arrangement." Private "deals" or "arrangements" involving the public trust are usually insidious, we have understandably come to feel. Their purpose is usually to inflict injustice of some kind on the mass of Americans excluded from them, either by skirting laws or flagrantly violating them. What is so remarkable about the aftermath of the circus fire, therefore, is how Hartford's tightly knit legal community actually worked *on behalf of* people, mostly from modest backgrounds, who could never have achieved so positive an outcome for themselves had they been forced to depend on an adversary procedure fought out in a traditional courtroom setting.

Of course, the Hartford legal community itself, sensing impending doom, had some compelling reasons to look beyond litigation to explore the benefits of arbitration. Without some vehicle for cooperation, they and their clients stood to lose *everything*. Even if the circus had remained solvent, would its assets and insurance have covered the huge award that courts would surely have issued? Could the Hartford Superior Court have handled the large volume of litigation, projected to last for at least ten years? Without cooperation, the circus was heading for certain bankruptcy, where the secured creditors, not tort claimants, would have first claim on the circus's assets after liquidation. There was no Chapter 11 procedure as we know it today, which would have allowed for a reorganization of the circus while the circus management remained a debtor-in-possession.

An equally striking aspect of the circus fire "arrangement" was the cooperation between Jewish and Christian attorneys. Anti-Semitism was still a significant force in American life in 1944. Even if their thinking was colored by the values and style of Hartford's insurance industry, then the pacesetter for the state's businesses, the men who hatched the idea of the circus receivership—Rogin, Schatz, and Weinstein—knew that their chances of obtaining significant positions within that industry were nil.

With this background, the scene in Willimantic on the afternoon of July 12 is particularly poignant: "As a gesture of good faith, Rogin then told Judge King that he would not accept a fee as the receiver unless and until all claimants were paid 100% on their claims. King thanked Rogin, put his arm around him, and said he would have signed the papers even without this guarantee." Cohn and Bollier are fully aware of the contrast this selfless professionalism offers to what are too often perceived as contemporary legal mores.

Indeed, even the Chapter 11 legislation that was so deeply influenced by the circus fire precedent cannot accomplish, in some cases, what the Hartford "arrangement" achieved. As the authors point out, "the city of Hartford and officers of the circus were targets of suits, along with the circus itself. But plaintiffs did not ultimately pursue them because the arbitration proved successful. In today's more litigious climate, however, Chapter 11 would not likely provide a 'global' solution because it insulates only one defendant, temporarily, from liability."

Guided by their shared understanding of and empathy for those victimized by the fire, all parties kept their differences in check and maximized their points of agreement. Personal tolerance provided a framework of trust and cooperation, and that framework, in time, yielded substantive results. It is somewhat less certain that such a happy result could be achieved in the Hartford of today, and the reasons for this may be worth exploring.

The scale of society. Though they were taking part, as citizens of the United States, in the most titanic war ever fought on this planet, these individuals were still inclined to think on a personal, human scale. A tragic tale recounted by a single person could influence their thinking, even when the money ultimately ran into the millions. That shared imperative of humanity made it possible for Rogin, as receiver, to become deeply involved in the nationwide business affairs of the circus in an attempt to maximize its profits and increase the likelihood that payments to fire victims would indeed achieve his goal of 100 percent compensation.

The relative absence of media hype. In the context of 1944, it would have been hard to imagine a reporter pushing a microphone in the face of a woman who had just lost her child while a television camera recorded her tears for the benefit of a voyeuristic "audience." Newspapers, supplemented by radio, were the primary vehicles of communication. Though they were no doubt regarded as fast-paced by the standards of the day, they were still sufficiently slow and reflective to allow human feeling its own rate of integration. They also encouraged the public to "stay with a story" as if the unfolding tale had long-term significance and consequences. The resulting sense of mastery was in fact based on the limited amount of information being flung at the public.

Today the weeping mother of the dead child would no sooner have "scored" on the seven o'clock news than something even more affecting or mind-boggling would displace it on the eleven o'clock news. Assaulted by a ceaseless stream of news and images, we have grown numb and distracted, a feeling that often masks a deeper, unarticulated panic.

A common moral language. As a university president, I can testify to the varieties of moral codes in contemporary society, as the furious debates over "what our students need to learn" amply illustrate. Everyone seems to agree that students need to learn about different national and cultural traditions—while also mastering the "basics" of writing and reasoning and developing a renewed commitment to ethical behavior. At that point agreement ends and debate begins: How important and relevant is John Stuart Mill when compared to feminist social critics who have never been admitted to the "core curriculum"? Should art history courses bestow lavish attention on Michelangelo and Rembrandt yet refuse even to glance at African, Asian, and women's art? Can ethics be more effectively studied through Aristotle than through *Manchild in the Promised Land?*

Consider, by contrast, the moral and cultural context within which the circus fire claims were resolved. The participants all shared virtually identical educational experiences, for which there was a broad social consensus. Jew or Gentile, they shared a deep awareness of the Bible, whose stories, in today's classrooms, often require detailed elaboration by instructors. The organizers of the arbitration process had passed through college curricula that demanded a basic understanding of Western traditions, and courses that were particularly attuned to issues of justice, morality, and choice. In this, of course, their education mirrored American society of the time.

The world of 1944 is not one to which any of us would willingly return. At the same time, that world had aspects that we dare not ignore lest we risk losing some of its most precious elements. It was a world that remained very open, particularly at the local level, to human initiative. Individuals could more easily make a difference.

As it happened, the initiatives launched by some of Hartford's most enterprising attorneys of the 1940s turned out to have many lasting national effects. Good, clear thinking tempered by human decency proved to be the most useful, successful way to proceed.

These days we so often tend to feel that our world has spun out of our control and that no personal initiative can do much to turn that process around. Henry Cohn and David Bollier, besides recounting for us the moving story of the Hartford circus fire, may help us to confront an even broader issue: How can we restore a sense of personal engagement and responsibility without which the world becomes a very insecure and even dangerous place?

STEPHEN JOEL TRACHTENBERG
PRESIDENT, THE GEORGE WASHINGTON UNIVERSITY, 1988–
PRESIDENT, UNIVERSITY OF HARTFORD, 1977–1988

ACKNOWLEDGMENTS

Many people played critical roles in helping us recover this near-forgotten episode of legal history from oblivion and interpret its significance in light of contemporary mass torts.

The first spark for our research came from U.S. Senator Joseph I. Lieberman, who for many years has been an ardent proponent of alternative dispute resolution (ADR). As Connecticut attorney general, Mr. Lieberman convened a Task Force on Alternative Dispute Resolution in 1984 to review the various methods of ADR and explore how the legal community could give ADR greater use and visibility. As part of this effort, Mr. Lieberman commissioned Henry Cohn, assistant attorney general, to investigate the ADR experience that resolved claims from the tragic Hartford circus fire of 1944. That report for the Attorney General became the core manuscript which, with considerable new research, reporting, and writing by journalist David Bollier, resulted in *The Great Hartford Circus Fire*. In providing the initial impetus for this project, we are particularly grateful to Joseph Lieberman, to his successor Clarine Nardi Riddle, and to the department head, Barney Lapp.

For Henry Cohn, this book represents the confluence of several personal projects and interests. In 1985, James Kennedy, then executive assistant to the attorney general, asked Cohn to research the life of Raymond Baldwin for the introduction of the attorney general's book of opinions he was preparing. In doing so, Cohn was surprised to find that among his many state achievements, Baldwin had served as governor in 1944 at the time of the circus fire and had even spoken to the junior bar concerning the settlement.

That discovery rekindled Cohn's interest in the circus fire. As a child he had heard that a relative of his, Edward Rogin, had been the "receiver of the circus." Many years later, attorney Jerome Caplan mentioned to Cohn that his partner, Rogin, had been praised in a court opinion for his actions as receiver. Now, having learned of Baldwin's involvement in the fire, Cohn decided to track down the court opinion. Instead of a decision dealing with plaintiffs and defendants contesting liability or damages, however, he found *Jacobs v. Ringling Bros. – Barnum and Bailey Combined Shows, Inc.*, a superior court case involving a dispute over the receiver's fee. Indeed, there were no reported cases involving any of the claimants; all had been settled out of court.

Propelled by both personal curiosity and professional interest, Cohn began to probe the "mystery" surrounding the aftermath of the circus fire. How had this remarkable settlement come to pass? What were the personal dynamics of the process? With these and other questions in mind, Cohn contacted people who had played prominent roles in the receivership and arbitration.

Arthur Weinstein and his former partner Michael Kulick shared their rich recollections and generously gave us access to Weinstein's files. We are also thankful to Edward Seltzer, Weinstein's assistant in 1944 and later his partner, for sharing his files on the circus fire. Edward Rogin, now eighty-three and a resident of West Hartford, was very helpful in recalling the personalities and events of the time. Joseph Kenny, an associate of Julius Schatz's in the 1940s, also provided us valuable background on the times.

The former state's attorney H. Meade Alcorn was kind enough to review his role in the fire's aftermath, and the late Judge Joseph Klau, a long-time member of the bar and a practicing attorney at the time of the fire, offered his views on why the cases settled out of court. Morton Elsner, whose father was author of the *Municipal Report*, discussed among other things his father's role as corporation counsel for Hartford. Gordon Hall of the attorney general's office provided useful insights into the connection between the Schneller report following the L'Ambiance Plaza collapse and the circus fire. United

States District Judge T. Emmet Clarie, in 1944 a member of the State House of Representatives and a well-regarded attorney from Danielson, described the colorful personalities of the time and the fire safety reform efforts in the legislature. Before his death in 1988, U.S. District Judge M. Joseph Blumenfeld, a young plaintiffs' attorney at the time of the fire, told us about the Ringlings, the Hartford legal community, and the circus fire settlement.

Several attorneys at Day Berry & Howard in Hartford—Thomas Groark, Ernest Ingles, and Olcott Smith—spoke with Henry Cohn about Cyril Coleman and the defense of the circus. Coleman's late daughter, Mary, recalled the hard work her father and Dan Judge had put into the case. Judge's daughter-in-law, Virginia, also shared her memories of Judge's role, as did Judge's long-time partner, John Mulvey. Judge, who for years lived in Florida and served as president of Honeycomb Corporation of America, a manufacturing concern, died in July 1990 at age eighty-eight.

As might be expected in an episode with so many facets, we relied upon the recollections of numerous witnesses to the fire and experts in specific areas. Dr. Milton Fleisch described his role in treating fire victims; Dr. Louis Harris recalled his knowledge of the medical community's response; and Elizabeth Hadley explained how local nurses and volunteers assisted the injured. Bruce Fraser, executive director of the Connecticut Council for the Humanities, directed us toward useful historical material on Connecticut in the 1940s. Peter Bartucca of the secretary of state's office was knowledgeable about the tent safety statute that was enacted after the fire. Rabbi Stanley Kessler described movingly how the fire inflicted deep scars on the Hartford community that persist to this day. Numerous other local residents, including Edward Daly, Joseph Hurwitz, Robert Klein, Gary Laurito, Paul Levine, Marianne Z. Lorenzo, Shelden Radin, Cornelius Shea, Leah Weiner, and Kenneth Wynne, shared their remembrances of July 6, 1944.

We were fortunate to have access to some fine legal minds in our exploration of the issues surrounding the circus receivership, arbitration, bankruptcy law, and mass tort litigation. Several scholars at the University of Connecticut School of Law—former Dean Phillip Blumberg, Professor Lewis Kurlantzick, and Professor Emeritus How-

ard Sachs—helped illuminate the legal complexities of the receivership and arbitration by pointing the way to old tort law books and
assorted books that referred to the Ringlings and the fire. We also
acquired more subtle understandings of numerous legal issues through
interviews with Alan Morrison, director of the Public Citizen
Litigation Group, Professor Harry H. Wellington of the Yale Law
School, and Senior Judge Robert C. Zampano of the U.S. District
Court.

On bankruptcy issues, Judges Saul Seidman and Robert Krechevsky
provided insights and recollections into Chapter X bankruptcy proceedings, confirming that the option was indeed a nightmare. Assistant Attorney General Joan Pilver provided a valuable critique of
our chapter on bankruptcy and mass torts. With respect to ADR,
Henry Cohn spoke with Donald Reder of Dispute Settlement, Inc.,
and Karen Jalkut of the American Arbitration Association.

Christopher Bickford, executive director of the Connecticut Historical Society, did us a great favor by referring us to Mark Jones,
archivist at the Connecticut State Library, who led us to a treasure
trove of documents about the fire. Cohn was the first to review documents released by the State Police in 1987. Numerous librarians
facilitated our research. Our guides included Hilary Frye, Marianne
Griffin, Denise Jernigan, Judy Kestell, Cheryl Schutt, Joanne
Turschman, and Theodore Wohlsen of the Connecticut State Library,
and Ann Biega, Barbara Karp, and Susan Miller of the attorney
general's office library. Professor Robin Glassman of the journalism
department at Southern Connecticut State University graciously gave
us access to the nearly forgotten archives of the now-defunct *Hartford
Times*, including many valuable photographs.

By providing us with many photographs from his personal collection and reproducing other images from the Connecticut State Library, Arthur J. Kiley, Jr., helped us recapture something of the
circus fire that lies beyond words. We are also grateful for permission
to use numerous photographs that originally appeared in the *Hartford Courant*.

A great many other people gave us invaluable help along the way,
including Valerie Ackerson, Joanne Chrisoulis, Maureen D. Regula,
Dan Gordon Judge, Jr., Andrew Kreig, Margaret Ryglisyn at Aetna

Life & Casualty, Cornelius Shea, and Captain Bernard Steadman of the State Police. Candee' DeFeo flawlessly typed the original report manuscript.

We are grateful to John Covell, our editor at Yale University Press, for sharing our vision of this book and shepherding it to completion. Jane Hedges, our manuscript editor, helped make the text sparkle.

One of the biggest debts incurred in writing a book is the support of one's family. For that, Henry Cohn deeply appreciates the help and suggestions of his wife, attorney Linda A. Cohn, and David Bollier is grateful to Ellen D. Bollier for sharing in the gestation of this book.

PART ONE • THE FIRE

Chapter 1

FIRE AT
THE CIRCUS

On April 18, 1956, Raymond Baldwin, then an associate justice of the Connecticut Supreme Court, addressed a gathering of the "junior bar" on what he called "an old, old theme": the lawyer's duty to serve the public. He cited worthy examples of public service drawn from both English common law and our own nation's two-hundred-year history.

One particularly shining example, Baldwin noted, was the dedicated response of the Hartford bar toward resolving the massive tort litigation following the horrific circus fire of 1944. He concluded that these Hartford attorneys had "affected for good the lives of many people and preserved a great American institution."[1]

The aftermath of the circus fire during the turbulent days of World War II provides a revealing glimpse of an American legal community grappling with an enormous tragedy that had complex legal ramifications. The story includes singular personalities, great pathos, a web of personal conflicts and professional rivalries, creative legal innovations, shrewd policy judgments, and a noble if slightly marred resolution to a complex, sad affair.

The physical and emotional suffering that resulted from the fire and its impact on an American institution, the circus, continues to tug at our sympathies and imagination, even today. In the pages that follow, we wish to illuminate a less fully discussed aspect of the

fire and one with arguably more importance today: the exemplary
response of the Hartford legal community and the more than satisfactory result of its efforts.

The first part of this book provides a history of the fire, its impact
on the Hartford community, and its legal aftermath. It sets forth the
circumstances of the catastrophe, the legal community's efforts to
settle numerous damage suits, the implementation and resolution of
a highly unusual receivership and arbitration plan to help the fire
victims, the special problems in managing the circus while such
arrangements were in force, and the enduring fire safety reforms that
the tragedy precipitated. Part I also contrasts the pretrial diversion
of the lawsuits and their eventual settlement with the one instance
of litigation that did develop out of the incident.

The second part of the book seeks to elicit general lessons from
the circus fire receivership and arbitration plan. To understand the
achievements of the circus fire case—the first modern example of
alternate dispute resolution (ADR) of a mass tort—it is necessary to
review the present status of mass tort litigation and its most commonly used alternative, the bankruptcy procedures set forth by the
Bankruptcy Reform Act of 1978. In this context, it becomes clear
why the would-be litigants of the circus fire found ADR to be an
eminently sensible, humane, and just alternative to traditional litigation. Although the circus fire settlement is in many ways a product of its time, a contemporary equivalent—a global settlement of
the Bridgeport L'Ambiance Plaza collapse claims—demonstrates that
the use of ADR in some varieties of mass torts is entirely possible
and worthwhile, given certain factual premises, judicial leadership,
and goodwill among all parties concerned. Finally, we conclude with
a general assessment of ADR as an innovative and effective tech-
nique in improving our court system while dispensing an equivalent
or superior form of justice.

Although one aspect of the circus fire—the fight for corporate
control—is still studied by law students, the resolution of one of
the nation's earliest mass tort cases contains other instructive lessons for lawyers today. The episode showed how a spirit of public
service and cooperation among lawyers can bear fruit; how a carefully crafted framework of arbitration can yield timely justice; and

how just compensation need not leave a blameworthy corporation crippled or destroyed. In our times, when mass torts are becoming far more prevalent, we would do well to study and emulate the humane, ingenious response of one community of lawyers nearly fifty years ago.

The Ringling Bros. and Barnum & Bailey Combined Shows, also known as the Greatest Show on Earth and the Big Bertha, came to Hartford in 1944, just as it had done every year since its formation and consolidation by the Ringlings in 1919.[2] Late in the morning of July 5, 1944, the circus train pulled in from Providence. The papers that day were full of war news. It was one month after D-Day, and headlines spoke of fierce fighting in Normandy and setbacks on battlefields in Italy. In state politics the popular Raymond Baldwin surprised his followers by announcing that he would decline renomination for governor at the upcoming state Republican Convention.[3] (He changed his mind a week later and was reelected in the fall.)

As usual the circus squeezed into the tiny Barbour Street fairgrounds, a lot that stood vacant except for an occasional victory garden and the yearly arrival of the circus. (Once intended for a new high school, the lot now contains Fred D. Wish Elementary School.) The tract, as was the custom, had been leased for three days in July from the city's Public Building superintendent for $500, in addition to the standard license fee of $150 a day. In keeping with past practice, the circus's agent, Herbert DuVal, left about a hundred passes to the show with the superintendent and the chief of police. Arrangements were made to station policemen at the circus tent; no formal notice was given to the fire department, and no city firemen or equipment were expected at the scene.[4]

Hartford was now the site of great industrial production. The *Hartford Courant* reported that the city had $137.6 million in armed services contracts for the fiscal year ending June 30, 1944. In 1939, the state had been muddling through a serious depression. A year later, huge orders for airplane engines, propellers, and submarines flowed in from the federal government. Pratt & Whitney boosted its work force from three thousand to twenty thousand in only thirty months, and Electric Boat and Hamilton Propellers experienced similar employment booms. Over the course of the war, Connecticut would reap more than $8 billion from U.S. munitions contracts, a sum amply supplemented by European munitions orders. From 1942 to 1944, the state had the highest per capita production of war materials in the nation—$3,000 for every man, woman, and child in the state.[5]

With such strong, sustained demand, workers flocked to the city from throughout New England and even Canada, 130,000 between 1940 and 1943. Wages were high and money orders flowed back to out-of-state homes. There was said to be rooming houses where three different shifts lived in one room. The scarcity of decent housing was particularly acute in Hartford, New Haven, and New London, where most of the newcomers settled.

The supercharged war economy caused its own set of strains on traditional values, as women joined the work force, children were left unsupervised, and a sense of social transience and instability reigned. Wartime dislocations caused sharp increases in juvenile delinquency, venereal disease, wartime profiteering, and rationing abuses.[6] Americans undergoing these social upheavals—along with the traumas of the war itself—welcomed the nostalgic diversion and carnival gaiety of the circus.

But the circus had changed, too, in these war years. In 1944 it was under the relatively new direction of Robert Ringling, a former opera singer and son of Charles Ringling, one of the founders of the circus. Beneath the surface calm lurked an ugly battle for corporate control between various Ringling factions, including one led by John Ringling North, the immediate past president. The Depression had put most circuses out of business. Now, in 1944, the War Production Board had imposed stringent wartime restrictions so that railroad cars, fuel, and other scarce supplies could be pressed into the war effort. The board limited the nation's rail circuses to three, shortened the lengths of circus trains, and limited the distances that they could travel. But since the circuses did boost morale in a war-weary nation, the government allowed them to survive. They even served as a valuable marketing vehicle for war bonds, which the Ringling Brothers circus sold as it traveled the nation; bond purchasers received free tickets.[7]

Wartime shortages, however, had imposed difficult new strains on the circus. The lack of civilian manpower was severe, prompting the chief wagon man to complain that he needed at least 15 more assistants and more experienced help. At one point that year, the circus staff of 424 workers was trying to do the work that 1,000 had previously done. To replace the men at war, teenagers were commonly hired to help with the heavy labor of assembling and dismantling the circus tents. The manpower shortage was so acute that the circus missed its scheduled matinee in Hartford on July 5, and barely had time to set up for the evening performance and the matinee the next day. Indeed, given the rush, many things received scant attention that day, including whether working fire extinguishers were unpacked and whether seats were secure and exits easily accessible.[8]

Perhaps the most dramatic impact of the war on the circus was the scarcity of needed materials. The armed forces had exclusive access to the only proven flame-retardant waterproofing solvent for use on their canvas tents—a solvent that the circus could otherwise have used on its big top. (Other circuses claimed to have found equally satisfactory and safe treatments; the Ringlings later claimed to have tested the available substitutes and found that they were quite flammable. The Ringlings also claimed that the substitute solvents easily scraped off when the tent was taken down and packed off to the next location.)[9]

Whatever the merits of alternative waterproofing treatments, there was no question what treatment Ringling circus crewmen did use—a time-honored method dating back to their grandfathers' time. In the winter months at the circus's Sarasota headquarters, laborers applied 6,000 gallons of gasoline and 1,800 pounds of paraffin to the big top. As one circus man described the process, "[Paraffin] comes in barrels like wax, and you have to boil that up and thin it out with gasoline in order to pour it on. You sprinkle it on and broom it and leave it there until it dries."[10] And that is what had been done.

Thursday, July 6, 1944, fell in the midst of a scorching heat wave, one of the worst in twenty-five years. The temperature outdoors was 88 degrees, hot and humid; inside the circus tent it felt like an enormous oven. (Weather experts in the scorching summer of

1988 frequently referred back to 1944 as the last comparable heat wave.) That day, there were more than seven thousand people in attendance, mostly youngsters and their mothers or grandparents; most of the city's men were in the armed forces or at factories. To this crowd, the circus was an old friend. Grandparents could return to their youth for an afternoon. Indeed, some of the old timers remembered how, as small children, they had "watered the elephants." The show began without incident at 2:00 P.M., as the band, under the direction of its well-known leader Merle Evans, led the audience in the singing of the Star-Spangled Banner.

The first performance was an acrobat dressed as a lion. Then came the real wild animal act — "a frolicsome forerunner of the magnificent display of perfectly schooled man-killers," as the program put it. On two steel runways about four feet high, enclosed at the top in a semi-circular hoop, trainers moved the wild animals from outside wagons to the exhibition cages in the center of the big tent. The spectacle included two veteran performers, Menelik, "king of the lion colony," and Paragon, "the largest and most beautiful Bengal tiger in captivity."[11] But this time, for budgetary considerations, the animal act was shorter than usual, and the trainers soon led the exotic menagerie down the runways to the cages outside the tent.

At 2:40 P.M. the dancing bear and the lions were just outside the main tent, and the Flying Wallendas were climbing up ladders to give the next performance. It was then that the first flame appeared on the canvas to the left of the main entrance. As one circus-goer, Morris Handler, later recalled, "I thought it would be no trouble being put out at that time because it wasn't an intense fire at all. It seemed to me that a simple hose would douse it immediately."[12] According to one report, band leader Evans spotted a tiny patch of flame "no bigger than a man's hand" and quickly had his twenty-nine band members switch from a dance tune to a fast-paced arrangement of "The Stars and Stripes Forever."[13]

Experienced circus people immediately recognized the band's sudden choice of that song as a secret signal of danger. The Wallendas immediately slid down from the aerial wire, and clowns and dancers looked around to see what was the matter. Things moved quickly after that. As one circus man later declared that day, "You ain't got the least conception of how quick a big top goes."[14] Eunice Groark, now lieutenant governor of Connecticut, was a six-year-old attending the circus that Wednesday afternoon. She recalled the next few astonishing moments: "It was amazing. It was as though someone punched a button and a light went on. I can still remember the whole place rising to its feet. There must have been a tremendous amount of noise, although what impressed me was the music, that you could hear the music over all of that."[15] Morris Handler remembers that "the band playing did, in one respect, give a little organization and let you know that there were people still inside that were doing their thing and hadn't just vacated the premises. I thought it was a noble act on the band's behalf."[16]

Kenneth Wynne, son of a former chief justice of the Connecticut Supreme Court and a naval student at Trinity College at the time, was attending the circus illegally that day: he and his buddies had gone AWOL. Because they were in uniform, they were admitted free. Sitting high up in the bleachers, they heard a rustle, saw some flames and instantly realized they had to get out, even though they never suspected the impending inferno. Without a moment's thought, they jumped down the back of the bleachers and went under the flap of the tent. They stopped, looked back and saw the tent explode. "We saw the panic and tragedy. The heat was intense, and then the tent collapsed in flames," Wynne recalled.[17]

Was it a mentally ill arsonist-roustabout, as *Life* later claimed?[18] Was it the circus's negligence in fireproofing? Was it a careless smoker in the men's restroom or in the bleachers? Whatever the cause or causes, the immediate result was horrific, as a Red Cross report later described it:

> Within a few minutes, the entire tent was a flaming mass. What had been a scene of gaiety and laughter a few minutes before now became a blazing death trap as tragedy struck swiftly. Many people were trapped in the arena as the flaming canvas fell upon them. Hundreds of others jumped from the bleacher seats and escaped under the tent's sides. Children were dropped to the ground by their parents and then tossed over the canvas wall to safety. Scores of persons reached the main entrance before the flames did.
>
> [The animal runways], still in place as the fire broke out, acted as

barriers to persons trying to escape from the arena. Some were successful in climbing over the runways, but as the panic-stricken crowd surged
forward a mass of humanity piled up and met death under flaming
canvas. Some persons undoubtedly were trampled to death.

Within an hour all that remained of the Greatest Show on Earth were
twisted metal poles which had fallen one by one as the supporting guy
ropes burned away, the metal animal runways and exhibition cages, and
the charred bleacher seats.[19]

At the time, John Stewart, Jr., a fourteen-year-old who later became Hartford's Fire Chief, was walking home with the circus passes
he had just earned for feeding and watering the elephants. Upon
seeing the fire break out, he rushed back to the scene. "The most
awesome feeling was when that tent collapsed. The poles had burned
and lost their tension and when it fell in the awful cries that you
heard were the people that were caught at the animal cage. That was
probably the most ghastly scene that I probably will ever witness in
my lifetime." Stewart credits the experience with shifting his career
goal from aviation to fire fighting.[20]

A resourceful thirteen-year-old physically disabled boy, Donald
Anderson, of Columbia, Connecticut, was credited with saving the
lives of more than three hundred people. When the fire broke out,
Anderson got separated from his uncle, with whom he was attending the circus. But the teenager managed to save himself by wrig-
gling under the sidewall canvas. Realizing that few other people
could squeeze under the canvas as he had, Anderson took out a
prized knife, which he carried at all times, and slit the canvas. As
the *Courant* described it, "First a trickle and then by the scores,
frantic men and women and children poured through the tear. Donald saw that his uncle, Mr. [Axel] Carlson was one of them, then he
ran further along the sidewall to where others were blocked and slit
other holes in the canvas for other hundreds to escape before the
flames could fell them." Unable to participate in other sports like
able-bodied boys, Donald had long wanted a knife to whittle. His
parents, who feared that he was not old enough to handle a knife
safely, had changed their minds only a few weeks earlier and allowed
him to buy it.[21]

Four months later, Governor Raymond Baldwin presented Anderson with the Connecticut Medal for his heroism. "What surprised me," said Anderson in 1984, "is nobody else thought about it. In other words canvas is canvas. It's not a brick wall. But in the confusion the people were trying to climb over the animal cages and pushing each other out of the way, and I mean, really accomplishing very little."[22]

A frenzied corps of reporters attending the circus immediately ran to phones and called their offices with the news, and word of the fire quickly went out over the national teletype. John Cleary, a *Hartford Times* correspondent whose mother-in-law died in the fire, later recalled: "By that time, the word had spread by the radio stations [eight minutes after the first fire alarm had sounded] and the demand for information was urgent. The city desk of the *Hartford Times* sent a 'flash' to the Associated Press. (A flash was a news item of the highest priority. The *Times* had never sent one before.) Telephone switchboards at both local newspapers, all the radio stations and police headquarters were jammed with calls from people frantic for word about relatives who had gone to the circus."[23]

As it happened, the state police commissioner Edward J. Hickey had attended the performance with his seven nephews. After safely leaving the tent, he made his way to a Hartford police car outside the tent and radioed police headquarters with the fire alarm. Then Hickey began to direct rescue operations and an inquiry. Also present at the circus with his son, daughter-in-law, and grandchildren, was Hugh M. Alcorn, the state's attorney from 1908 to 1942 and father of the state's attorney appointed in 1944, Hugh M. Alcorn, Jr.

The younger Alcorn and prosecutors James Kennedy and S. Burr Leikind began building a criminal case immediately—so swiftly that charges were brought that very day, July 6, against James Haley, vice president of the circus, George Washington Smith, the general manager, and three other top circus employees who had been present at the scene. (Robert Ringling, who had been in New York at the dentist, was never prosecuted.)[24] The Federal Bureau of Investigation, fearful that America's wartime enemies may have played a role, began an inquiry into possible sabotage by a circus employee. Amidst these accusations and rumors, a circus spokesman defiantly—and erroneously — declared that nothing combustible had been used on the tent.

Hartford was a city in turmoil. A woman recalled that as a fourteen-year-old she had bid her mother goodbye that morning with a remark that she and her cousin might take in the circus that afternoon. Instead the girls headed for the Colonial Theatre where their relieved mother tracked them down.[25] A father dropped off his children at the circus and left for work downtown. The children found the circus too expensive ($2 a ticket) and went instead to see the film, "Arsenic and Old Lace" at a local theater. (The film was based on a criminal prosecution by the father of the current state's attorney, Hugh M. Alcorn, Jr.) After hearing about the fire, the father spent several anxious hours looking for his children in hospitals and the morgue.[26]

Governor Baldwin quickly directed a mobilization of all emergency facilities. The immediate concern on July 6 was to identify the victims and treat the injured. Medical attention was dispensed under the direction of the Connecticut War Council (Connecticut's civil defense arm) and the American Red Cross at Municipal Hospital, a now-defunct facility located about a mile from the fairgrounds. The first patients were admitted at 2:45 P.M.

The chief resident at the Municipal Hospital, Dr. Milton Fleisch, who is now a Hartford pediatrician, remembers receiving a call that there was a fire raging on Barbour Street with injuries and that he should stand by; nothing further was said. Then the victims started to arrive. As he and his staff began emergency treatment, he quickly realized the scope of the tragedy and began deciding which patients would be sent to his facility and which ones transferred to Hartford Hospital or St. Francis. With the wartime shortage of doctors, Fleisch was already working seven days a week and was on call twenty-four hours a day. In the days following the fire, however, his lobby was swamped with doctors volunteering to treat the victims. Fleisch himself worked seven to ten days without stopping and later developed hepatitis from handling blood products and from his weakened condition. As he remembers it, everyone pitched in and "did not look at the clock."[27]

Within twenty-four hours after the fire 10,000 telephone calls had deluged the state armory seeking approximately 2,700 persons who had been reported missing. To help clear up the confusion, the war council dispatched a stenographer to help record the names and addresses of lost children who had been taken to the Brown School. Then volunteers undertook one of the happier tasks of the day — notifying relieved parents.

More than 1,000 volunteers, many involved in civil defense preparedness, mobilized over the next few hours. They came from the Connecticut War Council, Hartford War Council, Connecticut State Police, American Red Cross, State Guard, and Salvation Army. There were police and firemen, doctors and nurses, ambulance drivers and air raid wardens, telephone operators and messengers, and clergymen. Department store delivery trucks were used as ambulances. Help poured in from all over. Nearby towns sent police officers. Local factories let their workers out to help with the emergency. The navy furnished personnel and medical supplies. Governor Saltonstall of Massachusetts and Governor Wills of Vermont offered aid. Four Boston doctors who had treated victims of the Cocoanut Grove fire spent a day in Hartford advising on the treatment of the injured and the identification of the dead.[28]

The day was filled with shocking reports of mendacity as well. One woman living in a second-story apartment near the circus lot put up a sign — "Telephone" — in her window. When a long line of shaken people formed outside her door, she began charging everyone a dollar to use the phone. Another woman whose hands had been so burned she could not flex her fingers rushed to a nearby parked truck that had its engine running. She pleaded with the man to take her to the hospital, but the driver walked away. When she tried to drive the truck herself, the man came back, turned off the ignition, and took the keys.[29]

Reporter John Cleary reported that the pandemonium of the day gave rise to several mysterious, unverified events. "A woman wearing white hospital clothes and carrying a black bag volunteered her services at a hospital," where she worked several hours setting broken bones. Her work was so poor that at least two patients had to have amputations. Then there was the badly burned little boy whose uncle carried him into the hospital. When the family later returned, the boy's shoes were found in a heap of clothing in a corner but the boy was never found.[30]

Curtis Johnson, an old friend of Governor Baldwin's, recounted the day's travails in his biography of the governor:

> Baldwin had been up the whole night following the holocaust alerting and using the civil defense agencies to organize the forces of mercy in order to bring some comfort to the injured and to the bereaved families of those who had been burned to death in the worst catastrophe in Connecticut's history. The bodies of the dead, many burned almost beyond recognition, were taken to the state armory as a temporary morgue, and there, parents, relatives and friends came to identify loved ones. Ray spent the whole night in the armory, attempting in every way that he could to help those in the terrible and tragic task of identification. Leaving the armory after he had done all he could, he visited the hospitals of the city where the seriously burned were receiving emergency treatment.
>
> The war council, the state police, the Red Cross and all emergency agencies had done yeoman service, but for Ray Baldwin, a great-hearted and compassionate man, it was impossible for him to steel himself to the suffering and grief—especially where so many innocent children were involved.[31]

The Red Cross later detailed the tragic toll of the fire: "Four families were completed wiped out by the fire. There were 26 families in which the mother and one child lost their lives. Children of five families were left orphans. Several of the fire victims were in need of extended medical and nursing care and, in some cases, additional surgery."[32]

The death toll eventually reached 169, with at least 500 more injured. The "official" number of dead has ranged from 168 to 171 because of the great difficulty in finding and identifying all the bodies. Five bodies were never identified, and at least one was never found. Other serious fires have hit Hartford since then, such as the Christmas eve fire of 1945 at a convalescent home in which 19 people were killed and 36 others were injured. Nationally, fires that have taken large tolls include the 1942 Cocoanut Grove fire in Boston (443 dead), and the 1987 DuPont Plaza fire in Puerto Rico (115 dead).

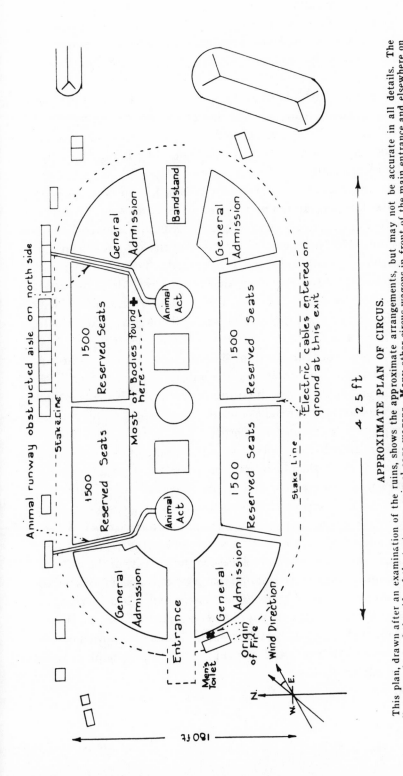

APPROXIMATE PLAN OF CIRCUS.

This plan, drawn after an examination of the ruins, shows the approximate arrangements, but may not be accurate in all details. The small squares beyond the side of the tent were animal cage wagons. Many other circus wagons in front of the main entrance and elsewhere on the grounds are not shown on this plan. At the right were performers' tents not involved in the fire.

Diagram of the Big Top.

Shocking as the Hartford blaze was, fire was not a stranger to circuses. The P. T. Barnum shows had been plagued by numerous fires over the years, including a devastating one in 1887 that demolished Barnum's circus museum in Bridgeport; in a Ringling Brothers fire in Cleveland in 1943 the exhibition animals were lost.[33] What made the Hartford circus fire so horrifying, besides the sheer magnitude of the human toll, was the tender age of so many of the victims. Fifty-six of the dead were children nine years old or younger, including one cute, blue-eyed eight-year-old girl who was never officially identified until 1991.

Her morgue tag read #1565 and she became known as "Little Miss 1565." Her face was not disfigured, and her picture was distributed around the world, and reprinted on numerous anniversaries of the fire. She was buried in Northwood Cemetery near the Windsor town line along with five other people who were burned so horribly they could not be identified. Over the years, the mystery of Little Miss 1565's identity came to obsess many people. Two Hartford police officers, Lieutenant Tom Barber and Detective Sergeant Ed Lowe, tried for years to identify the girl, without success. They became so personally involved with her tragedy that they used to take flowers to the grave of the girl on Memorial Day, Christmas, and the anniversary of the fire. With Lowe dead and Barber's health failing in the late 1970s, the Allied Florists Association of Central Connecticut vowed to continue the tradition of placing flowers on the little girl's grave, a promise still kept.[34]

Lowe and Barber had developed one unproven theory that Little Miss 1565 and her family had been transients traveling through the area when they decided to attend the circus. Another theory apparently held by Barber was that someone had identified the wrong child and never realized their mistake or never came forward to admit to it.[35] In 1981, Lowe's widow came forward, saying it was time to set the record straight; she claimed that her husband had learned the identify of the girl but that the child's family had requested that it be kept a secret so as not to revive their grief and heartache. The mystery took a strange twist in 1987 when someone anonymously placed notes on the six graves, claiming that the little girl was "Sarah Graham," that she was buried beside her male twin, "Michael," and that three other family members were buried in adjacent plots.[36]

Connecticut officials recently accepted the theory put forth by Lowe's widow. On March 9, 1991, the Connecticut medical examiner issued an amended death certificate identifying Little Miss 1565 as Eleanor Cook. A Hartford fireman and arson investigator, Rick Davey, had worked on the challenge of identification for nine years; his carefully documented report had convinced the authorities. It appeared that Eleanor's mother was reluctant to come forward because of a possible misidentification regarding Eleanor made by a relative at the time of the fire. Given the confusion of the day and the horrible burns and disfigurement of victims, it is not hard to imagine difficulty in making a positive identification. In any case, Eleanor's mother decided to let the matter rest and not cause the family further trauma. After the relative died in the late 1980s, Mrs. Cook, aged 85 in 1991, felt more comfortable discussing the matter with Davey and confirming the identity of Little Miss 1565.[37]

The state police files, now in the custody of the state archivist, indicate that Eleanor's photograph had been supplied to the state police as early as 1963. It is found in the same envelope as the morgue photograph that received worldwide circulation. Inexplicably, state police dismissed a 1955 attempt by Eleanor's brother, Donald, to identify the girl as his sister.[38] As Mrs. Cook told the story in 1991, she went to the circus on July 6, 1944, with Eleanor and her two sons, Donald and Edward. Mrs. Cook's severe burns required months of convalescence in the hospital. Donald survived. And Edward and Eleanor both died shortly after the fire.[39]

The precise causes of the fire and the subsequent casualties have never been fully determined. However, physical evidence and eyewitness testimonies point to a combination of factors: a careless smoker, flammable tenting material, blocked exits, inadequate exits (that is, actual fire escapes, not just normal aisles), use of loose folding chairs, and meager fire safety training and preparation. One account speculates that a monkey or chimpanzee jumping around in the upper portions of the tent, perhaps as part of an act, was carrying a lit cigar. Another conjectural culprit cited was the dry, dusty circus grounds, which included uncut grass.

And there has always been the possibility of arson. In 1950, a roust-about named James Dale Segee arrested in Ohio confessed to setting numerous fires, including the Hartford fire, as well as to four different murders. Much of the circumstantial evidence pointing to Segee was tantalizing: He had worked for Ringling Brothers in 1944 and was placed in Hartford in the days after the fire. Segee described moments of amnesia, set off by sexual experiences, during which he set fires. For psychiatrists, he drew pictures of burning circus tents and a hatchet-toting Indian chief in full war regalia, whom Segee said taunted him to set fires. (Segee himself was half-Indian. Psychiatrists traced Segee's drawings of Indians to an illustration used in advertisements by the National Board of Fire Underwriters.)[40]

Intriguing as all this evidence was, Hartford authorities felt they did not have enough evidence so many years after the fire to charge Segee, and he was never arrested. Nonetheless, the state of Ohio, with sufficient evidence to prosecute Segee for two other incidents of arson, put him in a home for the criminally insane in 1950.[41]

On March 9, 1991, along with the disclosure of Eleanor Cook's name, Lieutenant Davey declared that the fire was deliberately set, possibly by Segee. He contends that the humidity level inside the tent precluded the accidental start of the fire from a tossed cigarette—a conclusion affirmed by FBI arson investigators after an eight-hour, closed-door session with Davey. John Bailey, the Hartford state's attorney, after reviewing Davey's evidence in March 1991, declared that the case was still officially closed but added that his office would continue to review the evidence. Segee, now living in Ohio, refused comment and, as he has done repeatedly since 1950, repudiated his confession.[42]

Many people thought that the fire was the end of the line for the circus. "The disaster put the circus out of business for an indefinite period, probably for the duration of the war," reported the *Courant* on July 7, 1944. "It lost equipment which cannot be replaced in wartime, including the big steel cages where the wild animals perform and such irreplaceable items as manila rope, without which no circus can function."

But the equipment losses paled in comparison to the likely criminal prosecutions and civil penalties that the circus would face. Already people wondered how the circus could possibly survive the searing reckonings that would be meted out in court. In time, a few audacious attorneys with a seat-of-the-pants plan showed that many things are possible when everyone fervently hopes to "do the right thing."

Chapter 2

THE RESCUE OF
A CIRCUS

In New York City, William Dunn, the treasurer of the circus and vice president of Manufacturers Trust Company, knew that he had trouble on his hands as soon as word of the fire came over the news wires. For the next hour Dunn frantically tried to contact the circus's lawyers at the New York City firm of Engel, Judge and Miller to give them the news.[1]

From time to time, the circus's general counsel, Karl Loos of Pope, Ballard and Loos, a Washington, D.C., law firm, assigned contract cases and minor legal problems to Engel, Judge and Miller in New York City, which in turn usually assigned the cases to associate attorney John Reddy, Jr., aged thirty-three in 1944, a graduate of Yale College and Harvard Law School. But Reddy had entered the navy the previous month, so the miscellaneous circus legal work was inherited by Dan Judge, aged forty-one, a graduate of Fordham Law School and an experienced trial attorney. "We hadn't done very much, if anything, for the circus up until the time of the fire," Judge later said. "From then on I might say that I was very busy on behalf of the circus."[2]

When told of the fire, Judge immediate went to Dunn's office. "[H]e told me what had happened and he and I caught the next train to Hartford, which was 5:08, and got here about 8 o'clock. It was still light. I saw the shambles that was left of the fire and somebody told me the officials of the circus were over in the office of, I think, a gravestone cutting outfit next door [McGovern's Granite Yard]. We tried to get in but the state police barred us."[3]

Ringling's general counsel, Loos, wired from the west coast that Judge should continue to handle the circus's legal problems. Meantime, Loos's law partner suggested that Judge retain local counsel in Hartford. At the time, only Connecticut attorneys could appear in Connecticut courts; Judge would be permitted only to act as a consultant to that attorney. On recommendation, Judge chose forty-two-year-old Cyril Coleman to handle the civil litigation.[4] Coleman, described by friends as a shy, almost retiring man, was a graduate of Harvard Law School and a partner at the seven-member firm of Day Berry & Howard. An active Democrat in state politics, Coleman became a leader of the nonpartisan Citizens Charter Committee, a good government group that sponsored reformist candidates in Hartford city elections. In 1948, Coleman became Hartford's first mayor under the newly instituted city manager form of government. After two terms, declining to run again, he was appointed by Governor Ribicoff to several state posts.[5]

To defend the circus officials against the criminal charges, Judge and Coleman selected Lieutenant Governor William Hadden, an experienced criminal defense attorney.[6] (At the time of the fire, the Connecticut lieutenant governorship was a part-time position that did not ethically preclude a private practice. In 1945, Hadden was elected to a different part-time position, attorney general.)

The circus's civil liability was quickly apparent. An insurance adjuster, meeting with the Red Cross chapter chairman and area regional director, said that the circus carried over $500,000 in insurance and would faithfully meet its obligations as in the past.[7] But the *Courant* carried conflicting reports concerning the extent of coverage, and Hartford insurance executives speculated morbidly on which companies had sold how much insurance to Ringling Brothers. In any case, the insurance commissioner began to investigate the circus's insurance status, and the Ringling corporation opened a claims office in Hartford. Within a week this office had received several thousand claims.[8]

On Saturday, July 8 at 3:00 A.M., Deputy Sheriff Ralph A. Hager gave notice of the first lawsuits by attachment. Attachment was the common method of bringing a lawsuit in 1944, especially in cases where defendants were based out-of-state and the extent of their assets were uncertain.[9] A plaintiff's sheriff would attach stickers to the goods, freezing use of the defendant's personal property until a final judgment was rendered.[10] The first suit was brought by attorney Nathan Bergman for the death of Mrs. DiMartino, the mother of eight children. The suit sought the maximum $15,000 then allowed in wrongful death cases.[11]

Most death cases were not filed until the following week because they required more cumbersome legal work than personal injury cases, which were immediately filed in droves. (Wrongful death cases require an administrator to be named by the probate court, which can take several days or more.) The first personal injury case, filed by the law firm of Shipman and Goodwin, alleged one count of negligence and another count of nuisance. The most frequently named defendants, in addition to the circus corporation, were the officers of the circus and the city of Hartford.[12]

The typical liability suit alleged in part: "The defendant was negligent and careless in that although it was operating a circus to which the general public was invited yet nevertheless it failed to provide an adequate and safe place for witnessing of said performance." Specifically mentioned were the flammable nature of the tent, lack of attendants to control the fire, lack of proper exits, failure to have adequate fire extinguishers, carelessness in setting up exits from the tent, blocking exits, failure to comply with state and local laws, and finally, improper training of employees.[13] In the contorted syntax of law, this typical writ concluded: "By reason of the negligence and carelessness of the defendant as aforesaid, the decedent suffered severe, painful and disabling injuries and a severe traumatic shock to his nervous system, all of which caused his immediate death."[14]

Filing complaints was not always easy. The circus was not registered to do business in Connecticut, and therefore had no designated agent or street address. As a result, process-servers often had trouble finding officers of the circus upon whom to serve papers, as required by law. This prompted the secretary of state to declare the circus corporation qualified to do business in the state so that she could appoint a designated representative to accept the papers in the expected flood of damage claims.[15] In the end, most if not all of Hartford's personal injury bar filed lawsuits against the circus, for a total of $15 million in attachments. The superior court scheduled the suits to commence in its upcoming September 1944 term.

Although the civil suits posed an obvious long-term problem for the circus, a more immediate concern was the attachments, which prevented the circus from leaving town and continuing to operate. At the time attachments could be easily obtained by any plaintiff's attorney who, acting as an officer of the court, needed only to sign the attachment and serve it with the complaint in the suit itself. (Not until the 1970s did the United States Supreme Court declare that such attachments were an unconstitutional seizure of property without due process, a ruling that gave rise to a new "prejudgment remedy" procedure. Under the procedure today, a lawyer needs a judge's permission for each attachment. If such a fire were to occur in the 1990s, a judge would most certainly call a meeting of all tort claimants' lawyers seeking attachments in order to resolve their respective priorities to assets *before* signing the prejudgment remedy forms. If such a process had governed the circus fire attachments, it would have facilitated a more orderly court procedure and perhaps a settlement of claims, as illustrated in the L'Ambiance Plaza collapse case, discussed in chapter 10.) The properties under attachment were placed in the custody of the deputy sheriffs serving the legal papers. Once judgments were obtained in the civil suits, some years later, the successful plaintiffs would attempt to collect their funds, looking to the property seized and dividing it up among themselves according to the customary rule of "first in time, first in right."[16]

Since attachments obtained through the superior court could not extend outside the state of Connecticut, the only property of value to be claimed was the charred remains at the site of the fire and the menagerie.[17] As one court later described the attachments, "[T]he properties under attachment were little more than an assortment of burned-out and non-operative equipment and a collection of frightened and dangerous animals"—which is to say, claimants could seize

Ruth the elephant, Lotus the famous giant hippopotamus, and Gargantua the gorilla. [18]

Plaintiffs' attorneys also attached the circus's seventy-nine railroad cars located at the Windsor Street freight yards and tried, unsuccessfully, to attach any Ringling cash held in state. Subsequent events made the attachments on Ringling fire insurance policies moot. Frozen by the attachments on its property, the Greatest Show on Earth was trapped at the Barbour Street site. As a *Yale Law Journal* note of 1951 by Arthur Sachs declared, the "undestroyed earning assets of the business [were] immediately tied up by the personal injury claimants." [19]

It was a gloomy group of circus lawyers who met in New York City the Sunday and Monday following the fire. As Dan Judge later explained, "You must realize that a circus is nothing but an aggregation of independent acts. The circus burned down, a lot of people were killed and injured, and there was a very substantial problem as far as the circus was concerned of keeping our organization together, because there was a great despondency, as you may well imagine, immediately following the fire." [20]

As the attachments mounted, there was an additional concern, as circus folks put it, with "getting the show on the road." Yet the circus could not go anywhere unless its attorneys could remove all the attachments without forcing the circus into bankruptcy, or committing an act of bankruptcy. Under federal bankruptcy law at the time, the circus would either have to surrender total control of the circus to a court-appointed trustee or liquidate its assets entirely. Neither was an attractive option. Circus attorneys surely knew that there was another nasty possibility that would have been legal, if unconscionable—to sell the circus to a shell corporation, which could leave the tort claimants without any Connecticut assets to seize. A sale to a close friend of the Ringling family for a reasonable sum might well have survived an attack as a fraudulent conveyance, for example.

As the circus attorneys pondered their options, the situation at the scene of the fire rapidly deteriorated. Sanitary conditions at the circus grounds grew steadily worse, triggering a conference between the mayor of Hartford, William Mortensen, and the city health

officer, Dr. Alfred Burgdorf. Animals were roaming about the grounds
without proper supervision; some were dropping waste liberally about
the lot. Because of the attachments, circus roustabouts were not
allowed to gather up the remaining equipment; the salvage effort
stopped. So circus personnel languished day after day at the Barbour
Street site and railroad freight yards, attracting an unkempt crowd
of idlers and hustlers consorting with the motley crew of circus
laborers and performers.[21] The *Courant* described the desolate scene:

> The circus wagons housing the hundreds of animals stood idle on the
> massive Barbour Street lot Tuesday, while the hot afternoon sun beat
> down on the roofs of the animal cages. Mr. and Mrs. Gargantua, the
> giant apes, live in the only air-conditioned cage on the grounds.
>
> Food for the hundreds of animals "frozen" at the Barbour Street
> grounds ranged from milk and bread for the bears to red meat for the
> lions and tigers. As feeding time approached, the circus employees who
> had been sitting idly around all afternoon became active, carrying water
> and food to the dozens of cages. The animal cages, in plain view of the
> charred ruins of the "big top," are among the most valuable assets of the
> circus.
>
> Alderman Louis Kosoff of the Third Ward Tuesday afternoon told
> Mayor Mortensen he had received scores of requests that the animals be
> moved from the spot, and the mayor said efforts are being made to have
> them taken to another site, perhaps in the North Meadows.[22]

Hartford's legal community sensed impending doom. Even if the
circus remained solvent,[23] would its assets and insurance cover the
large awards that courts would undoubtedly hand down? Could the
superior court in Hartford handle the large volume of litigation that
would surely drag on for years? Most likely, the circus was heading
for bankruptcy, where the secured creditors,[24] not tort claimants,
would receive first payment from proceeds of a forced sale. There
was no Chapter 11 procedure for bankruptcy, as we know it today,
which would have allowed a "debtor-in-possession" to reorganize its
assets.[25]

Under the existing, inflexible Chapter X reorganization procedure, a trustee with broad investigative duties and obligations had
to be appointed when the debt exceeded $250,000; the probing
scrutiny of such trustees was an unpleasant ordeal for most debtors.

An expensive and time-consuming administrative burden was also placed on the debtor, who was required to send out notices to creditors and stockholders. Finally, Chapter X had legal restrictions that are now considered too cumbersome and complex—a "good faith" standard for filing the reorganization, an "absolute priority" that gave all creditors in the first class preferred treatment in the settling of debts, and a prohibition on asking creditors, by solicitation, to back a certain reorganization plan.[26] "All too frequently," concluded Patrick Murphy, a bankruptcy expert, "the patient died on the operating room table while the would-be doctors quarreled over the form of the operation."[27] It is no wonder that the bar could find no solace in federal reorganization proceedings and that Dan Judge consistently opposed them.

Although the circus was not eager to choose from among its unappetizing options, the plaintiffs' bar was not sitting idly by. Having recognized the difficult choices that lay ahead for both the circus and their own clients, several leading Hartford attorneys began to contemplate some creative alternatives. If existing law did not provide a clear and just resolution to this tragic situation, then somebody would have to *invent* one. The task fell to two friends, Edward Rogin and Julius Schatz, and to Schatz's law partner and friend, Arthur Weinstein.

Eddie Rogin, a resident of West Hartford, was a well-liked man of great competence and integrity, a man admired for his "coolness in judgment," in the words of one colleague. Born in Russia, Rogin immigrated with his parents to New Britain at the age of five. After attending Clark University and Boston University Law School, Rogin was admitted to the Connecticut bar in 1931. He had practiced law in Newington, served as a town judge, and in 1944 was sharing office space in Hartford with attorney Cornelius D. Shea.[28]

Rogin's close friend, a college acquaintance, was Julius Schatz, a man celebrated by his colleagues as a Hartford original. Schatz was well known among the bar as a bright man with impulsive moods, a proud bearing, a boisterous demeanor, and more than a little flamboyance. Always entertaining, Schatz was known as a bon vivant and raconteur whose booming voice could raise the roof.[29] He was also an ebullient rainmaker with a savvy business sense. Admitted to the bar in 1926, Schatz had achieved success by 1944 as a personal injury lawyer, and he had earned sufficient acclaim to encourage him to run—unsuccessfully—for attorney general and to compete—successfully—for the presidency of the Hartford County Bar Association.[30]

A third friend, Arthur Weinstein, would also play an instrumental role in the legal adventures that lay ahead. Weinstein, a graduate of Trinity College and Harvard Law School, was Schatz's partner and a talented wordsmith of legal documents. He was a calm, deliberate lawyer with a keen eye for legal detail.[31] In the months ahead, Weinstein's legal acumen and draftsmanship would help Schatz and Rogin navigate some treacherous legal shoals.

On the day of the circus, Rogin and Schatz were scheduled to take their sons to the show, but the unhealthy, humid conditions under the big top deterred them. Instead they decided to play golf that afternoon and were hacking their way through the course when the fire whistles blew. Weinstein had also passed up the circus that year because his son had seen it the year before and had no interest in going again. He left work early.[32]

During the next few days, Schatz, Weinstein, and Rogin were besieged by clients requesting representation in suits against the circus. Schatz brought one case on behalf of the family of Martin Marcus, a forty-four-year-old Hartford resident and owner of a local laundry who had died in the fire. Schatz had obtained an administrator for Marcus's estate as soon as possible—the Monday after the Thursday fire. But even then he was too late; numerous other suits against the circus had already been filed. Because of this routine procedural delay in obtaining an estate administrator, Schatz was in the unhappy position, along with other wrongful death litigants, of seeing his clients lose out to personal injury claimants who had been able to file their cases earlier.[33] Under the old "first in time, first in rights" rule, these earlier claimants had prior claims to any attached assets that might exist.

Since the flood of lawsuits began "before the embers had cooled," according to the *Hartford Times*, any suit filed after Saturday night or Sunday morning had virtually no chance of winning any money, even if a favorable judgment were obtained.[34] The federal bankruptcy remedy that was available, as discussed in chapter 8, would have led to a hasty liquidation, scant compensation for creditors, and probably nothing for tort claimants. With no other statutory remedies or means to resolve their claims, dozens of plaintiffs with wrongful death cases—and personal injury claimants who had filed too late—were left out in the cold.

Not surprisingly, the plaintiffs' bar was outraged. Rogin, Schatz, and Weinstein quickly set about grappling for a solution to the dilemma. In time, they came up with the idea of petitioning for a receivership for the circus, authorized by state law and supervised by the superior court. A receivership would place circus property under the control of the court and its duly appointed receiver and block any further attachments. More critically, under Connecticut law a receivership would sweep aside all the burdensome *prior* attachments to circus property and place all claimants on an equal footing. (In many states, some or all prior attachments are allowed to be carried over into a state receivership.) Finally, the court could block any new suits against the receiver, thus imposing a certain stability on the circus's precarious legal circumstances.[35]

There were problems in obtaining a state receivership, however. First, the circus itself or a secured creditor would have the right to object, and both would be inclined to exercise that right. A more decisive obstacle was the law's apparent requirement that a person be a "judgment creditor" in order to petition a court for a receivership. In other words, a mere claimant could not ask for a receivership; only claimants whose cases had gone to trial and been awarded damages could seek a receivership. Since this would take years, the plaintiff's bar found the receivership option seemed next to worthless; the circus would probably go bankrupt before it could be used.

Nonetheless, Rogin, Schatz, and Weinstein set about researching the law to see if they could find some ingenious legal detours around the problems. One possibility would be to find or create a "judgment creditor," such as a grain merchant unpaid for the feeding of the animals at the Barbour Street site. Such a person could quickly get a judgment on a breach of contract complaint, perhaps by default, which could then entitle the creditor to petition for a receivership.[36]

Meanwhile, other plaintiffs' attorneys were also searching high and low for a practical solution to their legal plight. In the confusing days following the fire, plaintiffs' attorneys were working overtime, and the personal injury bar was slow to grasp that the glut of litigation would soon collapse of its own weight; the circus's remaining assets would only satisfy a handful of claimants, if that. One attorney who saw the writing on the wall was Robert Butler, a U.S. District Attorney for ten years and, as was customary at the time, a private attorney as well. Butler's legal career had been illustrious from the very start: he qualified for the bar by reading law for three years. (Reading law to pass the bar, while serving an apprenticeship to a law firm, had its origins in the nineteenth century. Today only a few states sanction this method of entering the bar.) Butler had also served as corporation counsel for the city of Hartford and founded his own law firm.[37]

On the day of the fire, Butler was conducting a grand jury session in the United States Building on High Street. "I saw the trucks and ambulances and taxicabs come by with the bodies of the dead and injured," he later recalled. His private law office ended up filing twenty-two liability claims—including the usual attachments —against the circus. Despite his own role in suing the circus, Butler privately worried that "a great many writs of attachment were issued almost overnight" by the legal community. "[I]t was on the 11th of July, I realized that this whole thing was becoming a shambles and I telephoned Mr. Hadden, who was the only counsel for the circus whose name I knew at the time."[38]

Butler told Hadden that the circus was being destroyed and suggested that Hadden's client, Ringling Brothers, convene a meeting of the Hartford bar to "see if we couldn't find some formula for getting order out of chaos, getting the circus with its animals and personnel and equipment out of the city and on the road so that there would be something besides a total loss to everybody." Hadden replied, "That's a splendid suggestion, Bob." A meeting was set for Thursday, July 13 at 11:30 A.M. in the north courtroom of the Hartford Superior Court. Hadden promised to spread the word.[39]

Working separately, Rogin, Schatz, and Weinstein remained committed to their own scheme of obtaining a receiver and began to consider tactics for requesting the receivership. Because Connecticut courts took a summer recess in those days, only one judge was on duty for emergencies. The judge on duty during this particular period was based in Willimantic. Fortunately, he was Judge John Hamilton King.

King, appointed chief justice of the Connecticut Supreme Court in 1963, was called a "dictionary of the law." As Supreme Court Judge Alva Loiselle remarked of King, "Lawyers who appeared [before him] never ceased to marvel at his ability to cite legal precedent by volume and page from memory, the cases in some instances going back to colonial days."[40] A bachelor, King had practiced law with his father in Willimantic and had served as one of Connecticut's first assistant attorneys general until 1940, when he was appointed to the superior court. "King was a colorful trial judge," wrote one reporter. "He wore hand-knotted bow ties and, despite his severe expression, had . . . a dry, subtle sense of humor that frequently broke the courtroom monotony."[41] Thus Rogin, Schatz, and Weinstein were approaching an ingenious, creative jurist with an encyclopedic mind and a subtle understanding of the law.

Schatz planned to file for a receivership with King on Wednesday, July 12, the day before the scheduled meeting of the plaintiffs' bar convened by Butler and Hadden. On that Wednesday morning, Schatz finished drafting the papers requesting a temporary receiver. Schatz, Rogin, and Weinstein knew they had not resolved all the legal issues, but they simply decided they had done as much as they could to argue around the law. After stating that certain circus assets were now attached or threatened with attachment, their application concluded:

7. Said assets are in danger of being wasted and your applicant [the administrator of the estate of a circus fire victim] believes that the exigencies of the case demand the immediate appointment of a temporary receiver of said corporation in order that its assets may not be wasted and the interests of creditors and stockholders may be protected.
8. The Superior Court for Hartford County which has venue of all said actions is not now in session.
9. Your applicant therefore asks:

1. That a temporary receiver be forthwith appointed.
2. That such orders be passed for the government of said receiver and the management of the affairs of said corporation as may be judged necessary and proper.[42]

Although the legal argument was perhaps tendentious, given the letter of the law for receiverships, the situation was so desperate that the trio decided to take a chance anyway, file the request, and visit King in person.

Rather than choosing as the receiver a business associate, realtor, accountant, or someone who often referred cases to the firm, Schatz decided instead to ask Judge King to name Rogin as temporary receiver. The choice was inspired because King and Rogin had been friends for some time. What better way to smooth over the shaky legal basis for the receivership? Under other circumstances, Weinstein would have preferred a different receiver, but in the end he acquiesced to proposing Rogin.

With the papers completed, Schatz, Rogin, and Weinstein set off to Willimantic to see Judge King. At 2:00 P.M., they found him in his office on the third floor of the courthouse, sitting behind his desk and mostly hidden by it. (King was a short man.) After greetings were exchanged, the three explained the nature of their visit. King immediately replied that there were problems with the application because it had been made on behalf of an "unliquidated" tort claimant (a claimant whose case had not come to judgment and been given an award)—precisely the problem the three had anticipated.[43]

While the three attorneys stood there trying to think of a suitable response, King did something that impressed them for the rest of their lives. He stood up and, pushing a chair over to a bookcase, stood on it to retrieve a dusty old volume of *Connecticut Reports*. He swiftly turned to a case and began to study it. "You should rely on this case," said King to his startled guests. "In light of this, I will appoint the receiver."[44]

Although there is no definitive proof what case Judge King cited, it is likely that it was the 1903 case of *Cogswell v. Second National Bank*, which is found in volume 76 of *Connecticut Reports* at page 252. The case provides that a temporary receiver may be appointed where there exists *some* cause for doing so, but the judge need not decide the final merits of the case before making a temporary appointment. As was customary with motions seeking a preliminary order of receivership, no notice was given to the circus or to the other claimants.

King appointed Rogin as receiver, ordered him to post a $100,000 bond, and directed him to "take possession of all the books, papers, evidences of debt and property of said corporation, to collect all monies owing to it, and to take all lawful steps within his power to secure and preserve assets." A hearing on whether to make the appointment permanent was set for September 15, 1944, the day the Hartford Superior Court resumed its session.[45]

As a gesture of good faith, Rogin then told Judge King that he would not accept a fee as the receiver unless and until all claimants were paid 100 percent on their claims. King thanked Rogin, put his arm around him, and said he would have signed the papers even without this guarantee.[46]

Schatz now had his receiver order—a mutant legal vehicle for addressing hundreds of unresolved tort claims. The three men were elated as they drove back to Hartford. After years of striving to make a name for himself, Schatz, the ethnic outsider eager to impress his colleagues in the bar, had finally pulled off the legal coup of the decade. He was so excited that he kept banging on the car and trying to hug Rogin, who was driving. Rogin later confessed that he was afraid that Schatz would cause an accident.[47]

Upon his return, Schatz put out a press release announcing Judge King's order and Rogin's position as receiver of the circus. To the wrongful death claimants, perhaps the best news of all was that all claims would now be treated equally regardless of when an attachment was secured. The receiver, as an agent of the court, would inventory the prior attachments, supervise new lawsuits, and possibly arrange for the release of attached property in exchange for cash from the circus. Rogin, in the meanwhile, arranged for his bond.

If the triumphant Schatz, Rogin, and Weinstein had outmaneuvered everyone by obtaining the receivership, they also had a tough sell ahead of them. Would the circus owners, attorneys, and management go along with the novel scheme? Could they convince the plaintiffs' bar to accept the receivership?

When Robert Butler called Schatz to tell him of the bar meeting scheduled for the next day, he was stunned to learn about Schatz's unilateral action in obtaining a temporary receivership. Butler was also more than a little annoyed that his leadership of the circus fire plaintiffs had been so suddenly undermined and upstaged. Now his meeting the next day would address an entirely different agenda, one set by outsiders and not by himself.[48] Years later, the Hartford legal community would also wonder whether the Schatz-Rogin-Weinstein victory had sown the seeds of a bitter enmity that would burst forth with an ugly fury as the circus fire receivership drew to a close.[49]

Butler, of course, was not the only one surprised by announcement of the receivership. The circus, upon learning of the news, put out a statement that night pledging that "prompt steps will be taken to vacate the receivership."[50] The circus would have certainly been within its rights to object; so would any creditor. But any objections would also throw the circus into bankruptcy proceedings, and no one held optimistic hopes for the success of *that* course of action.[51]

Schatz and Weinstein personally broke the news to Dan Judge, who was staying at the Hotel Bond, one of the city's grand hotels at the time. They told him that the receivership order had been signed in chambers and asked him to furnish an officer of the corporation for service of the order. But Judge refused the request until he could consult with his Connecticut counsel. "I called Bill Hadden on the telephone and asked him what he thought of it, and he said, 'I don't think they have any right to get a receiver without notice at this juncture, and I wouldn't produce anybody for service.' So I didn't produce them [*sic*]."[52]

In an apparent attempt to convince Judge of the merits of the receivership, Schatz, Weinstein, and Rogin met with him at the men's bar at the Bond for several hours. According to Rogin, Judge was receptive to the plan but would not pledge the circus's cooperation or make any commitments.[53] Rogin met separately with Aubrey Haley, a chief stockholder of the circus and wife of Ringling vice president James Haley, to sell her on the idea of the receivership.[54] Aubrey, in turn, discussed the plan with the other chief stockholder, Edith Ringling, mother of the president of the circus, Robert Ringling. The two women, who had heard stories of little girls dying in the fire, were clearly sympathetic to the claimants' plight.[55] But the parties were unprepared to resolve anything at that late hour.

For Schatz and Rogin, however, it was important to achieve some sort of accord about the receivership before the meeting between the claimants' and circus's attorneys scheduled for 11:30 A.M. the next day, Thursday. So that morning at 8:30 A.M., Rogin set off to Willimantic again to meet with Judge King; he wanted to inform King that he had obtained his bond, as the order required. After returning immediately to Hartford to file the bond with the superior court, Rogin then met with Police Commissioner Hickey and Henry B. Strong, secretary to Governor Baldwin, to offer his cooperation. He also attempted without success to contact State's Attorney Alcorn to ask him which circus assets should be retained in police custody.[56]

Still, the big question remained unanswered: Would the circus consent to the receivership? Just before the meeting with the bar at the Hartford County Courthouse, Schatz, Rogin, and Weinstein met with circus attorneys Hadden and Judge. (Also present was Harold Mitchell, the Republican state committee chairman, who was connected with a Washington, D.C., law firm and was assisting in the circus's defense.) Apparently the Ringling family had acquiesced and accepted the idea of the receivership, for at this meeting Judge announced that the circus would not object to the receivership and would make a person available for service of the order.[57] Whereupon Schatz's sheriff, Sam Rosen, served George Washington Smith, general manager of the circus.[58]

For a few days now, Dan Judge had been looking forward to the plaintiffs' bar meeting. He was determined to arrive at an understanding with the claimants' attorneys. Even with a receiver appointed, a plan had to be formulated and accepted to deal with the crush of lawsuits. "I also felt—and in this regard I was ably seconded by the Ringlings and the people who ran the circus—that regardless of whether we had any liability or not, there was only one attitude to take, and that was that we were going to help the people who were killed and injured in this fire."[59]

The meeting was not a particularly pleasant one at first, if only because the recent turn of events had made many plaintiffs' attorneys suspicious and bewildered. Eight years later, Dan Judge described the proceedings as follows:

[W]hen we got to this meeting, Mr. Hadden had been more or less designated as our spokesman. He got up and explained our situation, but before he got started one of the lawyers in the group demanded that I tell them where the bank account of the circus was, and I told him that I didn't feel at that juncture that I was required to do it. I certainly didn't want any ancillary receivers appointed to go in and latch onto our assets in other jurisdictions.

Whereupon Mr. Cooney [a prominent Irish attorney of the Hartford bar] got up and proceeded to take me to task in a very substantial way for reflecting on the honor of the Connecticut bar that they would do any such thing. I tried to explain I had no thought of reflecting on anybody's honor, but at this juncture I was not making any disclosure.

Then Mr. Hadden made a statement and Mr. Butler got up and said he had given the matter very serious consideration and that he felt that a receivership—which as I recall now he talked about a Federal receivership—in any event, I so construed his remarks. As soon as he sat down about five other lawyers stood up, one after the other, and everyone agreed that Mr. Butler was right, the one thing that this called for was a receivership.

Well, I had been in a great many of these meetings and I realized that the meeting was getting away from us, that unless the bar could be made to understand what we really were trying to accomplish we might have all kinds of suits and all kinds of demands to precipitate a Federal receivership, and we sure had plenty of problems without having to contend with a Federal receivership [whose procedural complexity would have been ill-suited to resolve the crush of tort claims].

So I stood up and, as I recall it—and I have a pretty vivid recollection of what I said because it was a memorable occasion to me—I told the members of the bar that I was there as a representative of the Ringling family, who considered themselves the custodian of a great American institution and that my instructions were to help the people who had been hurt in this fire, that regardless of whether we had any liability or not we wanted to do everything we could to help them.

I then explained that I had a plan, which I was sure if I could satisfy the bar that it was in their best interests I could also satisfy them as to our good faith. I also advised them that we weren't going to consent to any Federal receivership, that there was nobody in the room that had any claim against us that could put us in receivership, that all the claims they were talking about were unliquidated tort claims which were not grounds for a receivership or reorganization, but that an attempt to put us in receivership might be fatal; a receivership *per se* might destroy the greatest single asset that there was in the picture, namely, the good name and the earning power of the Ringling Brothers—Barnum and Bailey circus.

When I got finished, Mr. Cooney, who not too long before was giving me a very difficult time, said he agreed with me, it would be a good idea to have a committee [to oversee the Rogin-led *state* receivership], and he moved that Mr. Lucius Robinson [president of the bar association] appoint one. Mr. Robinson wasn't in the city, but the motion carried and the committee that day was appointed, I believe by Mr. Robinson, over the telephone.[60]

Robinson appointed Robert Butler chairman of the Bar Disaster Committee and named Joseph Cooney and Julius Schatz as its two other members. A few months later, the superior court also appointed Schatz as attorney for the receiver, to file papers and handle various legal and procedural matters.[61] (Even though Schatz simultaneously represented several tort claimants while serving as the receiver's attorney, his two roles were not considered an unethical conflict of interest at the time.)

Dan Judge kept his word. After the meeting, without ever conceding that a receivership was justified, he began to cooperate with Rogin in his work as state receiver. Rogin traveled to the sites with circus manager George Washington Smith to take official possession of the assets at Barbour Street and the Windsor Street railroad yards. That same day, Thursday, City Health Officer Burgdorf pressured Rogin to remove the circus animals and personal property from the fairgrounds. Burgdorf had already issued an order that, due to worsening health conditions and neighborhood complaints, the circus

crowd would have to move to the North Meadows near the Connecticut River dikes by Friday evening.[62]

All this time, the circus's assets in Connecticut—railroad cars,
animals, auxiliary tents and poles, and other equipment valued at
$500,000—had lain idle. On July 13 Rogin met with Ringling
lawyers to negotiate an agreement to permit the circus to leave Hartford so that it could make use of its earning power and begin to pay
reparations to the claimants.[63] But that could not happen unless the
circus were allowed to substitute cash for the attached assets. (Also
present was an attorney representing the state of Florida because
John Ringling had bequeathed an interest in the circus to Florida.)

The negotiations continued into Friday, July 14. By the afternoon, the parties had agreed that the circus would surrender
$375,000 cash toward payment of claims, and an additional $5,000
for the receiver's expenses. The circus could also assign two fire insurance policies worth $125,000 to the receiver in exchange for a
release of its assets. By this time the insurance commissioner had
confirmed that the circus held a $500,000 indemnity policy with
Lloyds of London, the giant insurance concern, and that Lloyds was
prepared to pay any properly submitted claims. The circus agreed to
set aside all proceeds from this indemnity policy for claimants. The
final touches on the draft agreement were made by Arthur Weinstein,
from the claimants' group, and Cyril Coleman and Harold Mitchell,
the circus's local counsel and Washington, D.C., attorney, respec-
tively. The lawyers then traveled to Willimantic to meet with Judge
King and submit the agreement to the court.[64]

The hearing in Judge King's court began late Friday afternoon,
July 14 and ended about 6:00 P.M. with King signing an order
approving the agreement. King praised the bar association for a
"splendid piece of work" and called the agreement "the best possible
solution of a very difficult problem."[65] Once the agreement was signed
and the order to vacate issued, activity picked up quickly at the sites
where the circus was quartered. The *Courant* reported that immediately after 7:30 P.M., "the portable power plants which furnish elec-
tricity for the lighting at the grounds hummed as circus bosses
shouted orders to crews that were assembling the many wagons for
the short haul to the Pleasant Street siding."[66] At about 8:00 P.M.,

the *New Haven Register* reported, "A big black sedan pulled up with Florida markers on it. [Chief canvas man] Aylesworth stepped down from the big black car, and quickly word flashed through the yard."[67] The circus was leaving.

At 9:00 P.M. Friday, Rogin and the Ringling attorneys visited the Barbour Street lot with Dr. Burgdorf and Police Commissioner Hickey. Hickey had to determine what equipment and personnel would have to stay in Hartford to assist in the continuing criminal investigation and coroner's inquest. Most of the loading was completed by 11:00 P.M. and the final cleanup by 3:00 A.M. New Haven Railroad officials scheduled the train pullout for early Saturday morning.[68]

Despite the creation of the receivership, the attachments remained in force even though their actual legal effect was uncertain. Two new attachments were made that day as part of suits brought on behalf of deceased mothers and their young sons.[69] Eventually, Rogin certainly could have convinced the superior court to strike down these new attachments as null and void. He was concerned, however, that an attaching claimant would try to halt the pullout before the court could act. Therefore, he designated Schatz's favorite deputy sheriff, Sam Rosen, as his representative and escort to the circus cars until they were safely into New York State. Before the train left town, circus officials gave Rogin three checks totalling $380,000, the agreed payment for release of the attachments. (Some of the money was later put in government bonds.) Rogin conferred on that Saturday and in the following weeks with Judge King; Cyril Coleman, representing the circus; and various attorneys, regarding the plan for payment of outstanding claims.

Sheriff Rosen stayed with the circus as the crew loaded the elephants, camels, and stubborn donkeys on the cars. At 7:00 A.M., Rogin inspected the seventy-nine cars, and the red-and-yellow circus train began to roll out of Hartford, ten days after the fire. By 8:00 A.M., the last car had departed. Thirty-three persons to be questioned by State's Attorney Alcorn remained behind. Rosen recounted his journey with the circus to New York as "the assignment of a lifetime." He even brought his son, Bernard, aged fifteen, along for the ride. Bernard talked to the clowns, midgets, trapeze artists, and found "the circus folk are just like other people. They were all very sad about the fire and seemed to have suffered deeply for the people of Hartford." One young acrobat, said Bernard, recalled that he had "stayed in the burning tent as long as he could, literally picking people up and throwing them out an opening in the canvas." After the train had passed over the Newburgh Bridge on Saturday afternoon and arrived at the railroad junction of Maybrook, New York, Rosen and his son left the train. They traveled slowly back to Hartford by bus and train, arriving in Hartford about 3:00 A.M. Sunday.[70]

The Greatest Show on Earth was to return to its Sarasota home base, recuperate, take inventory, replace lost equipment—and then move on to the Midwest to perform again. For future performances, Dan Judge recommended that the circus play only at "open stadia," not under the big top:

> [This] was . . . due largely to the fact that when John Reddy [the former circus attorney] went into the Navy he was counsel for War Shows, Incorporated; the Government had a war show that they put around the country, and that gave me the thought that one place the circus could play—because it no longer had a tent, and we didn't think anybody would want to go in a tent, anyhow, after the fire—was to play in open stadiums. And considering everything, we did very well.[71]

The first shows after the fire were given at the Rubber Bowl in Akron, Ohio, on August 4–6, and then in Detroit and Chicago. Then depression set in. As Judge later described it, "We started out under adverse circumstances. We had terrific temperatures of about 104-degrees in Toledo and Akron. We came to Chicago and Jim Haley, as I recall, felt it was hopeless. We were losing money; people weren't coming to the show; we didn't have any advance sales and it didn't look as if the experiment would work; and Carl Loos [the circus's general counsel] sent me a telegram that Haley felt that we should fold it up and send it back to Sarasota."[72]

When Dan Judge got word of this advice, however, he immediately flew to Chicago to convince the board of directors that the show must go on. "[T]hey had to sell their tickets, rain or shine, just like at a football game." Judge's pep talk apparently helped get things moving again, as tentless performances resumed at stadia, fairgrounds, and baseball fields in the Midwest, Texas, and Louisiana. High-wire artist Karl Wallenda, appearing in the "open air" stadia later that summer of 1944, declared, "The awful fire has called up in all of us the spirit of the circus trooper." And Emmet Kelly, the clown, in words that might have come from a circus publicist, proclaimed, "We must forget the fire. We must entertain. In wartime, it's more important than ever. It's going to be great in open air."[73] By year's end, 1944, the circus had turned a corner; it showed a profit of $100,000 instead of a projected loss of $500,000. In addition, "it assured the people of Hartford that this circus had vitality and was able and willing to carry on and pay the claims."[74]

Fred Bradna, long connected with the Ringling front office, recalls how the circus first played again under the big top canvas the next year in Washington, D.C.:

> A management conference was called to consider how public confidence might be restored. I suggested that if a great public figure attended, the publicity might do more good than millions of dollars spent advertising the new unburnable canvas. An invitation to be present as guest of the circus was extended to General George C. Marshall. The war had just ended; during the conflict he had attended no public function; he was a great hero. The General not only attended but brought his grandson, Jimmy Winn. And a photograph of the two of them with clown Emmet Kelly appeared in almost every newspaper in the country the next day. There was no further fear among the public.
>
> "If the General thinks it's all right to take his grandson, I guess we can risk it, too," was a refrain we heard over and over again as the season progressed. It is quite possible that the General's action saved trouping under canvas in America.[75]

Although the circus had managed to get back on its feet, despite sagging morale, wobbly management, the loss of equipment, and acute wartime shortages, a still larger task lay ahead: the resolution of hundreds of liability claims.

Chapter 3

ANATOMY OF AN
ARBITRATION

Hartford attorneys would later describe it as a "love fest": the hearing on September 15, 1944, before the Hartford Superior Court, Judge P. B. O'Sullivan presiding, to decide whether the temporary circus receivership should be made permanent. The occasion provided a rare opportunity for mutual admiration and unanimous acclaim about the receivership by all parties—plaintiffs, the bar, the court, and, in more measured terms, the circus. Lucius Robinson, Jr., president of the Hartford County Bar Association, pronounced the events of the previous two months "a compliment to the bar." On behalf of the claimants, two prominent Hartford attorneys, Morton Cole and Arthur E. Howard, praised the receivership as a fair and effective solution to a difficult, tragic problem. Speaking for the circus, Cyril Coleman refused to concede that a receivership was needed but did not object to Rogin's appointment; a receivership would at least create a vehicle for settlement, Coleman believed, and therefore should proceed. [1]

With such broad backing for a permanent receiver, it is not surprising that the court confirmed Rogin's appointment, praising this "splendid program that has been adopted." Judge O'Sullivan gave the victims until July 6, 1945—a year after the fire—to present claims to the receiver.

The next major task for the Bar Disaster Committee, Rogin, and the Ringling attorneys was to draft an arbitration agreement allowing cases to be settled out of court. An agreement of this sort was considered preferable to merely substituting the receiver as defendant and allowing the suits to continue in court (an approach pursued nowadays under Chapter 11 bankruptcy proceedings).[2] Although Rogin and Schatz actively participated in drafting the arbitration agreement, most of the actual writing was done by Arthur Weinstein, Dan Judge, and Cyril Coleman (who Weinstein called a "prince among princes").[3]

The general idea of the agreement was that claims would be adjudicated by arbitrators; after collecting payments from the circus, the receiver would then disperse arbitrated awards to claimants.[4] Before this plan could take effect, however, many serious disagreements had to be settled. The circus did not want any lawsuits directed against its officers, but only against the corporate entity. Nor did it want claimants to win a seat on its board of directors, a demand pressed by many claimants' attorneys. Furthermore, the circus wanted to avoid repetitive lawsuits; claimants wanted the security of some final legal judgment and award. Finally, although the circus was willing to voluntarily pay out large amounts of money, it did not want those sums going to plaintiffs' lawyers first; so a fee schedule was adopted for the payment of attorneys' fees.

After some hard bargaining by the attorneys, Rogin was pleased to announce on November 17, 1944, that three separate drafts had yielded a basic agreement, subject to court approval. The *Courant* reported, "Submission to the arbitration agreement by the claimants is entirely voluntary, Mr. Rogin explained. But indications are that most of those who have retained counsel and filed suit against the circus in the Superior Court here will agree to it rather than face the long delay of a court trial."[5]

A meeting to explain the nineteen-page agreement between the Ringling Bros. and Barnum & Bailey Combined Shows and the claimants was set for November 24, 1944. The agreement began by affirming that there had been a fire during a circus performance, "as a result of which fire many persons were burned and/or injured and/or killed." It described the numerous claims pending against the corporation; the fact that Rogin was now receiver; and that certain funds had been paid over to him by the circus. The agreement also stated that the circus corporation "specifically denies liability" but that "a trial of each claim before the jury would result in many long trials, would consume the time of the Superior Court for a long period of time, and would involve a great deal of costs and expense to the corporation and the claimants, and to the State of Connecticut."[6]

The agreement, though lengthy and complex at times, provided an indispensable blueprint for the eventual resolution of claims. In broad terms, the agreement stipulated that both claimants and the circus would submit to arbitration under Connecticut statutes, and both would waive their right to a jury trial. The only issues to be arbitrated were the "actual receipt" of damage and the "amount of said damage." No arbitrated decisions could be appealed to a court, (except for instances of clerical errors, which could be rectified through a "motion to correct" to the arbitrators) [paragraph 1].[7]

Three arbitrators would settle the claimants' cases—one chosen by the Bar Disaster Committee, a second by the circus, and a third by the chief justice of the Connecticut Supreme Court. The amount of each claimant's award would be determined by a majority vote of the three arbitrators. The arbitrators were authorized to hire investigative assistants as needed, and formal rules of evidence were suspended unless the parties or the arbitrators requested that they apply. Once the arbitrators issued an award or group of awards, the superior court would then certify or reject it.

The arbitration agreement acted as a stay against other actions brought against the corporation or its officers, employees, or agents. Claimants were instead instructed to submit affidavits to the circus's local attorneys, Day Berry & Howard, naming the victims of the fire, the harm suffered, and the degree of damage. The corporation and a claimant had the option of stipulating, or agreeing, to an award and presenting it to the arbitration panel for approval; awards of less than $200 would not require approval. This section of the agreement concluded with a sentence that would later generate great controversy: "No award shall bear interest, except interest at the rate of 4% per annum beginning December 1, 1947" [paragraph 2].

The receiver was specifically ordered to comply with the terms of each agreement, a provision that tied the receiver into the arbitration agreement [paragraph 3]. He would pay out dividends after all claims had been adjudicated [paragraph 4]. In the event of violations of the agreement, one party was given fifteen days to notify the other. Disputes would then be resolved by the arbitrators [paragraph 5].

If the circus voluntarily or involuntarily entered into bankruptcy or failed to turn income over to the receiver, then the agreement would be terminated. In such an event, all bets would be off and "any party . . . shall be free to pursue any and all available remedies at law or equity" [paragraph 6]. On the other hand, once a claimant was paid an award, it released the receiver, the circus corporation, and its agents from any future claims [paragraph 7]. And to ensure that all financial dealings were above board, the agreement called for a series of accountants' reports for use by the receiver and claimants' attorneys. The statute of limitations for filing claims was retained as July 6, 1945, unless the agreement collapsed, in which case claimants would have an additional year to bring suit [paragraph 10].

If the circus were to pay the receiver out of its revenues, some agreement concerning what constituted legitimate circus operating expenses was needed. So in paragraph 8, a formula was adopted to define the circus's "net available income" for each year; any additional money would be paid to the receiver.[8] Under the agreement, the circus tentatively pledged to pay all yearly income above $750,000 to the receiver by each December 31st.

Out of special deference to claimants who had decedents—the "death cases"—the agreement would not take effect until at least 100 of the death case claimants specifically agreed to the arbitration [paragraph 11]. Other paragraphs of the arbitration agreement set forth basic understandings. The receiver's approval would be needed for any sale of assets by the circus corporation. The circus would forward to the receiver the $500,000 it anticipated getting from its Lloyds insurance policy. And the circus agreed to "resist vigorously" any suit brought to any court outside of the agreement [paragraph 12] and could deduct such legal expenses from its permissible net income.

As for the financing of this massive arbitration enterprise, the circus agreed to pay per diem fees for the arbitrators and their staff. The receiver's fees and expenses would be paid "from time to time," as ordered by the superior court [paragraph 14]. It is one of the enduring ironies of the arbitration that one of the seemingly simple provisions—the receiver's fee—of a fairly complicated agreement would later engender a controversy far more bitter than any claimant's case.

For the moment, however, the most critical provision of the agreement was paragraph 11, which required the consent of 100 death case claimants to effectuate the agreement. This became the next order of business. Clearly there were attorneys who did not want the arbitration to proceed, preferring to try the cases in court. To neutralize this predictable resistance, Rogin, the bar committee, circus attorney Coleman, and prominent Hartford attorney Robert Halloran got on their telephones and proceeded to coax and cajole any litigious lawyers to sign on to the agreement. Schatz and Weinstein were responsible for rounding up at least half of the signatures. Their efforts were greatly aided by strong public support for the arbitration as well as the claimants' fears that the court might frown upon any opposition to the plan.[9]

Rogin, who arranged for the claimants' attorneys and the circus to talk things over, later told of his missionary work for the agreement. The lobbying, in essence, consisted of

> talking, . . . arguing, . . . reasoning to different lawyers and pointing out to them the wonderful plan that had been arranged, the solution that had been arranged by everybody's cooperation, and attempting to get their cooperation in carrying out this arbitration agreement. . . .
>
> In my capacity as receiver, having been appointed by the Court, I received any number of telephone calls. I spoke with any number of lawyers who relied on me as receiver for my advice as to them having their clients sign the arbitration agreement.
>
> Of course, I was familiar with the arbitration agreement. It had to be explained to them. There were questions that they would ask me as to its import, as to its purport, as to certain specific clauses in the contract in the agreement, how it affected them. They asked my opinion as a lawyer how the arbitration agreement affected them. Lastly they would ask my advice as to whether or not they or their clients should sign.[10]

In the end, Rogin and the other architects of the arbitration obtained the requisite 100 "death case" signatures and 451 additional signatures from both death claimants and injury claimants. Each claimant signed a separate settlement agreement on a separate document. With the approvals in hand, the arbitration hearings began in late February 1945.[11]

In keeping with the agreement, three arbitrators were chosen. The bar selected Judge Abraham S. Bordon, then serving on the Common Pleas Court, who was widely recognized as a friend of the plaintiffs. Bordon had been one of Hartford's most prominent attorneys before coming to the bench and was responsible for giving many attorneys their start, including Abe Ribicoff, the future United States senator. In the 1950s Bordon was a judge for the superior court and, briefly, a state supreme court justice. After his retirement in 1961 he acted as a referee and settled countless cases. He proudly called himself "the settling judge."[12]

The circus, on Coleman's recommendation, chose Daniel Campion, a West Hartford resident, graduate of Syracuse Law School and head of the Aetna claims department since 1926. Campion, active in West Hartford civic affairs, was also a town judge. He was well liked by the bar and considered fair and reasonable.[13] For his part, Chief Justice Maltbie designated a distant relative of Raymond Baldwin's as the presiding arbitrator—Alfred C. Baldwin, seventy-three and a resident of Derby, Connecticut. At the time, Baldwin was a state referee who had served seventeen years, until 1942, as a judge for the superior court.[14] As it happened, the panel represented a wide spectrum of views: Bordon, originally a trial lawyer, was a Democrat and Russian-born Jew who had been raised in New Britain. Campion was defense-oriented, a Catholic, and a West Hartford resident. Baldwin, a Protestant Republican, was an outsider to the Hartford bar.

The fire had produced 551 cases requiring hearings. (In addition to 35 claims that were disallowed, 112 cases were settled by the circus without arbitration because their claims were for less than $200.)[15] The first case, in many ways typical, was that of the estate of a twenty-nine-year-old inspector at Pratt and Whitney. His attorney, Joseph Cooney, urged the three-man arbitration board to take into account the deceased's age, health, income, savings, and "initiative" in arriving at its award. Coleman, who represented the circus at the hearings along with Dan Judge, responded, "We are not trying to beat down any claimant. What we want is overall justice to all the claimants." The board awarded the inspector's widow the maximum then allowed under the wrongful death statute —$15,000.[16]

After a while, the cases began to fall into categories. Among injury cases, there were burns of a certain degree, scars, and injuries. Claimants filled out affidavits with information such as the age of the victim, injuries, prior health, and earnings, and if and how the injuries were related to the fire. Medical reports and pictures, if available, were requested. This material was sent to Coleman at Day Berry & Howard and to the arbitration board. The board would arrive at an award sum, and then add on any special expenses. As time went on, this procedure became routine and the arbitration became, in Weinstein's words, a "rubber stamp."[17]

Yet this procedure was not without its poignant moments. As *Hartford Times* reporter John Cleary wrote, "When the arbitration board awarded $100,000 to a young man whose face was badly scarred, a board member remarked to him, 'You're lucky to have $100,000 at the age of 19.' 'Lucky?' the young man said, 'Judge, look at my face. Do you think any girl will ever look at me without shuddering?'"[18] Examples of other awards included a middle-aged man who received $2,000 for burns to his face and loss of clothing in the escape. A woman who escaped with her two children and was burned on parts of her body received $2,500. An injured child received $2,800. There were also other large injury awards, including one of $100,000 to a professional dancer who was burned about her body, and an award of $90,000 to a young girl who spent more time in the hospital than any other victim. There were also a few awards in the $40,000 range.[19]

The death cases were in a different but not more complicated category. Again, claimants were asked to submit affidavits with such information as date of birth, the role of the fire in causing death, and the deceased's education, number of children, occupation, health, and current size of estate, for probate purposes. The more elaborate elements of damage used today (such as tax consequences) were not a concern then. Indeed, the chief criteria in determining the size of an award were the claimant's earning capacity and the size of his or her estate.[20]

In evaluating the value of a woman's life, the panel took into account "matters of education and social responsibility, such as her assistance to her husband in business." For the wrongful death of a child between three and seven, an award of $6,500 was typical. The estate of an elderly man in excellent physical condition received $8,500. A younger middle-aged man's estate received $12,000. A deceased child's estate received $6,000 and his mother's estate $13,000.[21]

Rogin, consistent with his duty as an officer of the court, attended a few of the arbitration hearings and kept a file for each claimant that included the arbitration award. Rogin would typically notify each claimant's attorney of the arbitrators' decisions, as in this letter regarding *Mary Hindle v. Ringling Brothers*: "In the above entitled case the award rendered by the arbitrators for the claimant in the amount of $25,000, having been reduced to judgment, is by virtue of the arbitration agreement allowed in the receivership matter. When dividends are declared by the Court, you will receive your dividend from time to time."[22]

The bar committee served as a watchdog for the proceedings, hosting several bar meetings to keep attorneys up to date on the arbitration. The committee also appointed auditors—Haskin and Sells—as required by the agreement. Of course, each member of the bar committee had his own cases before the arbitrators, an arrangement that would raise ethical questions by today's standards.[23]

At a time when minimum fee schedules for attorneys were routine and respectable (indeed, fixed fees were considered an ethical protection against "ambulance chasers") the bar in this case took the unusual tack of limiting its fees. Attorneys accepted 10 percent of awards in death cases, 15 percent of the first $5,000 in injury cases, 10 percent of the next $15,000 in injury cases, and no fees on awards larger than $20,000.[24]

The arbitration hearings, which lasted until March 1946, resulted in the assignment of $3,946,355.70 in awards to 551 claimants, making the average award $7,162.16.[25] As required by the terms of arbitration, the awards were then converted into formal superior court judgments. The entire process had taken slightly more than a year. Arduous as it had been, arbitrating the tort claims proved to be far less taxing than the job Edward Rogin had stepped into— reviving the beleaguered circus.

Chapter 4

THE FIGHT
FOR CONTROL
OF BIG BERTHA

As receiver of the Greatest Show on Earth, Edward Rogin did not have an enviable job. Somehow he had to ensure that the circus would increase its assets during his watch so that claimants could be paid. At the same time he had to steer the circus away from bankruptcy, stabilize its management, and ensure that performances around the country continued. If the show must go on, as entertainment folklore required, it would depend less on the performers' grit-and-by-golly than on Edward Rogin's financial acumen, diplomatic savvy, and raw determination to make the circus meet its obligations.

According to Cornelius Shea, the attorney who shared office space with Rogin, Rogin was obsessed with his mission of ensuring that all claimants be paid in full.[1] Rogin, it will be recalled, had graciously offered to serve as receiver for free until every last claimant was paid in full. He would soon learn the heavy price he would pay for his noble generosity: constant surveillance of circus management, finances, and litigation unrelated to the fire; previews of the new seasons' shows; and troubleshooting while the circus's top managers were imprisoned (as discussed below). Demanding as these many burdens were, Rogin's most urgent, difficult challenge would be keeping the company afloat while three warring factions of the Ringling family squabbled for control of the circus.

From the start, Rogin faced a grueling schedule and complex array of obligations. He attended meetings of the circus board of directors in New York City. He drove to Albany, where the circus was performing in July 1945, to prevent a disruptive management dispute between President Robert Ringling and Vice President James Haley. He traveled to Sarasota to ensure that the new shows were being adequately readied and costumed. He carefully reviewed the circus finances, scrutinizing weekly earnings reports and annual reports. He appeared before the superior court and probate court in Hartford to give periodic reports on the receivership's progress.[2]

Mindful of the fire victims' interests, Rogin was meticulous in monitoring how the circus used its limited resources. At one of its first meetings after the fire, for example, the board of directors decided to pay substantial legal fees to the circus's attorneys—$57,750 to Judge, $17,500 to Hadden, and $22,000 to others. Incensed that the circus attorneys should receive such liberal compensation before any of the claimants had been paid, Rogin and Schatz demanded that the fees be returned; eventually most of the fees were returned.[3]

From legal quandaries to tax problems to business negotiations, Rogin worked side by side with circus officials to keep the show rolling. In order to reduce the circus's tax burden, Rogin worked with Karl Loos, general counsel for the circus in Washington, D.C., to obtain large tax rebates from the Internal Revenue Service, citing the circus's loss of earnings due to the fire.[4] To help cut costs, Rogin urged the circus to enter into a long-term lease with Madison Square Garden, its opening venue each season. (James Haley nixed the idea because it limited the circus's flexibility but he nonetheless agreed to pay the difference in rents to the receivership.)[5]

After the war, the federal government approached the circus to sell it surplus railroad cars. Once again Rogin was called in to help work out the best financial arrangement for the purchase—$15,000 apiece for twenty-five steel, air-conditioned cars.[6] When the Hollywood mogul Cecil B. DeMille wanted to buy the movie rights to "The Greatest Show on Earth" for a film, Rogin negotiated the $75,000 fee for the circus.[7]

As receiver, Rogin also had to sort through a welter of technical and administrative matters to reestablish the circus's financial health. For example, it turned out that the circus's fire insurance policy required the circus to itemize its losses and depreciate the value of each piece of equipment. Thus, this policy did not yield the full $125,000 originally claimed by circus officials, but only $68,392. So the circus had to come up with the difference, some $56,608, and credit the payment towards the $750,000 payment due to the claimants' pool in 1945.[8]

Collecting its insurance money from Lloyds ended up being particularly complicated because the policy was an indemnity policy, which meant that the circus had to show proof of payment of $500,000 to claimants (by way of the receiver) before Lloyds would pay a matching sum of $500,000 in indemnity coverage. With Rogin's careful gathering of receipts and steady prodding, however, Lloyds eventually made good on its full payment.[9]

In addition to the fire victims' lawsuits, the circus was also beset by other litigation that required constant oversight. Many suits were routine trip-and-fall personal liability cases; other lawsuits were more unusual, such as the suits filed by spectators injured by a tornado that hit the circus tent in Dallas, Texas, in 1945. To assess the seriousness of the cases and how they would affect the circus's ability to pay the receivership, Rogin was called in to review thirty-seven lawsuits pending against the circus.[10]

In the midst of these complicated administrative matters, Rogin had to defend the legitimacy of his receivership on several occasions when challenged by claimants' attorneys. Although the historical details are unclear, Rogin spent considerable time fending off attempts to replace his receivership with a panel of three trustees, with a New York receiver, with a Florida receiver, and with a federal receivership. None of these maneuvers succeeded.[11]

As the arbitration and asset-collection process continued, the circus faithfully plugged along with its scheduled performances. On May 9, 1945, it strutted down the streets of New York City in its first street parade in many years, and at Madison Square Garden it raked in an impressive $7,600 per day.[12] It was a triumphant comeback. "Despite Hartford," a stubborn Robert Ringling told an interviewer, he was "never a quitter and was not going to be one now."[13]

To control costs, the circus itinerary from 1945 to 1947 was limited to the East, Midwest, and South. But in 1948, the troupe ventured once again by rail to the West Coast, performing in Los Angeles, San Francisco, Portland, and Seattle.[14] The end of the war initiated a period of rebuilding and revival, for both the circus and the nation. The American public was as eager as ever for the gaudy spectacle of the circus, which appeared on television for the first time on May 3, 1946.[15] Ringling Brothers even returned to Connecticut in 1948, mounting shows in Bridgeport, Waterbury, Plainville, New London, and New Haven. Hartford, predictably, was not on the schedule; four years after the fire, the wounds were still fresh.

Beneath the surface calm and apparent recovery of the Greatest Show on Earth, however, trouble lurked. One of the more disturbing problems was the criminal sentences that were handed down to six top circus officials. In his radio address of July 15, 1944, Governor Baldwin had pledged that if "any criminal negligence or neglect is involved, everything in the power of the state will be done to bring to justice those who may be responsible."[16] Based upon coroner and police reports, State's Attorney Alcorn proceeded with charges of involuntary manslaughter against James Haley, vice president; George Washington Smith, general manager; Leonard Aylesworth, boss canvas man; Edward Versteeg, chief engineer; William Caley, seat man; and David Blanchfield, chief wagon man.

In answering the charges, the defendants faced a certain dilemma in how to plead. Pleading guilty could hurt the circus's defense against hundreds of pending civil cases. Yet pleading not guilty, in the face of such palpable evidence of responsibility, would have scandalized the Hartford citizenry. In the end, all six ended up throwing themselves on the mercy of the court, pleading no contest.[17]

The coroner, Frank Healy, found that Haley and Smith, in their supervisory capacities, should have known of the dangerous conditions at the main circus tent. Canvas man Aylesworth was judged blameworthy for his inadequate supervision of the canvas waterproofing, distribution of fire equipment, and oversight of the fire watchers, who are supposed to be on the lookout for fire. As it happened, Aylesworth had left the Hartford circus site on the morning of the fire to prepare for the circus's arrival in Springfield, the next scheduled stop. For one reason or another, he had failed to return from Massachusetts before the ill-fated Hartford performance. Chief engineer Versteeg, in charge of distributing fire extinguishers, failed to distribute enough of them and to do so properly. Seat man Caley had failed to keep a lookout for fire. And wagon man Blanchfield had placed the wagons too close to the exits, thereby blocking escape.[18]

Unfortunately for Haley, he had been the most senior circus executive at the scene of the fire, making him the most likely candidate for a long prison term. Trained as an accountant, he had served as general manager of the John Ringling estate from 1933 to 1943, resolving numerous legal and financial problems in John Ringling's tangled $23.5 million estate. From that success, Haley moved on to become vice president of the circus and, in 1943, the second husband of Aubrey Ringling, one of the chief stockholders in the circus.

Judge William Shea, a gregarious Irishman whose politicking and connections had eventually netted him a judgeship, was charged with deciding what prison sentences to impose. Shea had been greatly impressed by the precedent of the Cocoanut Grove nightclub fire three years earlier, in which the culpable business executives were given stiff sentences. Perhaps inspired by that case, Shea on February 21, 1945, sentenced Haley to a minimum of two years in prison and gave lesser jail terms to the others. For its criminal negligence, the circus itself was fined $10,000.[19]

Upon announcement of the sentences, the citizens of Sarasota, hometown of Haley and the Ringlings, exploded. Florida newspapers and politicians loudly condemned the sentences as far too harsh, and letters flowed in to Judge Shea urging him to treat the circus managers with leniency.[20] Besides being appalled at the severity of the punishment, the Ringling family had another, more immediate concern: How would the 1945 season open in April, three months later, if the top circus managers were in jail?

Bowing to the massive protests and the legitimate concerns of the Ringlings, Judge Shea suspended the sentences for three months — with the approval of Rogin and the bar committee — so that the six convicted men could go to Florida and prepare the show for the upcoming season. State's Attorney Alcorn was more than a little irritated by the protests and political pressures from out-of-staters. He complained that the defendants wanted to have it both ways— extensions of their sentences *and* pleas of no contest.[21]

In April, just before the circus's grand opening in Madison Square Garden, the men returned to Hartford for a second hearing. Their lawyers had already asked the court to allow the men to withdraw their "no contest" pleas, a request granted without controversy. But the more provocative request was that the court suspend all the sentences on the grounds that each man was "indispensable" to the operation of the circus. Although Judge Shea did not suspend the sentences, he did lighten them significantly. Haley, Smith, and Aylesworth received prison sentences of a minimum of one year and one day to five years. Versteeg and Caley received lesser sentences. And Blanchfield, the remorseful wagon man who candidly admitted that he was not indispensable to the circus, was set free. (Blanchfield, significantly, was an old Connecticut resident who had helped the prosecution and reportedly charmed the judge.)

While the top circus managers were in jail, the board of directors and Rogin gave special scrutiny to the circus's operations. They were worried that the absence of key supervisors could result in mishaps on the road. And indeed, there were a few unfortunate incidents which, as it turned out, were more quirks of fate than the result of slipshod supervision. An aerialist fell to her death during a perfor- mance on May 9, 1945, at Madison Square Garden. The Dallas tornado that triggered several lawsuits by spectators also injured the acting general manager, Ed Kelly, and the equestrian director. To ensure that the substitute circus management could do what was necessary, Rogin consulted throughout this period with Robert Ringling and his mother Edith, a key stockholder. He also visited Haley at the Enfield prison farm to solicit his judgments on circus operations and financial decisions.[22]

Attorney Rogin, with no experience as a corporate manager, showed himself to be savvy and skillful in running America's premier circus. He dealt with both the everyday problems and unusual difficulties that might be expected to crop up in the course of transporting a troupe of 1,400 employees and 900 animals to 150 communities—

18,000 miles—over an eight-month season.[23] None of the normal challenges of managing a circus, however, would prove as difficult or serious as the "Ringing Wrangling," as *Fortune* wryly dubbed the problem. "The Ringling Brothers and Barnum & Bailey Combined Shows Inc. is a family shuttlecock entirely controlled by three incompatible sets of heirs who vote almost equal blocks of stock," noted *Fortune* in 1947.[24] Family fighting was almost a Ringling tradition, according to Dan Judge, who said that various segments of the Ringling family had "been fighting since they established the circus."[25]

The most recent round of bickering dated from the death in 1936 of John Ringling, the last of the seven Ringling brothers. (The brothers had one sister, Ida Ringling North.) John Ringling was a grand showman in the old tradition, a man who lived a life befitting a circus king—boisterous, sybaritic, ostentatious, reckless. When he died, childless, he left a 31.5 percent interest in the circus to his sister-in-law Edith Ringling and her son Robert Ringling. He also left an identical interest to his nephew Richard, son of his brother Alf T., whose voting interest passed to Richard's wife Aubrey when Richard died.[26]

Because of a family squabble with his sister Ida Ringling North and her son John Ringling North, John Ringling disinherited them both in a codicil to his will. But he had carelessly left them as executors of his will, allowing Ida and John North to reap substantial executors' fees. More critically, they became trustees of the circus stock left by John Ringling to the state of Florida and thereby acquired the right to vote 37 percent of the circus stock.[27]

The disposition of John Ringling's estate set the stage for a vicious, ongoing internecine battle that threatened to cripple the circus. Because there was no longer a circus veteran with the stature of one of the founding brothers and because the division of circus stock was almost an even three-way split, control of the circus was destined to devolve to the stockholder who could muster the greatest guile and daring in gaining a majority. Would it be Aubrey Ringling (later Aubrey Haley), the thin-faced, bespectacled widow of John Ringling's nephew Richard? Would it be Edith Ringling, the stout, implacable matriarch who was eager to use her influence to propel her son Robert to prominence in the circus, even though, as an operatic baritone, he was a dubious choice for the job by training and temperament? Or would it be John Ringling North, a born impresario who had flair, ambition, showmanship and, for good measure, a dollop of Yale education? (North matriculated at Yale in 1922 with the class of '26 but left college after two years.) As the circus receiver, Eddie Rogin was naturally interested in staying on top of the volatile feuding and in ensuring some degree of family harmony, at least until the fire victims were paid their just compensation.

If John Ringling's death inadvertently enriched the Norths and gave them a voting interest in the circus management, it also passed along enormous legal complications and a circus burdened by more than $1 million in debt. Yet as a shrewd and enterprising man, John Ringling North knew how to make the most of his fragmentary advantages. Through a complicated and clever financial restructuring, in which the circus borrowed money to pay off the debt held by John Ringling's estate, North managed to win voting control of the circus for himself in 1937.[28]

One key provision of the deal was a "voting trust" arrangement that entitled North to name three of the circus's seven directors. Three other directors were to be named jointly by Edith Ringling and Aubrey Ringling. The seventh and controlling director would be a representative of Manufacturers Trust of New York, which had put up the money for the restructuring. With the backing of W. P. Dunn, Jr., a vice president at Manufacturers Trust, North suddenly achieved his dream of presiding over Big Bertha.[29]

North wielded his newfound power with panache. After reorganizing the outstanding debt to John Ringling's estate, North upgraded the circus shows and brought in stylish new razzle-dazzle. In 1943, for example, he had two famous designers, John Murray Anderson and Norman Bel Geddes, modernize the circus's staging and decor. The composer Stravinsky was hired to compose an elephant ballet, and choreographer Balanchine blocked the dance.[30] To add the utmost touch of class to the spectacle, North had Peter Arno, the famous New Yorker cartoonist, draw cartoons for the programs. In his quest for a memorable show, North even went so far as to acquire two huge gorillas, Mr. and Mrs. Gargantua, paint their toenails, and exhibit them in a $25,000 air-conditioned cage.[31]

These changes did not sit well with Edith Ringling and Aubrey Ringling, the two chief shareholders. The women also objected to North's flamboyant, abrasive style and to his sense of superiority for having financially rescued the circus. As the women soon discovered, however, North's power over the circus had one significant vulnerability. The voting trust agreement that gave him control over three seats on the board of directors would expire when the circus's indebtedness to the estate of John Ringling was paid off—in 1943.

Anticipating this event and determined to oust North, Edith Ringling and Aubrey Ringling entered into a pact in 1941 that came to be known as the Ladies' Agreement. The two women agreed to vote their combined 63 percent interest in circus stock as a block for the next ten years. If they ever disagreed on circus matters, their attorney, Karl D. Loos, would arbitrate and decide how the stock would be voted. And if either lady wished to sell their circus stock, the other would have the first option to buy it.[32]

At a fateful January 1943 board meeting, the two ladies had a stormy showdown with North. Because of wartime travel restrictions and manpower shortages, North had wanted to close the circus that year and keep it at its Sarasota home base—a tactic that, not coincidentally, would help North stall Edith's efforts to promote her son, Robert, as president. But the ladies were determined that the show must go on, and with the surprise support of the seventh board member, banker Dunn, they prevailed over North.[33]

A few months later, North's voting trust arrangement expired, and the ladies were able to consolidate their victory by electing five of the seven members of the board of directors. Edith's son, Robert, was installed as the new president of the circus, and North lost control of his empire. As John North's brother, Henry Ringling North, sourly noted in his memoirs, "Thus the management of The Greatest Show on Earth was entrusted to Robert, who had made his career in opera; a certified public accountant [Haley] who had never ridden a circus train; a banker [Dunn]; and to two matriarchs who actually owned control of it."[34] When the Hartford fire struck some eighteen months later, North considered it a personal vindication.[35]

After being forced out, North lost few opportunities to criticize and carp and sow dissension. At the first meeting of the board of directors after the fire, on July 28, 1944, North tried unsuccessfully to remove Dan Judge from his position as supervisory attorney for all cases arising from the fire. In early 1945, North brought suit against the board of directors, claiming that they should be removed for dereliction of duty, because of their responsibility for the fire.[36] In his fruitless attempt to ground the circus during the 1945 season, North persuaded circus attorney Karl Loos to break ranks with the Ringling ladies. And in one of his more gratuitous and malicious attempts to stir up trouble, North sent his attorney, Leonard Bisco, to a bar meeting at the Hartford County Courthouse to urge the claimants not to sign the arbitration agreement. Arguing that the claimants would not be sufficiently protected under the agreement, Bisco created some modest resistance to the arbitration plan.[37]

At Judge Shea's sentencing hearing in April 1945, North's meddling took a particularly nasty turn. Stung by his recent ouster as president, North was only too happy to respond to his subpoena and testify that *none* of the convicted men was indispensable to the circus. He also took the opportunity to declare his utter lack of confidence in the management, a conviction amply underscored by his civil suit against the circus management.[38]

Meanwhile, Robert Ringling's testimony at the sentencing hearing inflamed the situation further and sowed new seeds of enmity that would have fateful consequences for future control of the circus. He told Judge Shea that managing the circus "would not be impossible but would be desperately jeopardized" without the six convicted executives.[39] James Haley, the man facing the most severe prison sentence, eagerly anticipated that Robert would help persuade Judge Shea to suspend or greatly reduce his sentence. But Robert, who was spared criminal prosecution largely because he had had the good luck to be sitting in a Manhattan dentist's chair the day of the fire, damned Haley with faint praise and simply said, "He [Haley] was a great help to me." During Haley's one-year prison sentence in Enfield, Robert Ringling did not write or visit him once.[40]

Although North did not testify in Haley's favor, he later saw a shrewd opportunity for himself if he could succeed in turning Haley against Robert Ringling. Haley, now a convicted felon and fall guy, spent his days in prison bitter and brooding, refusing to see some of his closest friends and associates. North made a special effort to visit him several times during his imprisonment. At one point North made a crafty offer to install Haley as president of the circus after his release in 1946, if Haley would agree that North could subsequently be president. North clearly had his eye on the stock held by Aubrey Ringling Haley, Haley's wife, whose votes could shift the balance of power back to North. For his part, James Haley yearned to rehabilitate his reputation after the fire and his imprisonment; a year-long stint as president, even if in name only, could give him a more honorable way to leave the circus.

At an April 1946 board meeting, North's ingenious scheme was put into effect. With Aubrey Haley's votes, North and Haley prevailed over Robert and Edith Ringling. Even in his moment of triumph, North could not resist a dramatic and malicious put-down of his rival. "When Robert appeared at the next show after the directors' meeting to direct the circus," according to one account of North's coup, "he [Robert] found that his seat had been replaced by a tub from the elephant act, and was asked to leave."[41]

Unfortunately for North and Haley, their collusion was illegal under the Ladies' Agreement of 1941 signed by Edith Ringling and Aubrey Haley, which had been designed to keep North in the minority. Each faction held enough shares to elect two directors, which they used to elect themselves—Edith and Robert Ringling, and Aubrey and James Haley. But to ensure that they jointly held sway over North, the Ladies' Agreement required both factions to vote for the same fifth director, Dunn, or to agree to whatever decision their designated arbitrator, Karl Loos, mandated. But North's scheme could be effectuated only if Aubrey Haley used her stock to vote only for herself and her husband—and *not* for Dunn. On the day of the 1946 board meeting, Aubrey Haley took ill, and James Haley voted his wife's shares in violation of the Ladies' Agreement—for himself and his wife, but not for Dunn. Edith Ringling was furious.[42]

To enforce the 1941 agreement, Edith Ringling brought suit in the Delaware Court of Chancery (the circus was incorporated in Delaware), with Dan Judge as her attorney. In late 1946, the court, in a decision written by Vice Chancellor Seitz, ruled in Edith's favor, holding that the 1941 agreement did not violate public policy and could be specifically enforced to require the shareholders to vote as in the past.[43] The ruling left Robert Ringling as president. Within three weeks North obtained a temporary injunction reversing the judgment and bringing Haley and him to power again; North also appealed the Seitz decision. Then, perhaps reeling under the stress of the litigation, which included North's suit against the circus owners for dereliction of duty, Robert suffered a stroke.[44] In the months ahead, as he struggled to regain control of his health, Robert became less and less interested in the struggle for control of the circus.

The constitutionality of the Ladies' Agreement under Delaware state law was finally decided in May 1947 by the Delaware Supreme Court.[45] It affirmed the basic rule that shareholder agreements *are* permissible. But the court modified the lower court's ruling by refusing to require that Aubrey and James Haley cast their votes for the directors stipulated in the agreement. Instead the court voided the Haleys' vote altogether. Although this left a vacancy on the board of directors, the court declined to rule on what the corporation should do about it.

Meanwhile, the tenuous Haley-North alliance was already beginning to fall apart. After his one-year term as president ended in 1946, Haley decided that he wanted to continue as president beyond the agreed term. At the same time, North found that he no longer needed the Haleys' votes to retain control. In 1947, he won his lawsuit against Robert Ringling for dereliction of duty and was awarded a $5 million judgment. Robert, ailing from his stroke and unwilling to fight North any longer, consented to a compromise. By October 1947, the litigation was dropped, North became president, and Robert assumed the titular roles of executive vice president and chairman of the board.[46] A key factor in the shift of power that gave North the majority interest, Dan Judge later explained, was the Ringlings' insistence upon a strict fiduciary agreement to prevent North from abusing his power at their expense.[47]

In November 1947, recognizing that the Robert Ringling–John

North alliance had beaten them, the Haleys sold out, giving North his long-coveted 51 percent control. Dan Judge and Leonard Bisco, North's attorney, became co-counsels for the circus. Robert, still in poor health, retained his official affiliation with the circus but was not very active. In 1950, Robert died from a second stroke, allowing North to completely consolidate control of the circus. Haley, now a hero-martyr among Sarasota residents, ran for the Florida state legislature in 1948. His popularity was so great that in 1952, he was elected to represent a newly created district in Congress, a seat that he held until 1972.

As a court-appointed receiver seeking profitability not control, Rogin viewed all the "feuding and fussing and fighting" with dismay.[48] Any managerial disruption could lead to a shutdown of the circus and certain bankruptcy. Naturally, Rogin wanted to do all he could to forestall such a scenario. As a friend of both the Ringling and the Haley factions, Rogin often shuttled between parties trying to keep the peace. When James Haley was annoyed with the Ringlings, as often happened, Rogin would try to soothe and mollify him. In a February 6, 1946, letter to Dan Judge describing a recent meeting with Haley, who had just been released from prison, circus treasurer Dunn spoke highly of Rogin's skillful interventions:

> Monday, January 28th, Ed Rogin and I spent about three hours with Jim Haley and he seemed to be in a much better mood and was much more affable than on Saturday. . . . If nothing else it fully came out that you [Judge] have some very good friends in Robert and Edith Ringling, Preston Cavanaugh [an associate of Karl Loos's] and Ed Rogin. Rogin exercised poise, coolness and judgment in an embarrassing situation and did not hesitate to say what a fine job you had done for your clients in keeping it out of Federal receivership. He is a very sound, capable lawyer and we are lucky to have him as a receiver.[49]

Rogin also tried to help the Ringlings respond to North's various maneuvers for control of the circus. As Rogin recalled, Edith Ringling was often "in a frenzy" over North's lawsuits in 1945 and 1946; after meetings of the board, Rogin would talk things over with the Ringlings until 3:00 or 4:00 A.M. if necessary.[50]

Needless to say, Rogin, who could "see what North was attempting to do," was not fond of North. Based upon North's suit against his fellow board-members and his resistance to the arbitration, Rogin later declared, "In my opinion, John North tried to do everything possible to serve his own selfish interests in bankrupting this circus." With North firmly in control after October 1947, Rogin no longer had an easy working relationship with the circus management.[51] Although the receivership had survived the turbulence of the corporate control battles from 1945 to 1947, Rogin's strained relations with North, as the new circus czar, made it more difficult for the receiver to extract the final scheduled payment to the fire victims.

Rogin had sent out the first payment, or "dividend," representing 25 percent of the judgments due, on June 26, 1946. He and his secretary, Miss Mitchell, had laboriously prepared the checks and a receipt of payment, to be signed by each claimant or representative. These receipts were used to document to the Lloyds indemnity officials that the circus had in fact made its own $500,000 payment to qualify for the indemnity coverage.[52]

Rogin prepared the remaining dividends with the help of an accountant, Allan Epstein. Epstein prepared a list for Rogin of the amount due each claimant. The second dividend (37.5 percent) was paid on January 23, 1947; the third payment (10 percent) was made on April 23, 1948. By that date, claimants had been paid 72.5 percent of their awards, or $2,861,107.[53]

On June 24, 1948, Rogin, delighted with the progress of the settlement, sent three copies of the arbitration agreement to Police Commissioner Hickey. In a cover letter, he wrote:

[N]one of the cases were tried but all were settled in accordance with the terms of the Arbitration Agreement by awards of the arbitrators. . . . The only expense to date, as far as the receivership is concerned, has been the cost of mailing checks, printing, and the premium of the bond.

This method of adjusting the public catastrophe, in my opinion, does credit to the Bar. I sincerely believe that it could not be done in many places outside of Hartford County. The cooperation of the claimants, the lawyers and the press made it possible for these poor sufferers to be compensated at least financially to the extent of 72−1/2 percent of their awards.[54]

Rogin then began a final push to secure the remaining 27.5 percent owed to the claimants. In January 1949, the circus paid an additional 5 percent to the receiver, and another 5 percent arrived in December 1949.[55] The final 17.5 percent owed to the receivership, however, was to prove elusive.

By the end of 1949, the circus's two attorneys, Judge and Bisco, had twice approached the bar committee and Rogin with offers to settle the remaining debt for less than its full amount.[56] North was financially squeezed from his acquisition of the circus, and he wanted to run the circus free and clear, without a receiver looking over his shoulder. But Rogin, Butler, and Schatz refused to settle for anything less than 100 percent and warned that they would oppose any proposals to negotiate a lesser payment. Rogin and the circus tried unsuccessfully to arrange a loan for the full amount of the final payment, $690,000, from the Connecticut Mutual Life Insurance Company.[57] But the company apparently did not want to take a risk on the circus and refused to make the loan.

If North was eager to terminate the receivership, Rogin had his own reasons for wanting to wrap things up. In April 1949, Rogin began to suspect a scheme to defraud the receivership. By comparing the circus gate receipts for the week ending April 11, 1948, with the receipts for the same week in 1949, Rogin discovered that the receipts had mysteriously fallen off by a large margin. Over the next few weeks, the same pattern of lower receipts continued. Could it be the weather? Less public interest in the circus? Or were there other, less savory explanations? As usual, Rogin was apprehensive about North's management.[58]

Suspicious of possible embezzlement, Rogin decided to investigate. He proposed to Schatz that the receivership engage Pinkerton's detective agency to look into the matter, and Schatz agreed. Rogin brought the matter up with the bar committee, soliciting their approval, and was finally given the go-ahead in September 1949 to hire Pinkerton investigators to resolve the mystery. The detectives traveled to a number of cities where gate receipts were traditionally strong—San Francisco, Los Angeles, Dallas, Houston—and made a startling discovery. In a report issued in the spring of 1950 with the help of Warren Brown, a certified public accountant from Hartford, Pinkerton's concluded that more people had entered the circus than the circus had in fact reported. Income loss was over $3,000 a day.[59]

Rogin concluded that the evidence warranted charging the North management with incorrectly reporting its daily receipts to the receiver; he suspected that the motive was to understate the economic health of the business to justify reduced payments to the receiver. Whatever the ultimate reason for the discrepancy between customers and gate receipts, this discovery prompted Rogin, the bar committee, and the presiding judge, James Murphy of Hartford Superior Court, to seek a prompt final payment from the circus in order to end the receivership. Using the Pinkerton report as ammunition, Rogin threatened North and his attorneys with a full hearing to investigate the matter and a possible takeover of the circus management. The circus attorneys replied that the report was more suggestive of theft at the box office than mismanagement.

When the circus came to Plainville, Connecticut, in June 1950, Rogin convened a meeting to discuss the final payment and termination of the receivership.[60] Held on the fourth floor of the Hartford County Courthouse, the meeting was attended by the bar committee, Dan Judge, Cyril Coleman, Edward Rogin, and, surprisingly, John Ringling North—a real coup, since North was often in Europe looking for new acts.

Butler set the tone for the meeting by flatly rejecting any discounted settlement. Judge Murphy was "no hick," warned Butler, adding that there might be grounds to find the circus in violation of the arbitration agreement. Sensing a hard sell, Judge and Bisco retreated to a more modest position—that the circus pay the $690,000 owed the claimants *without* the interest due to them on the awards, as specified in paragraph 2 of the arbitration agreement. This interest amounted to $140,000. Rogin relayed this suggestion to Judge Murphy, who seemed encouraged. Thence began a series of further meetings between the bar committee and Judge Murphy, who, like most participants, was eager to close the files on this arduous receivership. In July, Murphy wrote to Butler of the bar committee:

Dear Bob:

I am pleased to have your letter of the 12th concerning the optimistic outlook in the settlement of the circus fire claims. After the judges' meeting yesterday some of us were at Scoler's for lunch and Eddie Rogin told me that the situation looked quite promising. I am hopeful that it will work and will keep my fingers crossed until final word is received. Enjoy your vacation. From the accumulation of files upon my desk I can't see that the outlook at this end is at all promising.

Yours sincerely,

Jim Murphy[61]

After further conferences in Hartford, Bridgeport, and New York, the bar committee made an announcement on August 23, 1950, that a settlement for final payment had been reached that morning: "In order to complete the receivership and secure payment of the claims in full, the Bar Committee induced the circus to arrange to borrow a sufficient amount to pay the principal of such claims in full and will recommend to the claimants that interest accrued should be forgiven. . . . The Committee and the receiver regard the offer as an excellent one and unanimously recommend its acceptance."[62]

Why was it such a good deal to forfeit the $140,000 in interest to which claimants were otherwise entitled? According to the account in the *New York Times*, the bar committee feared that "the unpaid balance of the claims might never be forthcoming unless accepted at the present time. The world situation and the precarious financial status of the circus are factors involved."[63] With a surprising disdain for a substantial amount of money, the attorneys' announcement made light of the forfeiture of $140,000 by noting, "Actually, the amount of interest due to any individual claimant is relatively small." A more plausible explanation may be that everyone was becoming tired of keeping tabs on the wily business antics of John Ringling North.

In any case, the bar committee announced that a meeting would be held on August 31 at 10:00 A.M., at which claimants' attorneys and others could discuss the terms of the offer. Just as every claimant had had to agree to the original arbitration agreement, now every claimant had to agree to the waiver of interest due. Rogin rallied to the task and sent each claimant's attorney a "satisfaction of judgment" paper, to be signed and returned to him. The documents were to be held in escrow until all 551 were returned.

Remarkably, every claimant returned the agreement except one, who threatened not to sign and almost derailed the final payment. His attorney, Cornelius Shea, recalled that the dissenting claimant, William Derby, had faced "an extremely bad situation." His young daughter had been burned to death in the fire; his other child was badly burned; and his wife suffered terrible burns along the side of her face and around her neck. Their cases had been settled for approximately $100,000.[64]

Shea recalled in 1952 what happened when he sent the satisfactions of judgment papers to Derby. "He was out in Sandusky, Ohio, and I didn't hear from him at first, as I recall it. . . . Then he wanted a copy of the Arbitration Agreement. I sent it to him, and he was an intelligent young man and he was deeply hurt by this fire. At that time, as I remember it, there was an article in *Life* Magazine and John Ringling North about his mode of living, and he resented that."[65]

Shea talked to Derby on the telephone to interpret the legal papers, explain that he was entitled to interest from 1948 on, and that all 551 claimants would have to consent to the circus's offer. Still, Derby was not satisfied, and told Shea that he would wait until he got the interest money to which he was entitled. When Shea informed Judge Murphy of this latest development, Murphy suggested a face-to-face meeting so that he, Murphy, could impress upon Derby the significance of the offer to other claimants and the worrisome implications of the Pinkerton investigation. With a final settlement of the fire claims so close at hand, Murphy was not eager to let a single disgruntled claimant scuttle a deal that had taken weeks to hammer out—a deal that would finally put an end to a tumultuous six-year receivership.

After a two-hour meeting in Murphy's chambers, Shea recalls that Derby said he "would like to sleep it over and think about the thing." It was a difficult decision, Shea conceded, because "his wife, as I say, was horribly injured . . . and it was a bad case on the family." Rogin had waited in the hallway outside the judge's chambers and spent another half hour with Derby until 7:00 P.M. trying to help him see the importance of approving the circus's offer. Derby spent some time thinking about whether to capitulate to a high-living circus magnate whose enterprise had inflicted so much harm on his family. In the end, Derby agreed to go along with the other claimants and sign the satisfaction of judgment papers. The next morning Shea informed Rogin that Derby had given his approval.[66]

Throughout its negotiations to waive the $140,000 in interest due to claimants, the circus claimed that it needed a break due to lack of money. But now, with the satisfactions signed, the circus was prepared to pony up $340,000 in cash from its various bank accounts toward the $690,000 in principal due. (The circus might have extracted even greater concessions had not Rogin been intimately acquainted with the circus's finances—its bank accounts, the sums in each, and the accounts payable and receivable. Because Rogin knew more about the circus's financial status than even Cyril Coleman or Dan Judge, he had immense leverage in negotiating a fair settlement for claimants.)

Even with the satisfaction papers signed, however, the circus faced another problem: Who would loan $350,000 to an enterprise with such a troubled past and questionable finances? Even the circus's long-time bank, Manufacturers Trust Company, declined to loan the money. So did the First National Bank of Boston. In the end, Colonial Trust Company, one of Dan Judge's clients, agreed to lend the necessary $350,000.[67] At long last the circus could resume its fitful march toward financial independence after Rogin's long and vigilant stewardship.

On December 15, 1950, the circus made its final payment to the receivership, bringing the claimants' total receipts to $3,946,355.70. And when Rogin mailed the satisfactions of judgment to Coleman, the circus's local counsel in Hartford, the claimants' case officially came to an end.

For most claimants, receipt of the final payment resolved all outstanding legal issues. But nearly twenty years would pass before the final legal complication was settled. One of the fire victims, Charles Tomalonis, had apparently died without a will or any relatives. He had gone to the circus with the little daughter of a friend, and both had been killed. Although an estate had been created for Tomalonis to hold his arbitration award in escrow, no heirs could be located. In 1969, Judge James H. Kinsella of the Hartford Probate Court declared that in the absence of any legitimate heirs, Tomalonis's estate would revert to the state.[68]

From 1944 to the concluding payment in 1950, not one case had been returned to the superior court. As receiver, Rogin had performed a masterful job at shepherding Big Bertha through countless business decisions, management upheavals, performance preparations, scheduling and logistical problems, and marketing initiatives. He had mounted an energetic campaign of personal diplomacy to quell the family feuding and restore a modicum of stability. From the Pinkerton investigation to the hard bargaining over the final payment, Rogin had stayed on top of the finances, the personalities, the legalities, the deadlines. Amazingly, all of it had been resolved without litigation.

After working so diligently for the claimants' for more than six years, how much should Rogin now be awarded as receiver? The real irony of Rogin's receivership was about to become apparent, for the answer to this question would emerge only through a nasty, protracted process that had been kept at bay for so long: litigation.

Chapter 5

THE RECEIVER'S
JUST REWARDS

For seven years Edward Rogin had performed a daring high-wire legal act worthy of the Wallendas. The Hartford legal community had nervously held its breath, determined to maintain the precarious equilibrium Rogin had achieved. But by 1951, a store of powerful emotions, held in check for so long, could no longer be denied. Vanity, jealousy, greed, petty personal animosities: they all came tumbling forth in a terrible, splenetic rush, as if to compensate for years of saintly restraint and decency.

The awful paradox was that the man who had saved the circus, obtained just compensation for hundreds of fire victims and their families, and burnished the image of the Hartford legal community —all without resort to litigation or compensation for himself—was now in danger of going without reward.

Looking back on the situation five years later, Justice Baldwin told a bar gathering, "In this vast array of possible problems [stemming from the fire] only one issue reached the Supreme Court of Errors [later renamed the Connecticut Supreme Court], the question of the receiver's fees. This issue was not a matter of quibbling but an honest difference of opinion as to what the function of the receiver had really been and what his services were truly worth."[1] Participants to the battle, of course, hardly viewed the issue with such benign neutrality.

As the only dispute surrounding the circus fire to reach the courts, the battle over the receiver's fees is of more than passing interest. In a sense, the litigation was an organic outgrowth of the receivership and arbitration plan itself, as long pent-up passions came spilling forth to seek a resolution through the more customary modalities of dispute resolution: a lawsuit. The result, as we will see, is a somewhat anticlimactic coda and elegiac counterpoint to the triumphant success of the arbitration plan.

The terms of Rogin's receivership had been fairly clear. Under the temporary receivership order and the later permanent order, Rogin was given possession of "all the books, papers, evidences of debt and property of said corporation." He was to "collect all monies owing to [the circus] and to take all lawful steps within his power to secure and preserve its assets."[2] Paragraph 14 of the arbitration agreement directed the circus to pay Rogin all "fees and expenses" stipulated by the court from time to time. But Rogin was an honorable man. Not wishing to appear to exploit the tragedy, he declined to take the customary quarterly fee as he filed each report with the court. He asked, instead, to be awarded his fee only after all claimants had been paid.

By 1951, however, the spirit of cooperation and conciliation that had given rise to the receivership and helped it work was fast dissipating. After making the final payment, John Ringling North immediately stopped submitting business reports to the receiver even though he was under a court order to do so. North also announced that he would vigorously oppose any significant payment of receiver's fees. Rogin had feared that the North management might prove obstinate. As he later testified, "[W]ith the old management, I never anticipated any argument with reference to any fees by the receiver at any time. If I had, I probably would have kept much more accurate and concise records."[3]

As the mood of cooperation waned, Rogin anticipated other quarrels, particularly from the three-member bar committee whose members had grown irritated with Rogin's stunning success and public acclaim. From the start, Robert Butler, the committee's chairman, had been peeved that his early leadership in convening Hartford's personal injury lawyers had been preempted by the Rogin-Schatz-

Weinstein receivership plan. Butler was also unhappy that Rogin sometimes made decisions without the committee's approval. In 1948, for example, Rogin sent out a press release announcing that the circus was probably going to pay a "dividend" to claimants by Christmas. Butler, then counsel to the *Hartford Times*, called the *Times*'s city editor to stop publication of the press release.[4]

Schatz, too, had had a falling out with his old friend and ally, most likely because of professional envy. In the eyes of the public and much of the bar, Rogin was the individual responsible for the receivership. Despite his substantial contributions as counsel for the receivership, Schatz had never won similar public recognition. To claim his due share of credit, Schatz submitted his own fee request to the circus. (It was not necessarily noble self-sacrifice, as in Rogin's case, that caused Schatz's fee to be delayed until the end; it was customary for attorneys to be paid upon the completion of a project.)

In early 1951 Rogin began fee negotiations with North, but he quickly discovered that he was dealing with a tough bargainer with few scruples, little sentimentality, and no decency. In this judgment Rogin was not alone. Mike Burke, the circus manager from 1955–1956, recalled a meeting between North and George Woods, a director of the circus, at which Woods angrily declared, "Johnny, you're just a chiseler." Burke himself had once been stiffed by North when he failed to made good on certain promises about money and circus operations.[5] Given North's flinty disposition and determination not to pay Rogin's fees—or *any* bill he could avoid paying—Rogin was unable to reach an agreement on his fee, even with Weinstein's intervention. The last unhappy, unsuccessful negotiating conference took place on September 20, 1951.[6]

North formally made clear his intention to avoid payment on February 4, 1952, when he asked the superior court to terminate the receivership. The motion pointed out that final payment to claimants had been made ("except for the sum of $105, which for some reason a single claimant has neglected or refused to accept"). North also acknowledged that Rogin had been appointed receiver by the superior court and that he was "now acting as such." Without mentioning the need to pay any receiver's fees, the motion concluded:

5. The receivership no longer serves any useful purpose.

6. The defendant is anxious that the receivership be terminated before the end of the defendant's current fiscal year which terminates on March 31, 1952.[7]

And so the battle over the receiver's fee was joined. Rogin hired Hugh Meade Alcorn, Jr., the state's attorney who had prosecuted the circus managers, as his counsel. (Although father and son shared the same name, Hugh Meade Alcorn, and served sequentially as state's attorney, the elder Alcorn was known as Hugh and the younger as Meade. Rogin's attorney, Meade, was a prominent Republican activist with ties to President Eisenhower, eventually serving as chairman of the Republican National Committee from 1957 to 1959.) For its defense, the circus relied on Cyril Coleman and Dan Judge. Both sides prepared for a bruising legal battle to resolve what had theretofore been one of the biggest voluntary mass tort settlements ever achieved.

In his answer to North's motion, Rogin admitted that the receivership had effectively come to an end but that neither he nor Schatz had been compensated for their work. The heart of Rogin's answer argued: "The receiver has rendered services continuously from the date of his appointment on July 12, 1944, to date, which services occupied the greater portion of the Receiver's time to the exclusion of his private law practice. For said services covering a period of approximately eight years the Receiver has received no compensation and no reimbursement for his personal expenses."[8] Attached to the answer was a lengthy exhibit, prepared by Rogin's secretary, which set forth his activities over the eight-year period. Unfortunately, the summary did not include the time spent on each activity nor any details about what transpired in the meetings listed.

The trial began in June 1952. As fate would have it, Judge John T. Cullinan, described by Weinstein as "tall, gentlemanly and handsome," presided over the case. Cullinan was an able, highly respected jurist who moved freely in the elite circles of Connecticut law and politics. His supervision of the trial was reassuring to the litigants; it promised a fair result. Cullinan, like Rogin, had begun law practice in 1931. He came from Bridgeport and, after graduating from

Yale, worked in his father's law office. He then became a city prosecutor and later an assistant U.S. attorney; in 1941, at the age of
thirty-five, he was appointed to the Common Pleas Court; and Governor Chester Bowles appointed him to the superior court in 1949.
Retaining a behind-the-scenes interest in politics, Cullinan was mentioned in 1952 as a Democratic candidate for governor in 1954—just
as the receivership controversy was surfacing.[9]

When the trial began in June 1952 Rogin was the first witness.
He recounted the history of the receivership and its remarkable result
—payment-in-full for all tort claimants suing a virtually insolvent
business. Rogin also testified that he had received no compensation
even though the circus had benefited substantially from his actions.
Indeed, Rogin pointed out, management had often sought out his
advice. Dunn and Judge had praised him. Even Bisco, North's attorney, had contacted him days after the fire for his advice on whether
to retain Judge as counsel.[10]

To quell some of the smoldering resentments against him, Rogin
praised Schatz for putting together the receivership. He also com-
plimented the bar committee members for their great assistance over
the years. Still, Rogin pointed out that he *was* the receiver, and he
was due a satisfactory fee.

What fee did he demand? Schedule A, attached to his answer,
itemized two thousand hours. There were, however, an additional
three thousand hours of work—preparing dividends, obtaining signatures on the arbitration agreements, answering correspondence
—all of which were not reflected on Schedule A. Rogin's request
originally came to $225,000, but in light of the tragic circum-
stances of the fire, he agreed to settle for $175,000.

Was the amount fair and just? On cross-examination, Cyril Coleman, attorney for the circus, set out to prove that it was not. He
pursued a two-pronged strategy. First, he tried to prove that, as a
matter of law, the receivership had served little or no purpose after
the circus left Hartford on Saturday, July 15, 1944. Second, even if
one conceded the legal validity of the receivership, Coleman argued
that Rogin had not accomplished much as receiver. Seeking to establish that Rogin had played no active role in the circus management, Coleman suggested that Rogin had really been a nonoperative

receiver—an impotent stakeholder who passively represented claimants but held no meaningful authority. Rogin retorted that all he knew was that he had been appointed by the court as receiver.[11]

Coleman proceeded to question the need for many of Rogin's tasks. What purpose was served by stopping at Governor Baldwin's office on the day after being appointed receiver? What need was there to go to Sarasota, Florida? Did it really take so long to review the circus's financial reports? Some of this line of questioning failed because Rogin really had been instrumental to the circus's daily operations. Managing the Ringling circus was (and is) a highly complex enterprise. "It's extremely difficult to make it [the circus] profitable," the executive director of the Hartford Civic Center told the *Courant* in 1987. "It's a science, as far as I'm concerned."

Then there was the matter of Rogin's authority to perform certain functions. What right did Rogin have to invest money received from the circus? What gave him the power to obtain claimants' signatures on the arbitration agreements? To these questions, Rogin replied that he construed his appointment order as a broad mandate authorizing all of his activities; to the extent that his actions had been directly related to ensuring the circus's solvency, they were justified.

But Coleman suggested in his cross-examination that the Pinkerton investigation had been unnecessary to force full payment of the claims. He also questioned the need—and authority—for Rogin's intervention as peacemaker between the "Wrangling Ringlings." Finally, Coleman tried to show that Rogin's income from other legal clients had not especially suffered during his tenure as receiver. Although Rogin had managed to maintain his former income, he replied that his income had not expanded as it otherwise would have. He pointed out, furthermore, that his receivership duties during the first two years had been extremely burdensome and that he had conferred with Schatz and Weinstein virtually every day. The members of the bar committee may have volunteered their services, Rogin added, but they had also received ample compensation from the many claimants they represented on the side.

Alcorn resumed his presentation of Rogin's case by calling five witnesses—Cornelius Shea, Rogin's former associate; Lucius Robinson, Jr., Hartford County bar president in 1944; Joseph Cooney, a member of the bar committee; George Foster, a prominent receiver; and Louis Evans, a bankruptcy lawyer.[12] (Eager to protect his interest in a fee and still resentful of Rogin, Julius Schatz attended the trial. But he could not bring himself to attack his old friend; he never took the stand.)

Not surprisingly, Shea gave strong testimony in support of his old friend Rogin. He described Rogin's extensive involvement with the receivership and emphasized that he had not been a mere "escrowee." Shea continued:

> It was a situation that took a large amount of his time as a practicing lawyer, and I might add that, although there has been a misnomer about this being a stakeholder proposition on the receivership aspect of it, that was because of statutory difficulty in bringing this to a receivership, which Judge King well knows about. It was a real receivership as far as Attorney Rogin was concerned and for these several years, as I say, his time was largely occupied with receivership affairs.[13]

Robinson also praised Rogin and agreed that his fee request was reasonable. In a self-congratulatory vein, Robinson joked that he was glad the receivership had turned out so well, since he, as bar president, had had a hand in it.

In a deft move, Alcorn then called Cooney, a member of the bar committee whose appearance demonstrated that the committee was not united in opposing Rogin. Cooney, a gregarious old friend of Rogin's, testified that his own fee for serving on the bar committee would have been $50,000, had he not agreed to serve for free. Alcorn then called up Foster, the receiver, who cited several other receiverships in Connecticut to illustrate that Rogin's fee request was entirely reasonable.

Some of the most important testimony came from Louis Evans, an experienced New Haven bankruptcy lawyer who described what formal criteria should be used in setting a receiver's fee. Quoting from *Matter of Osofsky*,[14] Evans cited six factors:

1. The time which has fairly and properly to be used in dealing with the case; because this represents the amount of work necessary.
2. The quality of skill which the situation facing the attorney demanded.
3. The skill employed in meeting that situation.

4. The amount involved, because that determines the risk of the client and the commensurate responsibility of the lawyer.

5. The result of the case, because that determines the real benefit to the client.

6. The eminence of the lawyer at the bar, or in the specialty in which he may be practicing.

Applying these principles to the case at hand, Evans concluded that Rogin had duties to enforce payment by the circus, to pay the claimants, and to report to the court. He had put in substantial hours. He had shown business acumen. Further, "this whole situation could have gone into bankruptcy at any moment either as a result of a fight [among the Ringlings] or as a result of the decision on the part of the circus not to operate so that it could eventually pay off all creditors in full, and that situation had to be met with considerable skill and tact."

In light of the amount actually distributed to claimants—nearly $4 million [or about $20 million in 1990 dollars, after adjusting for inflation]—Evans concluded, "I can't conceive of a better result that could have been attained in any receivership than this matter, to have paid off in full all judgment creditors, being the people who were either killed or injured. That is the maximum result that could have been attained."

If the circus had gone into bankruptcy instead, Evans speculated, "It would have been picked up at the auction block for 'x' amount of dollars, certainly less than $4 million, and that limited fund [less legal expenses] would have been available to the claimants" only to the unlikely extent that they would be able to recover anything from the bankruptcy proceeding. Evans also noted that Rogin's gentlemanly delay in seeking payment for himself was a costly sacrifice. Had he taken a fee every quarter, he would have earned considerable interest on his remuneration.

Based on this analysis, Evans found that Rogin's demand for $175,000 was "a very reasonable request." He expanded this assessment with a burst of praise:

I want to say that it was nothing short of a stroke of genius that caused this receivership to be filed by Julius Schatz. And the wisdom of Judge

King, a classmate of mine in both college and law school, was extremely important and is borne out by the results accomplished by this entire proceeding. There is an excellent article in the *Yale Law Journal* of December 1951, and as it points out, this is the second receivership of this in a mass tort. [word(s) missing in original court records]. Any judgment creditors could have knocked out this receivership right at the start.

Evans then proceeded to shoot down Coleman's attempt to portray Rogin as a "mere stakeholder."

I assume he did everything necessary and required of him under the order to ultimately put into the coffers of this receivership the full amount of money to pay the judgments. . . .

[Rogin had] to write letters, to set up the files, to handle conferences in this office, telephone calls, to spend 5,000 hours as he has testified, to live with this type of receivership, as you must. . . . You can't close your file and desk on this receivership at 5 o'clock whether you like it or not. You wake up in the morning and in the night you think of something you may have overlooked or feel you should do, and it is with you most of the time.[15]

The circus receivership was unique and ingenious, Evans reminded the court. Rogin had shown "courage" in telling King he would not take a fee until all claimants were paid in full, because "it has been my experience that one case in one thousand pays off in full in a receivership proceeding." With this stirring testimony to Rogin's integrity and legal savvy, Rogin's case was concluded.

Now it was Coleman's turn to argue John Ringling North's position. One key witness was Dan Judge, who testified about his own role in bringing about the receivership and arbitration agreement. Judge recalled that when the agreement was drafted, he did not expect the receiver to draw a large fee:

I took the position with the [Bar] Committee that I wasn't going to have a big overhead expense for distributing our money. I've had a great deal of experience in reorganizations and with receivers, and I was well aware as to what kind of claims could be made on behalf of receivers. I was assured by Mr. Coleman and I was assured by everyone else that I didn't have anything to worry about, that in fact the State of Connecticut was notorious for the small amounts of fees it handed out to receivers, and that there wouldn't be anything that I would have to worry about in that regard, and that everybody recognized that Mr. Rogin was in effect a disbursing agent.

Still, Judge conceded that Rogin had not been a mere technician:

Well, we went along, we put the agreement together, and in fairness to Mr. Rogin, I felt that in addition to whatever he might get as a disbursing agent, he was cooperative and he did do a number of things which ordinarily we don't think of a receiver doing, like going out and being helpful in getting the claimants to send in their arbitration agreements. [16]

Despite this admission, Judge stressed that Rogin had not been a voice for the claimants; that Schatz, not Rogin, had forced further payments by the circus; and that Rogin had not brought about a peaceful accord among the warring Ringling factions.

This testimony was weakened, however, when Judge admitted on cross-examination that it had been Rogin who pushed extensively to obtain the final payment. Rogin knew the financial situation of the circus well and had advanced settlement discussions by threatening to dig deeper into the revelations of the Pinkerton report. Although Judge's testimony was supposed to minimize Rogin's role, he concluded by admitting that he and Dunn had agreed in 1946 that they were lucky to have Rogin as the receiver.

Coleman's second witness was Reese Harris, Jr., vice president of the Bank and Trust Company in Hartford, Connecticut. Harris testified that a stakeholder-custodian for his bank would receive $5 per hour. For two thousand hours, Rogin would receive only $10,000. Alcorn swiftly challenged the comparison as misleading. Isn't a stakeholder-custodian—essentially a bank clerk—an inappropriate comparison? What does, say, a receiver of rents who goes door-to-door receive? Twenty dollars an hour, Harris replied. Isn't it also true, Alcorn persisted, that a 5 percent fee is not uncommon when serious responsibilities are involved? Harris agreed. Well then, Alcorn concluded, by that reckoning Rogin would be entitled to about $200,000!

Coleman's surprise witness was Robert Butler, chairman of the Bar Disaster Committee, who had decided to break with Rogin and support John Ringling North. It was a stunning, dramatic development. In a June 26, 1952, article, the *Courant* described how "the turmoil which has lain beneath the surface during the eight years of receivership is being revealed." The headline trumpeted: "Circus receivership strife is revealed."

In Butler's view, everything commendable had been accomplished not by Rogin but by the bar committee and Schatz. The committee, not Rogin, had settled the liability insurance hassles. Schatz, not Rogin, had pressured for more rapid payment by the circus. The tax rebates had been obtained by Karl Loos, not Rogin. The Pinkerton investigation Rogin had instigated had nothing to do with obtaining the final payment. Nor had there been any point in Rogin's peacemaking trips to New York and Florida.

According to Butler, Rogin had been told repeatedly that he was not a "conventional receiver," only a "disbursing receiver." Butler recalled seeing some material on the receivership in 1944 or 1945 in the *Courant*. "I called Mr. Rogin and asked him, and he said, yes, he gave it to the press. I asked him by what authority. He said, 'I'm the receiver.' I told him, 'Well, you are the receiver in a sense, but you are merely a stakeholder.' I told him it was intolerable to have that situation, and [dissemination of information] must stop." (Dan Judge had testified to the same effect, that he had told Rogin of the limited nature of the receivership.)

And then there was the circus board meeting in New York City in April 1945, when the receiver's representatives demanded that the circus attorneys return their fees. As Butler recounts the story:

> The conversation was pretty hot, Your Honor, on both sides and I finally arose and stated—and this I think was the only statement that I made, as chairman of the Bar Committee—that the circus authorities might not realize it but they were closer to a receivership of their circus than they had ever been, by this act, and that they were in very grave danger. Mr. Schatz arose and repeated that, and said, "You are on the verge of a receivership and we are going back to Hartford and take steps to have a true receivership of this circus."
>
> I meant a real receivership of the entire circus and not the type of receivership that is involved here, which was the type that I had told Mr. Rogin in this unpleasant telephone conversation he was working under.

Then it was time for cross-examination. What occurred was a titanic duel between the former U.S. Attorney Butler and the former State's Attorney Alcorn. It was a strange and startling spectacle because the two men had known each other for years and had even discussed the criminal cases against the circus executives when Alcorn had been the prosecutor. Now the two men assumed new roles: Butler-the-witness was somewhat cool and formal in his manner; Alcorn-the-interrogator was constantly on the attack.

Alcorn pressed Butler for more details about the fiery board meeting of April 18, 1945. He tried to demonstrate that Rogin had also protested the circus lawyers' fees—and thus was as aggressively involved in overseeing the circus as Butler purported to be. Then Alcorn shrewdly tried to undermine Butler's damaging testimony by pressuring him to question Rogin's integrity as well:

ALCORN: Do you recall [the fight over the attorneys' fees] having happened?

BUTLER: Not in precisely the way it is stated there [in Rogin's notes]. I don't mean to suggest that Mr. Rogin intentionally misstated it.

ALCORN: I wouldn't think you would suggest that. He is a member of the bar and you regard him highly, don't you?

BUTLER: Your Honor, must I . . .

THE COURT: I will allow the question.

BUTLER: Do we have to go into that?

ALCORN: Don't you regard him highly?

BUTLER: In some respects, yes.

ALCORN: Capable lawyer, isn't he?

BUTLER: I think so.

ALCORN: You wouldn't suggest that he would misrepresent in his own records what happened in a conference with you, would you Mr. Butler?

BUTLER: I don't suggest he did willfully, but I think there is always possibility of human errors.

ALCORN: We all make mistakes, and you might make some.

BUTLER: Indeed, I have made many, Mr. Alcorn.

ALCORN: I want to see if you have.

Continuing his counterattack, Alcorn got Butler to admit that he had not known about Rogin's meeting with the Ringlings after the formal board meeting concluded on April 18, nor about the board meeting of May 2, 1945, at which circus finances and management had been discussed. In other words, Alcorn suggested, Butler knew little more about the receiver's actual duties than the formalities and had been ignorant of Rogin's considerable behind-the-scenes involvement. Butler shot back that Rogin's attendance at the May 2 meeting had been gratuitous, because his counsel, Schatz, had been there and could have represented the claimants' interests perfectly well.

Alcorn and Butler sparred, also, over the importance of the Pinkerton investigation. Butler claimed it had not hastened the circus's final payment and that he had been aware of the circus's finances from the beginning of the receivership until the last dollar was paid. But Alcorn subverted Butler's claims of punctiliousness by bringing out that Butler had taken lengthy summer vacations and had missed an important conference on the Pinkerton report held with Judge Murphy in July 1950. The battle continued:

ALCORN: You don't have any objections to having a receiver paid for his services, do you?
BUTLER: No, not at all.
ALCORN: You like to see lawyers pretty well paid for their services?
BUTLER: I like to see them fairly and adequately paid, yes.

Alcorn then asked Butler whether he had ever advocated a federal receivership of the circus, which the Hartford legal community had expected Butler to propose at the meeting he called for Thursday, July 13, 1944. Indeed, Alcorn pressed, had not Butler himself aspired to become the federal receiver? Butler replied, "Oh no, not under any circumstances, Mr. Alcorn." But based on remarks that Butler had made in 1944, most attorneys familiar with the circus fire, even Dan Judge, believed that he had wanted a federal receivership.

When Alcorn presented Butler with Judge Murphy's letter praising Rogin, another testy exchange ensued:

ALCORN: Do you regard Mr. Rogin's part in effecting that compromise [on the circus's final payment] as having been important or unimportant?
BUTLER: Why, certainly, it was important.
ALCORN: As a matter of fact, he played the major role, didn't he,

in bringing that about, very much as Judge Murphy has described
it?

BUTLER: I don't think so. I have never thought so.

ALCORN: You disagree with Judge Murphy?

BUTLER: Yes, for the reason that Judge Murphy did not have all the
facts.

ALCORN: Do you know whether Judge Murphy had all the facts?

BUTLER: From that letter I know that he didn't have all the facts.

ALCORN: You really don't know what Judge Murphy knows about this,
do you?

BUTLER: I had quite a long discussion with Judge Murphy in chambers,
he and I, about the matter.

ALCORN: I understand, but I am asking you if you know everything
that Judge Murphy knows about this receivership.

BUTLER: Of course not.

ALCORN: You really don't know what was in his mind when he wrote
this letter.

BUTLER: No, but I knew if he had had all the facts he certainly wouldn't
have written the letter in that way.

Alcorn questioned Butler about the *Hartford Courant* articles that
Rogin had inspired and forced Butler to admit that Rogin had performed a public service by making news of future payments to the
claimants available. But Butler countered that Rogin had not been
authorized to release that information and that even the court could
not authorize such disclosures.

ALCORN: The gist of the situation is this, isn't it: That you and Mr.
Rogin just didn't get along very well?

BUTLER: That is not correct.

In his final series of questions, Alcorn explored the difference, if
any, between an operating receiver and a nonoperating receiver. What
about the five thousand hours of work logged by Rogin?

ALCORN: You think he should be compensated for those functions or
acts which he did in connection with the receivership which would
be beyond the call of his duty, so to speak?

BUTLER: No, I don't think he should be so compensated.

ALCORN: There is no doubt in your mind, is there, that Mr. Rogin performed the duties of the receiver here as you regard the appointment?

BUTLER: Yes, he did. Among the things he did, he performed the functions of the receiver as I regard it and understood it to be.

ALCORN: But as I understand the questions asked of you and your answers on direct examination, you regarded Mr. Rogin has having done more than he had to do, isn't that right?

BUTLER: Yes.

ALCORN: In other words, he did too good a job, in a sense.

BUTLER: Not at all, Mr. Alcorn.

ALCORN: Well, for what he did do, which was in your view of it proper under his appointment as receiver, you feel he should be compensated reasonably.

BUTLER: Certainly, Mr. Alcorn.

Alcorn concluded his cross-examination by making the point that the bar committee was merely a sedentary watchdog committee and that the real responsibility for overseeing the circus's day-to-day operations and financial health lay with the receiver. On re-cross-examination, Alcorn brought out a devastating admission of conflict-of-interest on Butler's part.[17] It was already known that Butler's firm had handled twenty-two claims against the circus, an act that might raise eyebrows today but was considered acceptable then. But the more damning conflict-of-interest, even by the looser ethical canons of the time, was that Butler had "represented Mr. Haley at the request of Mr. Loos as counsel for the circus, in contacting members of the parole board to obtain for him a parole at the earliest possible moment and if possible before Christmas in 1946." Butler had been paid $1,500 for his services.

Under Alcorn's questioning, Butler admitted that he had held two conferences with Haley and interviewed other circus defendants in prison. Furthermore, Butler had "talked or saw every member [of the parole board]. One or two I talked to on the telephone where it was inconvenient to see them at a particular time and discuss the matter with them on the telephone." The aroma of influence-peddling was clear when Butler conceded to Alcorn, "They [parole board members] knew who I was . . ."

With this revelation, Butler's testimony was completed and the matter of Rogin's fee now lay in the hands of Judge Cullinan. The trial had opened up many bitter animosities that had been repressed during so many precarious, worrisome years. It also provided an ignoble capstone to an otherwise stunning legal achievement. Rogin and his friends hoped that, despite the traumas of the litigation, Judge Cullinan's verdict would yield some shred of justice for a job well done.

On August 27, 1952, Cullinan had concluded his deliberations and rendered his opinion, which began, characteristically, with a dramatic, well-written summary:

> Following Hartford's catastrophic circus fire of July 6, 1944, the fortunes of the circus corporation reached a perilously low point, creating doubt of its ability to rise from its ashes to reestablish itself as a medium of national entertainment. One hundred sixty-nine persons lay dead in morgues; 382 persons lay tortured and suffering with painful, critical and permanent injuries; an additional 112 persons sustained less serious but nonetheless distressing injury; legal actions with attachments aggregating fifteen million dollars appeared to plague circus management; internal factional dissension beset the corporation; several of its officers were under arrest charged with criminal negligence; public confidence in the organization had been shattered; and the corporation's future, viewed from any angle, seemed desperate.[18]

After reciting the history of the receivership, Cullinan noted that "the circus corporation, which has obligated itself to pay the item [Rogin's fee], quarrels violently with the proposed figure, contending that it cannot be substantiated in fact or in law; that it represents a grossly excessive demand; and that the duties of the receiver were largely those of a stakeholder rather than of an active receiver of a going concern."

Turning to the nature of the receivership, Cullinan had little trouble concluding that Rogin held a "true receivership" albeit for a limited purpose. For only two days—until the circus left town— Rogin had had the circus assets in his custody. After Saturday, July 15, 1944, Rogin's chief duties had been asset retrieval and payment of claims and, as an officer of the court, ensuring compliance with the arbitration agreement. "Such accountability involved time, thought, ingenuity, imagination, and effort for which fair and reasonable compensation must be paid."[19]

As the test for payment of a receiver, Cullinan endorsed criteria similar to those set forth by Evans in his testimony. Then, citing a Hartford Superior Court case of *Bassett v. City Bank Trust Co.*, Cullinan wrote:

> There is no rule of thumb by which compensation of a receiver and his counsel may be measured but each case must be controlled by its own circumstances considering such factors as the amount of cash and other assets handled by them, the time and effort they have expended, their ability and effectiveness as officers of the court as indicated by results obtained, the difficulties encountered in conserving and administering the insolvent estate, and the care and fidelity with which the difficulties have been met and surmounted.[20]

In applying this test, Cullinan found that the receivership had demanded a great deal from Rogin in 1944, especially in "navigating in unfamiliar waters" and dealing with "warring factions" of the Ringling management. The years 1945 and 1946 were also busy for Rogin as he "steer[ed] an even course" between the claimants and corporation. But from 1947 to 1952, the receivership duties had been more routine. Rogin had achieved "singular success" in obtaining full payment of the $4 million, said Cullinan, acting with skill, tact, and intelligence. The claim of five thousand hours, however, was overblown, asserted Cullinan. Although finding Rogin sincere, the judge believed that Rogin had become too close to his work to be dispassionate. He had "magnified his worth."[21]

Looking at the matter impartially and in the proper perspective, the figure of two thousand hours had to be allowed, Cullinan agreed. But Cullinan noted that Rogin had suffered no loss of income from his private legal practice from 1944 to 1951; indeed, his income had increased every year. An equitable receiver's fee, Cullinan concluded, was $60,000. In the finding, drafted after the memorandum of decision, Cullinan allocated the receiver's fees year by year, as follows:[22]

1944 (2d half)	$ 8,000
1945	14,300
1946	14,000
1947	5,300
1948	5,600
1949	5,300
1950	5,900
1951	1,100
1952	500

Cullinan concluded by commending the Ringling Brothers Corporation for recognizing its "deep moral obligation" and, by making full monetary reparation, for having met its duty "foursquare."

> This laudable spirit of management has been matched by the dignity and exemplary conduct of the legal profession of Hartford County. What might well have been an unseemly, grasping and sordid approach to a dreadful tragedy has been, on the contrary, an exhibition of lawyers at their professional best, acting with restraint and high-mindedness and with consuming zeal for justice to all concerned. The lawyers of Hartford County have honored their profession. It is a pleasure to pay tribute to them in this public manner.[23]

On the day that Cullinan handed down his ruling, just a few days before Labor Day, Rogin was at the beach. When he heard of the sum that Cullinan had decreed—$60,000—he exploded in rage at the miscarriage of justice. John Ringling North, for his part, could not have been happy with the result either, even though it was nearly one-third less than what Rogin had requested.

The decision was so perplexing and unsatisfactory to both the circus and Rogin that they appealed the ruling to the Supreme Court of Errors. Coleman threw himself into the appeal, writing two briefs and conferring with John Ringling North in Hartford and Florida. He reiterated his contention that Rogin was merely a stakeholder:

> Receivers can be "active," "passive," "liquidating," "foreclosure," "operating," "dry," "statutory," "temporary," "permanent," "limited," "provisional," "special," "general," or of many other types and varieties, depending upon the orders affecting them. . . . Mr. Rogin was clearly

a narrowly limited receiver whose duties were entirely ministerial in nature.[24]

Citing Butler's testimony, Coleman argued that after the circus left Hartford on July 15, Rogin had become a custodian only and should be compensated only as a custodian. Coleman argued, furthermore, that the arbitration agreement specifically vested the bar committee and the arbitrators—not Rogin—with the authority to compel the circus to take certain actions.

Then there was the matter of services that Rogin claimed he had performed. Coleman charged that these were "recklessly exaggerated" and beyond the scope of his assigned duties. If Rogin had spent 850 hours mailing out dividend checks, as he claimed, then he was working 18 hours a day at some points, Coleman scoffed. Rogin should be paid for 500 hours at $20 per hour, said Coleman. Ultimately, it had been the skillful management of the circus, not Rogin's prodding, that had enabled the circus to successfully pay off the its debts and liability claims.

In addition to attacking specific charges that were said to have taken too long, to have been unauthorized, or to have accomplished nothing, Coleman was especially critical of Rogin's role as a peacemaker. "[T]he evidence in the case nowhere proves that any such intervention was necessary or desirable or had any effect on the defendant's performance of the arbitration agreement and ultimate payment to the claimants." Rogin was not a court-appointed "guardian angel."

Alcorn's brief in reply was short and to the point.[25] It declared that Rogin was a receiver in every sense of the word. Although the physical assets may have left Hartford on July 15, 1944, "by the nature of the receivership as extended by the Arbitration Agreement, he had many duties to perform and his compensation is dependent not upon some fancy name with which the defendants might seek to label him, but upon the services, in fact, performed by him."

The Connecticut statute makes no distinction between types of receivers, Alcorn pointed out; it looks only to the work done and the results accomplished. The fact that Rogin did not have full control over the circus does not vitiate his claim, Alcorn asserted. He is not asking to be paid for eight years as chief executive officer. What is important is that the receivership had allowed the circus to avoid an insurmountable crush of litigation and save its business. The case marked a milestone in legal history for which the receiver was justly entitled to a respectable fee.

Alcorn attached two tables to his brief. One gave support for each paragraph of the findings made by Judge Cullinan. The other table was used to show that there were additional facts that should have been found. (Judge Cullinan, for example, had not even mentioned the Pinkerton incident.)

Evans and Foster, the bankruptcy experts, had supported Rogin's claim for $175,000, noted Alcorn; the defense had not produced a single expert to undercut this figure. And banker Reese Harris, Jr., had stated that even a receiver of rents was entitled to 5 percent of the final liability payment, which in this case would amount to nearly $200,000. The $175,000 fee was justified, Alcorn continued, because the "receiver, in fact, devoted an enormous amount of time and ingenuity to his task, undertook a very large degree of responsibility and accomplished an exceptionally fine result." Rogin kept the circus going and made sure that the payments, particularly the final one, were made and not diverted elsewhere. Under all legal tests the full fee was justified.

In his conclusion, Alcorn debunked the circus's claim that Rogin had benefited at the expense of the claimants who, after all, had been paid in full. Alcorn also pointed out that the circus had paid its own attorneys quite handsomely. Now the circus should live up to its agreement to pay a reasonable sum to the receiver, who had saved both the claimants and the corporation from disaster.

Alcorn and Coleman argued the case before the supreme court on January 7, 1954. Two months later, on March 16, the Honorable Raymond Baldwin, associate justice, delivered the court's opinion.[26] It was a strange symmetry for Baldwin to have the final word on a tragic case for which he, as governor, had made so many decisions ten years earlier. He had been at the scene of the fire, directed much of the emergency response, and supervised many activities in the fire's aftermath. Baldwin had gone on to be reelected as governor in November 1944 and moved on to the U.S. Senate in 1946. In April

1949, at about the same time Judge Cullinan was elevated to the superior court, the new Democratic governor, Chester Bowles, made the startling announcement that he would appoint Baldwin, his Republican rival, to the Connecticut Supreme Court. In his political history of Connecticut, *The Legacy*, Joseph Lieberman tells of the surprise that the Bowles appointment caused:

> The state's strongest Republican vote-getter had been eliminated from active politics and Bowles was free to appoint a Democrat to replace him [in the U.S. Senate]. For [party chairman] John Bailey it was too good to be true. So good was it in fact that when Bowles told Bailey of the development, he did not believe it. In Bailey's school of politics, you made your breaks or you took a slight opening and expanded it to your advantage. You were not given major strategic victories without some work. To the Republicans, of course, the move brought pain and no doubt contributed to their ill-temper during most of the rest of the 1949 session.[27]

Baldwin accepted the appointment, according to his friend Curtis Johnson, because he felt ineffectual in Washington as a liberal Republican. Despite his aspirations for a greater leadership role and a presidential nomination, his party had passed him by. On a personal level, Baldwin's wife was unhappy in Washington and wanted to return home. He also needed to support three sons, all of college age, for which the income of a justice would go much farther than that of a senator. Even if the Republicans considered Baldwin a traitor for relinquishing his preeminent elective post, how could they oppose the appointment? The former governor had been the most successful and popular Republican of the past fifty years. So Baldwin took his seat and eventually became chief justice, retiring at the age of seventy to become a state referee.[28]

In reviewing the appeal of Judge Cullinan's ruling, Baldwin brought his broad range of personal involvement, political knowledge, and judicial wisdom to the case. He began his opinion by noting the "black prospect" facing the claimants following the fire. Yet the ultimate resolution had been as happy and successful as could possibly be imagined—"one of the finest examples of effective cooperation between lawyers, litigants and the trial courts in attaining justice that has come to our notice from the legal annals of this or any other state," he declared.[29] But the question here, Baldwin hastened to note, was whether the trial court award to the receiver was appropriate. Baldwin began his answer by describing Rogin's varied activities as receiver—a list that reflected somewhat more favorably on Rogin than the similar list drawn up by Cullinan.

The court ruled that the arbitration agreement did not supersede the receivership but was instead a supplemental authority. This decision was a point in Rogin's favor, a point that had been hotly contested by Coleman and North. Then Baldwin enumerated the receiver's other accomplishments: settlement of fire insurance proceeds, settlement of the Lloyds of London claim, and the securing of tax rebates to offset the circus's losses. Baldwin also credited the receiver for being "instrumental in preventing [the] conflict" between the directors of the circus from interfering with the circus's performances. Again, Coleman had fought this conclusion and lost.

Baldwin noted how the receiver had conferred with attorneys, distributed dividends, and set up files, sometimes working late into the night and on weekends. He specifically mentioned the Pinkerton investigation. This too exceeded Cullinan's findings and Coleman's contentions and boosted Rogin's hopes for a reversal. In his brief, Coleman had whittled down the two thousand hours that the trial court had found appropriate. Now Baldwin, even though he had enumerated many more receiver's responsibilities than Judge Cullinan had mentioned, reaffirmed the two-thousand-hour figure as appropriate.

In light of his diverse responsibilities, the court held that Rogin's had been a "true, though a limited receivership." He had not been just a stakeholder. Although Rogin had had the help of various people, he remained the court's agent. Much depended on him. He had used "industry, integrity, skill and tact" in carrying out his duties. Both court and counsel for the circus had recognized his contributions.

Having said all this, Baldwin was unwilling to raise or lower the $60,000 award made by Judge Cullinan. The amount was a "question of fact," a determination properly made by the trial judge and one that the supreme court had no jurisprudential basis for overturning. Given his generous rendition of Rogin's achievements, Baldwin probably believed that Cullinan's award had been too paltry. But as a matter of law, the trial court's finding of fact could not be swept aside on appeal; Baldwin had no choice but to affirm it.[30]

The final matter to be resolved was the fee due Julius Schatz for his services as counsel to the receiver. In light of Baldwin's decision, there was little point in an extended battle between Schatz and the circus. In any event, as a secondary issue, Schatz had not had as many conflicts with North as Rogin had.

On June 5, 1954, Judge Cullinan held a conference in Bridgeport to resolve this last bit of business. Attending were Schatz, Weinstein, Coleman, Butler, and Judge's law partners, John Reddy and Robert Thrun. (Having been paid, Rogin had nothing to do with the fee received by his estranged friend.) At the end of the meeting it was announced that the circus, after consulting with North, would consider paying a "reasonable fee" to Schatz to avoid another costly bout of litigation.[31] If no agreement were reached, a full hearing would be held on July 6, 1954, in Hartford—the tenth anniversary of the fire. As it happened, no hearing was necessary. On July 6, the parties agreed, and Judge Cullinan approved, a fee of $100,000 for Schatz.[32]

The outcome of the receiver's fee dispute left a bitter aftertaste. The ultimate denouement was perplexing and disappointing to much of the Hartford bar, even though a certain minority erroneously believed that the attorneys for the circus fire, including Rogin, had made out like bandits.

As a legal matter, the dispute amounts to little more than a blemish—a disappointing conclusion to Rogin's admirable stewardship of the circus during very difficult times. It is ironic that even though the machinations of litigation are meant to be meticulously fair and dispositive, Cullinan's decision cast a cloud over the fee verdict that persists to this day. Rogin's detractors charge that he had been lucky to be named receiver, that he used his position to justify vacations in Florida, and that the reputation he gained as receiver enabled him to obtain lucrative business contracts during his term as receiver. Rogin, for his part, remains bitter about the resolution of the fee dispute, particularly in light of Cullinan's decision, which certainly did not credit his evidence as fully as Justice Baldwin did. Rogin is especially annoyed by the charge that he profited from his position. Dr. Fleisch, a physician who had treated fire victims, recalls attending a party at a country club several years after the receivership terminated at which someone hinted that Rogin had benefited from the assignment. Rogin shot back an icy stare.

Perhaps the messy dispute simply illustrated the limits of sustained cooperation among lawyers. The fire had occurred in a war-weary society with a different mood and temper. By 1952, the tumult of wartime and its awful memories, of which the circus fire had been a part, had receded from the public consciousness. Without such fearsome realities binding the American people—and even contentious lawyers—together, could anyone expect such big-hearted succor and decency to continue indefinitely? In that respect, the disintegration of the novel receivership, borne aloft more by common need and hope than by the letter of the law, was inevitable. And its demise also heralded the elegiac ending to a gentler, more humane era of legal practice and the dawning of a new, more contentious one that continues to hold sway today.

Chapter 6

FIRE SAFETY REFORMS

When the first flickers of flame edged up the side of the big top that hot July afternoon in 1944, a new era in fire safety preparedness dawned in the United States. Public catastrophes have a tendency to focus the attention of government officials and galvanize reforms. The circus fire was no exception. It triggered enactment of stringent fire safety requirements for public functions, establishing a higher threshold of protection that remains largely intact today.

How did state and local authorities come to appreciate the shortcomings that had contributed both to the fire and to the human toll? The first order of business was to try to determine the cause of the blaze. As mentioned in chapter 1, eyewitnesses suggested that a careless smoker had inadvertently ignited the flammable tenting material. Another tantalizing theory pointed to a mentally ill roustabout with a penchant for arson. But neither explanation could be satisfactorily verified, and the precise origin of the fire remains a mystery. Given the confusion resulting from the catastrophe, it is easy to understand why investigators were unable to identify the source of the first flame.

In a sense, the source of the blaze is almost beside the point; the real culprit, as later investigations would show, was the multitude of contributing factors that made the human toll far worse than it needed to be. The carelessness was systematic. Charles Perrow, professor of sociology at Yale University, coined the term *normal acci-*

dents to describe catastrophes caused by the unanticipated interplay of "safe" components in high-risk technologies.[1] Although his analysis of complex technologies is obviously not relevant to the circus fire, the principle of "normal accidents" might be reasonably applied. For here was an unanticipated interplay among many parties —circus management, roustabouts, animal performers, police and fire departments, the city council, and others—whose individual actions, taken in isolation, did not seem particularly dangerous. But when their respective inadequacies came into unanticipated interplay, the resulting catastrophe had all the trappings of inevitability. It was "a disaster waiting to happen."

Most of the 169 fatalities occurred at a tent exit that had been blocked by a four-foot metal chute, which served as a passageway linking the animal cages outside the tent to the performing ring. Hundreds of other casualties were caused by falling, burning canvas; by the toppling of tent poles when guy ropes burned; by the obstruction of loose chairs; by the trampling of a panic-stricken crowd fleeing the tent; and by spectators jumping from heights to places of safety.[2]

Although these sources of harm were fairly self-evident, there were obviously more serious culprits to be identified in the workings of Hartford's fire safety establishment. It fell to an official municipal board of inquiry, appointed eleven days after the fire, to determine what exactly had caused the fire, assess how well it had been handled by city agencies, and issue recommendations to prevent similar disasters in the future.[3] It was not empowered to recommend any civil or criminal penalties.

At the same time, State Police Commissioner Edward Hickey, in his capacity as state fire marshal, issued his own report on the fire.[4] His findings provided evidence for the arrest and prosecution of the circus managers and prompted the State Legislative Council to issue a series of legislative recommendations. The council was a state body composed of senate and house members whose mandate was to propose bipartisan "good government" reforms in state law, a function now served by the Legislative Research Office.

The five members of the Hartford board of inquiry were a diverse, highly respected group consisting of Monsignor William Flynn, chancellor of the diocese of Hartford; George Long, Jr., president of Phoenix Fire Insurance; W. Ross McCain, president of Aetna Fire Insurance; Walter S. Paine, a nationally known safety engineer; and Solomon Elsner, city corporate counsel and first cousin to the owners of the G. Fox department stores, who served as chair. The board quickly began its investigations into the response of city agencies, starting with the Public Building Commission, which had leased the city-owned Barbour Street fairgrounds. Alarming practices came to light immediately. The lease had been drafted by Ringling Brothers, not by the Hartford Corporation Counsel. Not surprisingly, this lease made few demands of the circus. The board of inquiry found that the lease "contains no reservations whatsoever with respect to safety and sanitation. Even the elemental need to clean up the premises after occupancy, with its accompanying deposits of cook-tent refuse and human and animal excreta, was left to a verbal understanding in the expectation, presumably, that fear of reprisal in subsequent years would be a sufficient effective sanction to compel a clean up."[5] Nor did the lease mention insurance coverage; the certificate of coverage, bonding the circus for any liability, was never furnished. Remarkably, the Hartford Corporation Counsel had approved Ringling-drafted leases in 1941 and 1942 when the circus had come to town. Inexplicably, no city review or approval had been made of the 1943 and 1944 leases.

Given the slippery contractual arrangements, it is not surprising that the Public Building Commission had no formal guidelines on its books directing its superintendent how to lease city properties; he was guided only by informal directions "given from time to time as an occasion arose," according to the board of inquiry's report. Perhaps one reason for the commission's casual approach to the lease was a modest emolument: twenty-five to thirty free passes to the circus given to the superintendent.[6]

There was still another reason why the Public Building Commission was more likely to grant unsafe leases of city property. It was authorized to do so without consulting other city departments —police, fire, health, and building—departments that might need to know about nongovernmental uses of city land. Such an interdepartmental review might have alerted city authorities to the inadequate size of the Barbour Street lot for a circus, prompting them to take special crowd control and fire safety precautions.

The board of inquiry next turned its attention to the police department, which had issued the license allowing the circus to operate in the city. Like the leasing process, the granting of the business license, at $150 per day, was a dreary formality given little serious attention. Part of the reason, no doubt, was that the city council had enumerated no specific criteria for granting or refusing licenses. Still, the police chief should have asked the council to specify criteria for the granting of licenses for "public amusements," especially since all other licenses granted by the police had specific criteria. If the license had required a lot of appropriate size for the big top, or if other city agencies had been notified of new licensees, then potential health, safety, and fire risks might have been anticipated. On the other hand, even clear guidelines for licenses probably would not have improved the judgment of a police chief who, like the building commission superintendent, accepted the circus's gift of forty to fifty free passes to the show, which were passed along to favored friends and associates.[7]

The board of inquiry also found that there simply were not enough police officers in the big top. State law required that police be on duty at large gatherings at theaters and auditoriums. Yet here was an outdoor exhibition with a seating capacity larger than any Hartford auditorium and which, furthermore, was "an itinerant enterprise" with no stake in the community. The police chief had detailed thirty-six officers for the first day's performance, and forty-five for the second day. Another ten or eleven controlled traffic at points where circus wagons were unloading and at intervening streets. Yet none of the officers at the circus that day were stationed *inside* the tent except for a few who had wandered in "of their own volition," according to the board of inquiry. And no officers had been assigned to ensure that exit corridors were established and kept clear—a statutory responsibility for police at large *indoor* gatherings. The only police protection within the circus grounds was at the moneywagon and dressing tent—to protect against pickpockets and to safeguard circus property and personnel.[8]

State law required the police chief to determine how much police protection was needed "at places of amusement" and to ensure that the exhibiting corporation paid for the service. In this case, the police chief ignored the law altogether, neither determining how many officers were needed, based on some objective standard such as seating capacity or square footage, nor billing the circus for the police protection. The police chief's inaction did not arise from "deliberate defiance," concluded the board of inquiry, "but rather out of an inertia that we have found characteristic of other relationships between the city and the circus, and which found expression over and over again in variants of the excuse, 'It was always done that way before.'"[9]

As chance had it, when the fire first broke out, four police detectives were at the main entrance to the circus looking for a parolee suspected of being among the circus workers. But even this serendipitous timing was unavailing. "At least two of the four detectives," the board of inquiry found, "reported to their superiors that they saw the fire in its incipient stages but hesitated to give alarm for fear of causing a panic."[10]

Although the police department had failed miserably in its administrative and preventive functions, its response to the catastrophe, the report found, "was in the best traditions of the service and, in many instances, approaching the heroic. The on-duty force devoted hours to the work of rescue and the grimmer tasks incident to such a holocaust. The off-duty squads volunteered in great numbers."[11]

The health department, charged with licensing all food sold at the circus and reviewing the living conditions of performers and animals, also came in for criticism for its poor oversight. The board of inquiry found that the cursory health inspection before the performance had consisted mostly of blindly following the precedents of previous years. Of course, after the fire, the health department was overwhelmed with problems, ranging from the living conditions of circus personnel to disposal of abundant animal waste. The report recommended new regulations to help deal with toilet accommodations for circus patrons and better disposal practices for animal waste.[12]

Another city agency that failed in its oversight responsibilities, said the board of inquiry, was the Building Commission, which was charged with enforcing municipal building and zoning codes. The building supervisor claimed that the zoning laws did not apply to circuses, and thus he was blameless. Yet he conceded that, as a matter of custom, he had assigned a deputy to check the safety of the tent, seating supports, and exit arrangements. The deputy's inspection proved to be of little value, however. Using vague standards that relied on the customary practices of previous years' circuses, the deputy found that everything was fine—even the blocked exits.[13] According to State Police Commissioner Hickey's report, the building inspector had gone to the circus grounds at 11:00 A.M. on July 5, but the big tent had not been set up yet. When he returned at 3:45 P.M., he stayed for only an hour and later reported that he "was satisfied that erection of tent, construction of seats and exits complied as in previous years."[14]

The board of inquiry also found the inspection process entirely too slipshod: "Here again is the picture of a distinct void in the legal prescriptions covering transient hazards, which are neither periodic nor infrequent, as contrasted with the lengthy and meticulous rules laid down for indoor amusement places. Here again we have a situation where responsibility, insofar as it attaches at all, is spread over several departments, without any coordinating medium."

This was one of the most damning findings of the board of inquiry. "Officially the fire department did not know of the presence of the circus in our city," said the local fire marshal. "To my knowledge this department has never been consulted nor informed as to requirements for permit or license."[15]

The truth is, no one at the circus or the fire department gave much thought to the importance of fire preparedness. The only members of the fire department's "fire-prevention bureau" were the deputy chief, a fireman, and a clerk, and occasional off-duty firemen who served without pay. Whether the fire hazards at the circus grounds should be attributed to this light staffing or the department's complacency, many more modest preventive measures could certainly have been taken. For example, at the fairgrounds, there were no telephones, fire alarms, or fire hydrants to deal with an emergency; the closest hydrant was 300 yards down the street. Of nine exits from the big top, one was obstructed by animal wagons and equipment vehicles, another by a fence protecting the victory gardens.[16]

In the main tent, wood shavings were strewn on the ground along with dried grass cut two days earlier. No fire drills had been held; the circus had no fire chief; and none of the employees were trained in fire fighting. There were a few items of equipment: fourteen pails labeled "for fire use only," a few fire extinguishers, and four mobile water trucks. But the extinguishers had not been distributed, and the water trucks had been used to get water to the animals and performers and to hose down the dusty grounds, not to fight fire. Two men in the "Blue Bleachers" had been assigned to watch for fire, but due to the shortage of manpower, they had been detailed away from this task to disassemble the animal chutes. At the cry of fire, they returned to the "Blue Bleachers" where two other employees were dumping three water pails on the fire, with no noticeable effect.[17]

The Hartford fire department's lax attitude toward fire prevention stood in contrast to the practices of neighboring towns, many of whom had been chastened by Boston's terrible Cocoanut Grove fire in 1942. Some safety-conscious cities, such as Bridgeport, had made it a practice to run hose-lines from a fire hydrant to the big top and to inspect the tent, just to be on the safe side. In Waterbury, the city fire marshal inspected the circus before and after each performance and remained at the site with a two-way radio during performances. He also had circus employees hose down the area around the main tent and menagerie after each performance. In Hamden, both police and fire details stood duty during performances.[18]

Hartford authorities, alas, had not considered such precautions. And even if they had, there probably would not have been time to implement them that July 6, given the mad rush to set up the tent in time for the performance. It would be hard to find a more poignant symbol for the lack of fire preparedness than the lone pail of water—still full—found at the spot where the first flames had appeared.

The fire department did have some statutory authority to inspect the circus site and structures for fire hazards. But because there were no specific legal requirements for tents, seating arrangements, exits, fire-fighting equipment, and so forth, the department made no inspections and held no consultations with circus authorities. According to Police Commissioner Hickey's report, "The executive officers of the Hartford Fire Department could not recall or produce any records to indicate that [onsite inspections] had ever been furnished to any circus appearing in the City of Hartford for the past 30 years," despite several serious brush and grass fires at the site over the preceding six years, including two in April 1944.[19]

But even if the fire marshal had inspected the site and tried to stop the show, how would the public or city authorities have greeted such a decision? Not enthusiastically, one might assume. As Mayor William Mortenson later admitted, the public considered the circus "an ancient, glamorous institution . . . a harmless never-never land" and would not have welcomed the spoilsport intrusions of a persnickety city official.[20]

A vigilant fire marshal would probably have encountered similar resistance to any efforts to prohibit smoking at the circus. Smoking was a popular habit in America of the 1940s, a custom considered suave and sophisticated. Even though theaters had "no smoking" rules, would the circus management and the public consent to such a rule at a boisterous outdoor spectacle? And how could the fire department enforce such a rule, in any event, without sufficient personnel? The "smoking culture" of the time made fire prevention that much more difficult. It was considered quite daring for the *Hartford Times* to editorialize in favor of a limit or outright ban on smoking at outdoor public gatherings.[21] Despite the fire department's deficient performance before the fire, the report found that it had performed quite admirably during and after the fire.

Having enumerated the myriad failings of various city departments, the board of inquiry stepped back to determine why. Much of the blame, it concluded, must lie with the city council. A new city charter, adopted in 1941, had stipulated that various implementing ordinances be enacted by the city council. But the council had failed to give power to the departments to inspect and regulate outdoor events—as the charter stipulated—and agency heads, for their part, had failed to ask for such authority. It is not entirely surprising that agency heads were ignorant of the 1941 charter revision; three years after its ratification, an indexed version had yet to be published. To deal with the gross lack of coordination among city agencies, the report recommended a "clearinghouse for the exchange of pertinent information among the various municipal agencies having to do with health and safety." Before any city property is rented or a license issued for public assemblies, all city agencies should be notified, the report urged.[22]

To prevent an "itinerant performance company" such as a circus from flouting local laws, the report urged that no organization be granted a business license (or a lease, if the performance involved public property) without agreeing to comply with all local codes and posting a performance bond to cover any liabilities. By establishing such a contractual relationship with the city, it would be more difficult for a licensee to challenge the enforcement authority of city agencies.

The report made two other administrative recommendations. First, it urged the city council to develop standards to govern the issuance of parade permits. Parades, after all, can choke main arteries with crowds and prevent fire trucks from reaching their destinations. Second, the report urged city agencies to discontinue their age-old practice of accepting free passes from applicants for licenses. Even if no venal intent existed in this case, the appearance of impropriety was too great.

Finally, the report endorsed a series of technical fire safety guidelines issued by the American Standards Association in the wake of the fire.[23] The new national code, drafted with the assistance of the Hartford building inspector and several Hartford insurance executives, stipulated minimum fire safety standards for "circuses, fairs, carnivals, exhibitions, contests, gospel meetings, auctions or other public assemblage." The guidelines covered such issues as the minimum number of exits, exit and aisle passages, fastening of seats, flame-proofing materials, combustibility of wood and wires, amount and location of fire-fighting equipment, training of personnel, use of ventilators to draw off heat and gases in the event of a fire, and emergency lighting systems to ensure against panic during power failures.

The report urged the city of Hartford to adopt the recommendations at once, as drafted, so that they could go into effect immediately. The day the report was issued, the city council convened a
special meeting to start working on the new ordinances. Not surprisingly, the council did adopt the report's recommendations, as
drafted. Several months later, after making minor refinements, the
council incorporated them into the municipal code. These ordinances
have survived essentially unchanged to this day.[24] The day after the
report was released, the *Hartford Courant* editorialized that it evinced
a "meticulous regard for accuracy" and "carefully reasoned" conclusions. According to *Courant* editorialists, the report's principal criticism was directed at the city council for failing to enact ordinances
implementing the new 1941 city charter.[25]

The board of inquiry recommendations spurred a wave of fire
safety reforms nationwide. According to a 1944 report by the National Institute of Municipal Law Officers, cities throughout the
country began reviewing their codes to bring them up to the latest
standards. Cities which adopted new codes in the wake of the fire
included Salt Lake City, Utah; Sacramento, California; and New-
port, Rhode Island. San Francisco and Los Angeles, with no insurance requirements or mandatory fire marshal inspections, began the
process of developing new regulations.[26]

As municipal fire reform proceeded apace, the Connecticut legislature began its own review of *state* fire safety standards, to ascertain
what improvements should be adopted in light of the circus fire.
Police Commissioner Hickey's report provided the factual foundation for a series of recommendations by the State Legislative Council, whose members in 1944 included Representative T. Emmet Clarie
(now a federal judge), Representative Raymond Thatcher (later a
state comptroller), and until August 8, 1944, Representative Harold Mitchell, the Republican State Committee chairman. Most of
the detailed technical work that went into the legislative recommendations was performed by a fire hazards advisory subcommittee
chaired by Representative Leon Riscassi, a Hartford attorney who
represented fire claimants. Other subcommittee members included
Captain Walter Stiles of the state police and William Goltra, a plaintiffs' attorney. The subcommittee's findings—the Riscassi Report[27]

—were issued in November 1944, two months before the 1945 session of the General Assembly began.

The Riscassi Report's chief conclusion was rather simple and straightforward: "Our present laws do not contain sufficient specific regulations for assembly in tents, particularly those used for amusement purposes." The solution: State legislation to require the local mayor or his designee, such as the police chief, to confer with the local fire marshal and building inspector. In turn, no license could be issued "until they certify that the premises and equipment to be used are reasonably safe for use. This would fix responsibility in the event of a catastrophe such as the circus fire."

When the Riscassi Report reached the 1945 legislature, the Public Health and Safety Committee promptly held a public hearing on a proposed bill, on February 27, 1945.[28] Fire chiefs' clubs around the state, recognizing the need for "control and guidance in governing the safety facilities of travelling shows," quickly endorsed the legislation. The bill applied to any circus tent having the capacity to shelter one hundred or more persons. A license had to be obtained from the state police commissioner, who could issue the license only if he determined the amusement "reasonably safe" for public attendance. The police commissioner could also make and enforce regulations regarding seating, exits, lighting, fire-fighting equipment, smoking on the premises, police protection, and other safety-related conditions. Failure to comply with the statute or its regulations could result in a $500 fine or six-month jail term.

When popular legislation is on a fast track toward enactment, it is sometimes difficult to interject worthwhile modifications to it. Fortunately, Insurance Commissioner Ellery Allen seized the opportunity to argue that licensing authority ought to be vested with the *state* fire marshal, not local fire marshals. This would ensure greater rigor and uniformity in safety reviews before any licenses were granted, Allen argued persuasively. Allen also urged legislators to authorize the state insurance commissioner to review the indemnity bonds required to be filed by any traveling circuses. After the fire, Allen recalled, "It was well over a week before I could determine whether or not there was any insurance existing covering the loss, and what form that was. I only found out by cabling London several times and going to a great deal of difficulty in trying to find out if there was any insurance."

At that point in Allen's testimony, Senator Lynch interjected: "In other words, a man comes in town with a circus and applies for a permit to run the circus, and that person would have to send that permit to the insurance commissioner for approval of the form of indemnity bond." Allen replied, "The bond [is] to be approved by the Insurance Commissioner before the permit is issued. In my opinion it would avoid a great many misunderstandings. There are indemnity bonds and indemnity bonds, and it requires experts to find which is a good one. I might add, our department has them." Allen's proposals, placed on the legislative calendar on the last possible day, ultimately prevailed. The state fire marshal and insurance commissioner would have augmented powers.

The bill was reported out of committee to the senate floor just a few days before adjournment. The record of debate in the senate has been lost; the house debate occurred on June 6, 1945. "Debate," in truth, is a somewhat misleading term for the acclaim heaped on the bill. It passed unanimously, and became law on July 1, 1945.[29] Years later, journalist John Cleary reflected on the reforms, "Did any good come from the fire? Yes. The laws governing large assemblies of people under *tents* and indoors were strengthened and given teeth. The responsibility of officers and employees of corporations toward the public was clarified and underlined."[30]

The current statutes—Chapter 532 of Connecticut General Statutes—are virtually the same as those enacted in 1945, with three minor exceptions. To take account of new tent technologies, the definition of a tent now includes "air-supported plastic or fabric." Another amendment to the law was added in 1953; it requires circus proprietors to designate the secretary of state as the proper agent for service of legal documents in the event of a lawsuit against a circus. (This change, of course, was inspired by the confusion that occurred in 1944 when the plaintiffs' bar could not find any agents of the circus on whom papers could be served.) Finally, the adequacy of a circus's indemnity bond is no longer left to the discretion of the insurance commissioner, as the original law specified. It is now set forth in a table that specifies precisely how much insurance coverage is required, based on tent size. (The largest tents—those covering 30,000 or more square feet—require $6 million of liability insurance.)

The more stringent safety and insurance requirements for the tents of "itinerant performance companies" have had a sobering impact on the business, as one might expect. Brian and Debbie LaPalme, a Willimantic couple traveling with one of the last touring outdoor tent shows in 1986, complained that circuses are going indoors and being transformed into a different beast entirely. "A real circus is outdoors, with the tent flapping," with the audience close to the action, said Debbie. "Ringling Brothers is more like a Broadway production." When the Roberts Brothers circus performed in Wilton, New Milford, and Sandy Hook, Connecticut, they could not perform under their big top canopy because of the prohibitively high insurance rates.[31]

The Clyde Beatty–Cole Brothers Circus of De Land, Florida, almost came to Bristol, Connecticut, for a performance under a big top in June 1987. But the circus quickly discovered that it could not afford the insurance coverage required by state law. In 1985 the circus had paid $150,000 for $6 million of coverage, enough to satisfy state law. But two years later the same premium bought only $1 million of coverage. At the time, Connecticut's liability requirements were six times higher than those of the seventeen other states where the Beatty-Cole circus performed. The poignant irony in this instance concerns the group that hoped to bring the circus to Bristol: the town's police and fire mutual aid associations.[32]

For reasons having less to do with flammable tents than with the larger arenas and modern amenities, the Ringling Brothers' circus has abandoned the big top and taken its spectacle indoors. Given the marginality of the remaining touring tent circuses, the state statutes dealing with outdoor amusements have a certain archaic ring to them. Yet they are not without relevance.

The reforms enacted after the circus fire guided and inspired contemporary lawmakers in the wake of the collapse of the L'Ambiance Plaza in Bridgeport, which killed twenty-eight workers on April 23, 1987. The special panel appointed by Governor O'Neill to investigate the L'Ambiance tragedy, the Schneller Committee, urged that state building inspectors be authorized to overrule local building officials in interpreting and enforcing state building codes. Schneller based his recommendations on the Riscassi Report, which urged more thorough inspections of buildings in the central cities. His recommendations also relied upon Insurance Commissioner Allen's judgment that the state fire marshal should have superior authority over local fire marshals and codes.[33]

The emotional trauma of public tragedies tend to wash over communities with a stunning force and then slowly dissipate with time, as memories grow dim. The most meaningful residue and the most enduring legacy of a preventable tragedy, therefore, can often be found in the law, a medium by which one generation can transmit its hard-won lessons to future generations.

1. Emmet Kelly entertains children before the afternoon performance of the circus on July 6, 1944. Within hours, scores of people would be dead and hundreds injured.
2. Dozens of people trying to flee the fire would be trapped by the caged runways (foreground), through which animals were brought into the center ring.

3. Before the performance began, a mother and child (foreground) gingerly climb over the animal runways. The arrow, inserted by the *Hartford Times*, marks where the first flames appeared.

4. By slicing open the tent canvas with a pocket knife, Donald Anderson, a resourceful thirteen-year-old, is credited with helping more than three hundred people escape the flames.

5. In moments, circus gaiety turned to terror. "It was as if someone punched a button and a light went on," recalled one survivor.

6. To calm the panicked crowd, the circus band heroically played on through the first minutes of the fire.

7. Apart from its tent and equipment, now utterly lost, the circus had few tangible assets that fire victims could hope to seize.

8. Dozens of firemen converged on the circus site to put out the flames.

9. Clown Emmet Kelly carries water to douse the flames. Fire investigators would later blame a shortage of emergency buckets, among other inadequate precautions.

10. Given the wartime scarcity of men, the circus hired dozens of inexperienced teenaged boys to set up tents and equipment. Unnecessary fire hazards may have resulted.

11. Besieged by hundreds of attachments on its assets, the circus was stranded at the Barbour Street fairgrounds. Neighbors became enraged by poorly tended animals and a rough crowd of malingerers.

12. Only charred bleachers and a few circus wagons remained after the devastation. The Fred D. Wish Elementary School now stands on the fire site.

13. As if for a wartime disaster, civil preparedness officials quickly organized a makeshift morgue at the state armory.

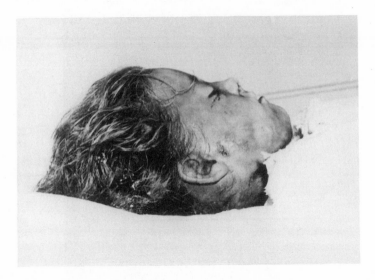

14. For forty-seven years the identity of this eight-year-old girl who died in the blaze—Little Miss 1565—remained a mystery. In 1991 Hartford arson investigator Rick Davey disclosed that the girl was Eleanor Cook.

15. Worried families flocked to the armory by the hundreds to check the whereabouts of loved ones.

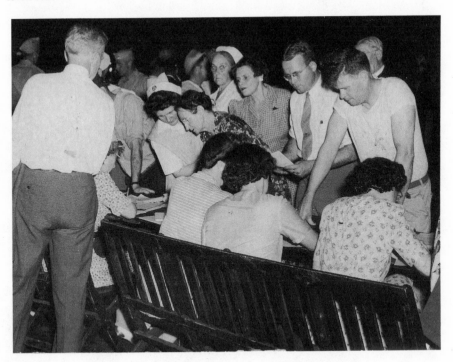

16. Dale Segee, a twenty-one-year-old drifter with a history of mental illness and arson, confessed in 1950 to setting the circus fire. Citing insufficient evidence, Hartford authorities declined to prosecute him.

17. Involuntary manslaughter charges were brought against (from left to right) George Washington Smith, general manager; James Haley, vice president; Edward Versteeg, chief engineer; Leonard Aylesworth, boss canvas man; David Blanchfield, chief wagon man; and William Caley, seat man (not pictured). Circus attorney Dan Judge is seated at right.

18. Judge John T. Cullinan presided over the only litigation resulting from the circus fire, on the size of the receiver's fee. The trial was divisive, and the ruling controversial.

19. Judge John Hamilton King, renowned for his encyclopedic recall of legal cases, authorized the novel circus receivership. King would become Chief Justice of the Connecticut Supreme Court in 1963.

20. The signing of the arbitration agreement in the winter of 1944 brought the leading attorneys together: The trio who secured the receivership (from left to right) Julius Schatz, Arthur Weinstein, and Edward Rogin; Hartford bar committee members Robert Butler (seated, with pen) and Joseph Cooney (seated, right); and circus attorneys Dan Judge and Cyril Coleman (standing, right),

21. John Ringling North, the flamboyant impresario determined to gain control of the circus, lost few opportunities to sabotage the receivership and arbitration.

22. The Ringlings gather to attend a circus performance on April 12, 1943. Aubrey Ringling, later married to circus vice president James Haley, sits to the left of Edith Ringling in front row. Robert Ringling and his wife sit in back row.

PART TWO · MASS TORTS AND THE ART OF CREATIVE SETTLEMENT

It is a rich irony that the creative legal aftermath of the Ringling Brothers' circus fire is a virtually unknown story among contemporary students of mass torts.[1] Because the disputants were able to pursue an innovative settlement scheme and forgo the byzantine and usually inconclusive rituals of mass litigation, no court opinion for the case exists. As a result, no readily available corpus of facts or legal analysis concerning the case can be found,[2] and even researchers predisposed to learn more have trouble getting the facts right.[3]

This obscurity, however circumstantial in origin, says a great deal about our contemporary legal culture and its modest regard for alternative dispute resolution (ADR). Few legal commentators give serious attention to ADR as a worthy vehicle for dealing with mass torts, even though mass torts often result in gross contortions of tort law and civil procedure; awesome court costs; inappropriate use of court resources; and lengthy delays, inequities, and highly unpredictable outcomes.

To be sure, the applicability of ADR may be limited in settings in which the scientific evidence is speculative or there are hundreds or thousands of dispersed claimants, all of whom may not even be identifiable for years. Indeed, ADR may well be more suited for mass accidents, in which victims and causation can be more easily ascertained, than for mass toxic torts, which are characterized by long latency periods before the bodily harm becomes manifest. Still, the very fact that most toxic torts are resolved through settlement anyway, after years of costly discovery and procedural maneuvering, suggests that the value of traditional tort litigation is reaching its limits. Perhaps a more deliberative system of ADR, pursued before the mass litigation process is too far advanced, could yield results that are far less expensive, much faster, and more just to the victims and their families. That, at least, is a key lesson to be learned from the circus fire settlement and from a more contemporary variant, the settlement of the L'Ambiance Plaza collapse achieved in 1988.

Drawing upon the lessons of the circus fire, Part II explores the possibilities and limits of ADR as a strategy for resolving mass torts today. Chapter 7 begins by sketching the disturbing state of mass tort litigation today: the costs, procedural complexities, and implications for justice. Chapter 8 provides an assessment of the merits of Chapter 11 bankruptcy proceedings as a vehicle for settling victims' claims and reorganizing companies beleaguered by mass tort litigation.

Against this backdrop, we then consider what role ADR strategies might play in resolving mass torts. Starting with the circus fire, chapter 9 explores why the Rogin-Schatz-Weinstein settlement scheme was able to succeed. What factors make it an aberration and what factors make it a potential model for contemporary mass tort ADR? The enduring lessons of the circus fire settlement can be more easily identified when compared to a more recent, equally remarkable mass tort settlement, the L'Ambiance case. By analyzing this special settlement and exploring other ADR techniques used in mass torts, chapter 10 provides a rudimentary introduction to a seldom explored field of legal inquiry: the promise of ADR in resolving mass torts.

Apart from their lessons for ADR, the settlements of claims arising from the circus fire and L'Ambiance Plaza collapse offer pungent critiques of our current legal culture, which often regards settlements as inherently inferior or dismisses them as "exceptions that prove the rule" of the normative value of adversarial litigation.[4] This attitude is surely one reason why many mass torts prove intractable.

Too many attorneys glorify epic litigation as heroic and consider compromise a cop-out for weaklings.[5] Many judges, schooled in the discipline of formal adjudication, understandably fail to appreciate the benefits of ADR. For their part, plaintiffs, the ones who pay the bills and suffer the harm, are hostages to a system that clearly does not serve them well. Yet to the extent that plaintiffs see their "day in court" as their only salvation, they too must adopt new attitudes toward dispute resolution if ADR in mass torts is to be possible.

One inestimable benefit of history over academic speculation is the actuality of the former: *Certain events happened*. In a legal climate crying out for innovations, much can be learned from the success of these two settlements. We believe they hold untapped lessons for future mass tort litigants.

Chapter 7

THE MASS TORT
MESS

When describing mass tort litigation, legal scholars who normally write in dry, measured tones suddenly explode into colorful, almost lurid language. The system of adjudicating mass torts is a "bizarre structure," concludes Judge Alvin B. Rubin, a federal judge for the Fifth Circuit Court of Appeals, in a major law review article on the subject.[1] The former dean of the Yale Law School, Harry H. Wellington, who once served as a mediator between asbestos companies and insurers, calls the asbestos litigation "extravagantly expensive and grotesquely inefficient."[2] The judge overseeing the Dupont Plaza Hotel fire litigation, Judge Raymond Acosta, described his responsibilities in the case as "a nightmare,"[3] and the First Circuit Court of Appeals has called the case a "litigatory monster."[4]

Mass torts are not an entirely new phenomenon. Over the years many catastrophes have resulted in dozens or hundreds of lawsuits against one or more companies or the government.[5] But mass torts are now occurring with greater frequency, and they often involve staggering sums of money and latent harm that will not be manifest for years or decades. They present complex difficulties in gathering and retrieving documentation,[6] new quandaries for judges trying to provide fair adjudication,[7] and novel procedural dilemmas.[8]

There is no single reason for the proliferation of mass tort lawsuits, of course, but it is entirely reasonable to suppose that the growing frequency of such suits parallel the pace of technological innovation and the increasing size of mass markets.[9] One might also surmise that mass tort litigation is increasing as more consumers are aware of, and assert, their legal rights.[10] Victims' lawsuits are setting new legal standards of accountability for corporate behavior that was previously hidden from public view.[11] (Whether the court system provides the most efficient or equitable instrument of accountability is another question entirely. Federal regulation, a system of rigorous prevention rather than ad hoc deterrence, is surely more cost-effective and humane.) Whatever its wellsprings—and they are too deep and complicated to delve into here—complex litigation, which comprises mass torts and other major civil disputes, is posing "a very real crisis in modern jurisprudence," argues U.S. District Court Judge Spencer Williams:[12]

> The long arms of these "big cases" . . . have ensnared virtually thousands of courts in this country in costly and repetitive litigation, threatening to last well into the next century. These cases are but the harbinger of the judiciary's role in an increasingly complex society, with huge multinational corporations peddling their mass-produced consumer goods and drugs by instantaneous satellite communication. In such a society, it is not an overly pessimistic prediction that, absent some legislative or judicial solution, our attempt to try these virtually identical lawsuits, one-by-one, will bankrupt both the state and federal court systems.[13]

In the realm of mass torts, a significant conceptual divide separates mass accidents (physical catastrophes that occur suddenly and harm identifiable victims) and toxic torts (substances that cause diseases whose precise causation and victims cannot be easily identified and whose symptoms may not appear for many years). In the case of mass accidents, where liability can be easier to determine, litigation often centers on how to allocate damage claims among codefendants. In toxic torts, by contrast, it can be extraordinarily difficult to prove causality and thus to hold a defendant liable, let alone devise practical and equitable remedies for compensation.

Even within these two main categories of mass torts, however, there are significant variations in the physiognomy of cases. Salient differences include the number of plaintiffs and defendants (ranging from dozens to tens of thousands); the possibility of plaintiffs' contributory negligence; the probability of defendants' liability and perceived self-interest in settling; the amount and types of insurance coverage; the anticipated extent and cost of pretrial discovery; the geographic dispersion of litigants; the demeanor of the trial judge; and many other factors. Given these variables, in short, mass tort cases are predictably unpredictable.

Yet mass tort cases are not sui generis either. They usually share several common attributes, as Judge Rubin points out: "[Mass torts] result in the filing of many suits; they produce high litigation costs; they are generally resolved only after great delay; they affect not only the litigants but other users of the court system; and their total human and economic costs affect all of society."[14] The incidence of huge multiparty, multiforum litigation has become so common, in fact, that the American Law Institute (ALI) is conducting a major inquiry into how the courts might better respond to this litigation. "[T]he time has come," writes the ALI Complex Litigation Project, "to replace *ad hoc* innovation with procedures developed specifically for complex cases. This especially is true because the essential features of complex litigation are predictable, and the number of cases is bound to increase."[15]

The Complex Process of Mass Tort Litigation

To understand why mass torts present such intractable difficulties for the courts and why ADR techniques might provide superior alternatives in some instances, it is necessary to explore the common dynamics of most mass tort litigation.

A tort case today, involving multiple casualties, injuries, or illnesses, is generally pursued the way that tort cases have been pursued for the last two hundred years. A suit with two or more plaintiffs is filed in state court, and a jury renders a verdict. But most mass tort cases quickly assume very complex dimensions and are pursued under elaborate procedures outlined in *Manual for Complex Litigation*, the "bible" on the subject issued by the federal courts.[16]

The *Manual* first recommends that all related litigation be consolidated before the same judge, at least for the major issues of liability and damages. The judge becomes the "manager" of the case, shaping it for trial by defining the issues and controlling the terms of the discovery process. As a matter of practicality and efficiency, attorneys for the plaintiffs and defendants are organized into groups, with one attorney or law firm assuming the role of "lead counsel." As Judge Rubin explains the process:

> An elaborate structure of committees is created, including lead counsel and teams of discovery counsel. . . . [D]efense lawyers are also using regional or national management schemes to share information and trial techniques. The defendants themselves are coordinating their strategy in order to present a united front. On both sides, specialized counsel are more frequently appearing as trial counsel in suits that once would have been tried by less experienced local counsel.[17]

Sometimes there are plaintiffs' attorneys who refuse to go along with the committee, hoping to present their own case in a particular style or to earn a higher fee.[18] Other times there are defense counsel who cannot agree to act by committee, claiming that their respective legal concerns are too dissimilar to the majority.[19] Where the court can achieve a consolidated approach, it designates one or more attorneys to speak for all the plaintiffs or defendants and to conduct discovery of witnesses. The lead counsel may also serve as a conduit to distribute documents from the court to defendants, or from one side to the other. The costs of these committees are shared pro rata by all the parties.

Because it is quite common in mass torts for new claims to arise over time, particularly in toxic tort cases, the court must also set up a procedure for adding new parties. There must be a master file developed with standard pleadings, motions, and orders. Certain pleadings and orders may be deemed applicable in all cases, including newly filed ones. To streamline the process, the court must see that key points of contention are identified at once. Where various state and federal laws apply, the court must sort out claims and defenses to ascertain which body of laws should hold.[20] Major disputes over insurance coverage, which can frustrate the resolution of mass tort suits, must be addressed at once.[21]

The first stages of discovery often center on general issues of defendant liability; individual and particular matters are reserved for a later stage. General forms are used to prevent as much repetition as possible during discovery. Attorneys seek to identify any government reports that might have some bearing on the tort, from such agencies as the National Transportation Safety Board, the National Institute for Occupational Safety and Health, and the Environmental Protection Agency.

Because the circumstances of causality and culpability are so critical in mass tort litigation, the court must set up a schedule for deposing key experts, whose opinions provide a factual framework for the case. In toxic tort cases, in which experts must testify about events that occurred decades ago, discovery can be an especially arduous process. As this process proceeds, the court sets deadlines for submitting final expert reports. If the reports raise some questions of judgment or bias, the court may decide to order an independent expert to review the evidence as well.

Class actions are not typically used in mass tort litigation because the factual circumstances of each case usually vary too greatly.[22] But some court decisions suggest that class actions may become acceptable as a means of deciding major issues of liability.[23] Cases have been decided both for and against granting class action certification to consider punitive damages against a defendant.[24] "At the moment," concludes Judge Rubin, "efforts to increase the effectiveness of class actions focus on situations in which a limited damages fund is available."[25]

The pretrial discovery process and procedural jockeying for advantage play a major role in the litigation of mass torts, introducing a bewildering new set of procedural quandaries, expenses, and logistical difficulties. The rigors of this process can be seen in the litigation arising from the Dupont Plaza Hotel fire on New Year's Eve 1986, described by the *ABA Journal* as "the most deadly fire on American soil in more than 40 years."[26] The fire, set by a disgruntled employee in the midst of a labor dispute with the hotel, raced through a second-floor casino, killing more than one hundred people. The day after the fire, numerous plaintiffs' attorneys were winging down to San Juan to set up shop, protecting their clients' (and would-be clients') interests. Their immediate concern was gaining access to the fire scene, which the defendant hotel resisted on grounds that multiple inexperienced attorneys rooting around the charred site could disturb valuable evidence. (The hotel surely also worried about generating negative publicity concerning its operations.) Plaintiffs countered that there was an equal likelihood that premature cleanup by the defendants could disturb or destroy important evidence.

An initial suit sought merely to settle this issue of accessibility. After the judge issued a five-day freeze on the cleanup and appointed a plaintiffs' committee, a plan for access to the fire site was developed. Plaintiffs were given five days of access; no evidence was to be "withheld unreasonably" or removed without the consent of the defendant; and any evidence removed was to be placed in a joint storage area accessible by two keys, one held by each side. The hotel also promised not to remove any luggage or clothing until each room had been videotaped. This taping might enable experts to trace the path of the fire and find its cause. The defendant also agreed to keep the hotel, appraised at $40 million, free of encumbrances. (There was only $1 million of liability insurance, hardly enough to satisfy liability claims.)[27] These arrangements were only the beginning of a massive investigatory process that involved more than two thousand depositions.

In time, more than 2,300 claims were filed seeking $1.8 billion in damages against more than 180 defendants.[28] The complexities of adjudicating the mass tort were so extreme that Judge Raymond Acosta divided the case into five separate trials, each to determine different facets of liability.[29] To manage the more than one million pages of court papers that had accumulated over three years, a special depository had to be built. To accommodate the army of lawyers and their documents at trial, a makeshift courtroom also had to be built.[30]

If the actual courtroom was bursting the normal physical limits of legal tradition, lawyers' ethical considerations were also facing new pressures. Lured by the promise of big money and pressured by the brisk schedule of pretrial activity set by Judge Acosta, some attorneys reportedly solicited fire victims while they were still recuperating. Other victims were hounded at home with tales of great wealth awaiting them. Melvin Belli and a law partner were fined $5,000 for filing a claim on behalf of a dead relative of one fire victim, a mistake that Belli attributed to the need to file claims quickly for more than one hundred relatives of victims.[31]

It was not entirely surprising that three years after the fire, and two months after the first of five consolidated trials had begun, the major parties to the fire litigation announced a settlement worth $147 million.[32] The case had become too unwieldy, too complicated, too costly; it had become a caricature of normal litigation. It is still too early to know what legal and court expenses had accrued by that point, but the experience of the MGM Grand Hotel fire in Las Vegas — in which the defense costs of $200 million were about the same amount that was paid out to plaintiffs in damages — probably provides a reasonable benchmark.[33]

The odyssey of pretrial discovery and procedural maneuvering can become particularly complex in toxic torts, in which conflicting scientific theories must be sorted out and decades-old evidence exhumed.[34] The special problems posed by toxic torts are too complicated to examine here; there are, however, numerous book-length treatments of such mass torts as Agent Orange,[35] asbestos,[36] and the Dalkon Shield,[37] and the legal literature on the subject is rapidly growing. No consensus has yet crystallized on how the traditional tort system should be modified to handle mass torts. Yet there is widespread skepticism that the current process can truly yield justice and preserve its legitimacy. Legal journalist Edwin Chen voices a sentiment held by many thoughtful legal analysts:

> Does it really make sense to have the compensation awarded to those whose health was injured turn upon exhaustive investigation and trial of the question whether a particular manufacturer or user knew or should have learned about the dangers of working with asbestos twenty, thirty, and forty years ago? After exhaustive inquiries and protracted trials, will the verdict and judgment really turn upon careful, reasoned findings upon such questions? Is the method developed for negligence of the nineteenth century suited to such cases? Have we done anything but make it more cumbersome and more expensive with the outcome more uncertain?[38]

The Problems of Adjudicating Mass Torts

At first blush, it seems to make sense to stretch and modify conventional tort adjudication procedures in order to accommodate mass disasters. After all, the chief difference seems to be merely the scale of the harm, and this hardly seems reason enough to abridge certain due process rights that individual tort litigants customarily enjoy. Yet legal commentators are beginning to agree that the sheer size of mass torts are making such litigation untenable; the courts, defendants, and plaintiffs simply cannot withstand the manifold strains much longer. However "rational" received legal procedures and doctrines may be, their actual implementation on a large scale is becoming too unwieldy and even antithetical to basic fairness.

Adjudicating mass torts is typically plagued by astronomical legal and court costs, extraordinary delays, knotty procedural quandaries, judicial intervention, gross inequities, and—despite all the hurdles heroically overcome—highly unpredictable outcomes.[39] Appreciating the magnitude of these problems requires a brief elaboration.

LEGAL COSTS

With quiet nobility, Edward Rogin agreed to forgo his fees for serving as receiver until all claimants in the $4 million circus fire arbitration had been paid. He and most of his colleagues in the Hartford bar had a sense of seemliness and proportion about their fees; they did not want to reap huge personal windfalls from a horrible community tragedy.[40] By the 1980s, of course, this sense of proportion had been supplanted by a brash sense of entitlement among attorneys.[41] When combined with an interminable legal process of Dickensian dimensions, the chief beneficiaries of mass tort litigation would seem to be the lawyers. (Indeed, a 1987 Rand Corporation study found that in the massive array of asbestos lawsuits, plaintiffs received, on average, only 37 percent of the total expenditures to settle each claim; the rest was consumed by defendants' and plaintiffs' legal fees and expenses.)[42]

The legal costs of the asbestos cases, "the unchallenged giant of complex litigation" according to the American Law Institute,[43] will not soon be surpassed. A 1983 study by the Rand Institute for Civil

Justice found that defendants spent an average of $2.71 for every dollar that was ultimately awarded to injured plaintiffs.[44] To put this in a broader perspective, Rand explains, "The average total compensation per claim paid by all defendants and their insurers was approximately $60,000 and total defense litigation expenses were $35,000 (58 percent of total compensation). Thus, the total costs to defendants and their insurers averaged about $95,000 per closed claim."[45] These sums have probably increased since this study was completed.

There are many reasons for such gargantuan legal sums, apart from the hourly fees of defense lawyers. The unprecedented scale, procedural complexities, and duplication of efforts that occurs in trying mass torts quickly runs up the legal bills. Wellington points out, for example, that each case has "an average of 20 defendants in every case—each with its own team of lawyers."[46] Multiply the legal fees from a single case times the ultimate number of personal injury cases that Manville expects it will pay claims on—between 83,000 and 100,000 cases[47]—and it is easy to see that the total legal bill will run into the billions of dollars. Wellington cites a business school dean who puts the final estimate at $64 billion.[48] (This sum, one might add, does not include the many lawsuits seeking to determine responsibility for removing asbestos from buildings.)

To take another example: By June 30, 1985, the Dalkon Shield litigation had cost the A. H. Robins Co. and its former insurer, Aetna Life & Casualty Co., $378.3 million to dispose of cases. It spent another $107.3 million for legal expenses, and nearly $25 million in punitive or exemplary damages.[49] Legal fees in the Agent Orange case had consumed roughly $100 million by 1986, more than half the $180 million final settlement sum.[50] Even mass disasters, which are usually less complex than toxic torts, can generate legal defense bills of $200 million, as we saw earlier.

The numbing expense of litigating mass torts, by itself, shows how warped the current system has become. Professor Robert L. Rabin of Stanford University Law School, referring to the Agent Orange litigation, puts it succinctly: "When process costs become the dominant characteristic of a system designed to allocate liability on corrective justice principles, tort law has lost its bearings. When closer inquiry suggests that the system is no longer even pursuing corrective justice ends, tort law has lost its *raison d'etre* as well."[51]

PROCEDURAL QUANDARIES AND DELAYS

The procedural rules that govern a normal tort trial become, in the context of a mass tort, a complicated puzzle of Kafkaesque dimensions. Judge Acosta, the federal judge presiding over the Dupont Plaza Hotel fire litigation, explained the nearly overwhelming nature of his responsibilities:

> It's a nightmare trying to keep up with everything the parties are doing, the evidence, the discovery, the jurisdictional issues, third-party actions, who are the proper party defendants and all the rest. There are millions of documents. I deal with it by referring to the *MCL* [*Manual for Complex Litigation*]. I have a magistrate ruling on discovery. And I try to anticipate what's coming down the road.[52]

Even with the *Manual for Complex Litigation* and conscientious management of the case, mass torts have a tendency to present novel procedural issues. In the Dupont Plaza case, for example, plaintiffs' attorneys claimed attorney-client privilege for their document-management system. As a federal court explained, "The plaintiffs argue that they have sifted through millions of pieces of paper in order to locate and identify relevant documents and that, although the documents themselves are not protected work product, the identification protocol requires the plaintiffs' lawyers to reveal their mental processes and opinions. These, they argue, constitute 'opinion' work product which should enjoy absolute protection." In 1988, the court ruled against the plaintiffs.[53]

Judge Acosta might take some consolation in the fact that his case involves a mass accident, not a toxic tort. With "only" forty-six complaints involving 2,000 plaintiffs suing more than 180 defendants, the issues raised by the Dupont Plaza fire are relatively simple, compared to those raised by toxic torts such as Agent Orange or asbestos. After 600 plaintiffs had filed suits in the Agent Orange case, the federal court certified a plaintiff class containing an estimated *2.4 million* members! To complicate matters, some 2,440 individuals decided to opt out of the plaintiff class (600 of whom later changed their minds and rejoined the class). The twists and turns of the Agent Orange case, says the American Law Institute, "is a perfect example of the inadequacy of our traditional procedural system to cope with mass disasters or the demands of modern substantive law."[54]

The length of mass tort trials also says a great deal about the ills of the current system. Asbestos litigation has been going on since the late 1970s, with no end in sight. More than 14,000 Dalkon Shield cases, begun in the early and mid-1980s, were not resolved by the end of the decade. The prospects of delay, in and of itself, present a serious obstacle to many plaintiffs who need timely compensation and time to heal their emotional wounds. Mary Beth Kornhauser, a Dalkon Shield user who underwent a radical hysterectomy at the age of twenty-five, decided not to go through two to five years of litigation "never to [be] able to put the pain behind me, wondering when I would have to completely relive the experience in a trial situation. . . . I had had enough pain caused by them."[55]

JUDICIAL INTERVENTIONISM

Because of the size of most mass torts, trial judges are sorely tempted, or virtually forced, to assume an activist role. They must aggressively manage and lead, not simply adjudicate, the case. They must guide the participants through the investigation and the pretrial maze and try to encourage comity among plaintiffs and defendants, lest the case spin out of control. Although several judges have been praised for their activist leadership in managing mass tort cases, many commentators are also uneasy with such behavior.[56] Judges, after all, are supposed to play a neutral, somewhat remote role. Their essential purpose is altered if they seem to make public policy rather than merely enforce or interpret it; if their powers are used to supravene the powers customarily enjoyed by plaintiffs and defendants; or if their rulings have few plausible precedents or statutory bases behind them.

Chief Judge Jack Weinstein of the U.S. District Court for the Eastern District of New York has attracted considerable controversy for his handling of the Agent Orange case.[57] The judge was sympathetic to the Vietnam veterans allegedly injured by the spraying of dioxin, a defoliant, but strongly doubted whether Agent Orange had actually caused many of the veterans' medical problems. He therefore launched a crusade to obtain a settlement, and early in the case, with the investigation barely underway, set a trial date of May 7, 1984. He hired a consultant to develop a settlement plan and, in April 1984, appointed three special masters to assist in the process. Two days before the scheduled trial date, Judge Weinstein ordered the parties to appear with their "toothbrushes and full negotiating authority" to conduct marathon settlement talks. After nonstop sessions that periodically featured "pep talks" by the judge, the case was settled, just before jury selection. The settlement created a fund with a balance of over $200 million to compensate the veterans' claims.[58] Although most observers applaud the settlement, many worry that Weinstein was too zealous and even coercive. On the other hand, the miasma of complex litigation awaiting all participants would have been highly unpalatable as well.

One is tempted to pity judges of mass tort cases for being ensnared in a conundrum. Even with the *Manual for Complex Litigation*, they often have little practical guidance or clear precedents for the dilemmas they face. Yet when they exercise imaginative leadership in trying to manage or settle a case, they are often criticized for overstepping the boundaries of judicial authority. Commentators may agree or disagree with the behavior of a Judge Miles Lord in the Dalkon Shield case (who aggressively forced disclosure of damaging documents from A. H. Robins and chastised Robins executives for "corporate irresponsibility at its meanest") or a Judge Lambros in the asbestos cases (who pioneered the summary trial innovation to expedite settlements). Whatever the merits of their behavior, there are grave implications for justice when judges, perforce, assume more interventionist roles in adjudication.

GREATER UNCERTAINTY AND INEQUITY

We have already cited many of the factors that make mass tort litigation a highly problematic enterprise. The scale and complexity of the process creates a special burden for plaintiffs, who must often endure grievous physical and emotional disabilities, family stresses, huge legal fees, and anguishing delays as the arcane machinery of litigation grinds on. Defendants may not suffer the personal traumas and can more easily afford the expenses and delays. Yet they too face extraordinary expenses, uncertainties among investors, and a cloud of public suspicion and disdain. The process, concludes one account of the asbestos litigation, "was a crapshoot for both sides. Some victims won huge awards or managed to wring sizable settlements from asbestos producers; others got little or nothing. The only ones for whom the dice were always hot were the lawyers. Producers had retained 1,100 law firms around the U.S. to defend them by the mid-1980s; thousands more lawyers specialized in representing victims."[59]

Much of the uncertainty in mass torts stems from the diversity problem, in which dozens or hundreds of cases are tried simultaneously in different jurisdictions. This can lead to such problems as "inconsistent outcomes, whipsawing (from the ability of defendants in separate litigation to point to a nonparty as the one truly liable), and uncoordinated scrambles for the assets of a limited fund."[60] Inequities can also arise from the highly variable punitive damages that different juries may award for similar harms.

The "race to the courthouse" syndrome is a major source of potential injustice. In such scenarios, the earlier plaintiffs manage to recover some money from the defendant-company whereas "latecomers" find a bankrupt company and recover nothing. The circus fire receivership was expressly created to short-circuit this problem by providing an orderly framework for equitable compensation for all plaintiffs. Protecting latecomers in toxic torts, in which the anticipated disease does not manifest itself for years, remains a serious problem with no easy solution.

Clearly the first step toward solving these myriad problems and bringing order to a disaggregated mass tort is to consolidate all related cases into one jurisdiction, a central goal of the American Law Institute's Complex Litigation Project. But even with such a reform, the litigated resolution of a mass tort will probably involve considerable uncertainty and inequity. Although ADR techniques have many obvious limitations, their use in appropriate settings might help restore a measure of predictability and self-determination to the litigation process that usually leads to a settlement in any case.

There is no small irony in this fact. At some point in the litigants' odyssey through the mass tort maze, after years of costly discovery and pretrial maneuvering, the case ends by being settled. "These cases are like walking up a pitch-black, winding staircase, and you never know how much further you have to go in total darkness," said Bud G. Holman, the chief attorney defending the Union Carbide Corporation after the settlement for the Bhopal disaster was cinched. "Then, all of a sudden it's light, and it's over."[61] It is plausible to assume that the fruits of discovery may play a role in any ultimate settlement, but an equally if not more persuasive factor, evidence suggests, is sheer exhaustion with the litigation process. Either the judge or the lead plaintiffs' attorneys or corporate defendants decide that enough is enough and choose to use their powers to help achieve some sort of acceptable closure on a long, nasty, complicated, expensive ordeal.

Can such litigation sagas be prevented? As we explore in chapters 9 and 10, the answer could more frequently, and with certain qualifications, be *yes*, particularly in mass catastrophe cases. But before embarking upon that inquiry, we must first assess a hybrid forum for resolving mass torts that has become one practical if unwieldy alternative: bankruptcy court.

Chapter 8

THE BANKRUPTCY "SOLUTION"

It is a periodic drama in the evolution of law: A novel set of circumstances recurs again and again, rendering a received body of law confusingly complex and impractical and creating bothersome quandaries and a discomforting sense of injustice. Although litigants caught in this twilight zone may sense that "there's got to be a better way," many of them already have too much to gain through the existing set of rules. They realize, furthermore, that a new consensus about how to proceed in a more just, enlightened, or functional way has not yet crystallized. Dispute resolution becomes a matter of muddling through.

The Ringling Brothers circus stumbled into this sort of twilight zone of the law in 1944 as it groped for a better way of dealing with its mass tort than the bankruptcy laws of the time permitted. The solution devised by the Rogin-Schatz-Weinstein trio and accepted by the circus was an equity receivership granted by the state court.[1] Even though it was a legal innovation with scant precedent for dealing with mass disasters, it proved to be an effective vehicle for keeping the circus afloat while settling victims' claims in an orderly fashion.

Many contemporary mass torts seem to be caught in a similar sort of twilight zone of the law. Respected legal commentators and judges decry the deficiencies of existing law for resolving mass torts, particularly toxic torts, noting the excessive costs, delays, uncertainties, inequities, and related factors mentioned in chapter 7. Yet until new legal vehicles for resolving mass torts emerge, bankruptcy law will continue to be pressed into service by many tortfeasor companies. Bankruptcy courts may in fact be able to provide an organized, equitable, and final resolution to mass tort claims, while preventing outright liquidation of the company. But bankruptcy courts were never really intended to serve that function. The laws they administer are focussed, after all, on the contractual relationships between debtors and creditors; mass tort claimants are uninvited guests to this alien body of law. So until a better vehicle is devised by Congress or the courts, bankruptcy law can serve tortfeasor corporations in the same manner that the equity receivership served the Ringling Brothers circus—as an imperfect but functional legal alternative for muddling through.

This chapter examines the evolution of bankruptcy law as a way to manage mass tort litigation, noting its advantages, limitations, complexities, and inequities. The bankruptcy laws that prevailed at the time of the circus fire were radically reformed in 1978, so a new legal structure came into existence just as a wave of unprecedented mass torts—asbestos, the Dalkon Shield, Agent Orange, DES (diethylstilbesterol)—crashed down on the courts. Indeed, the reforms in bankruptcy law are one reason why so many tortfeasor corporations have sought refuge in Chapter 11.

Examining the origins of the circus receivership is useful, nonetheless, because it illustrates one way the courts successfully supervised a corporation beset by scores of tort claimants and creditors while avoiding the special burdens of bankruptcy reorganization. The circus receivership also helps illustrate why the bankruptcy reforms of 1978 were so necessary: the previous bankruptcy code was simply too rigid and arbitrary whereas the new law, however flawed with respect to mass torts, is far more flexible and practical. If the circus fire had happened today, Chapter 11 would probably have been able to accomplish what the equity receivership did (even if an arbitrated settlement with claimants might be more problematic). Yet even the new bankruptcy law is not well-equipped to deal with toxic torts, one of the most explosive areas of law, as we will see below.

Origins of the Circus Receivership

As recounted in chapter 2, the equity receivership for the circus was the joint product of some enterprising plaintiffs' attorneys, an astute judge with an encyclopedic knowledge of relevant case law, and a community consensus that conventional legal alternatives (that is, the bankruptcy law of the time) would simply not help the circus or the fire victims. Rogin and his colleagues proposed the receivership, and Judge John Hamilton King obligingly provided the legal justification—an obscure 1903 Connecticut case, *Cogswell v. Second National Bank*,[2] which provides that a temporary receiver may be appointed where there exists *some* cause for doing so, but the judge need not decide the final merits of the case before making a temporary appointment.

A few months later, pleased with the initial success of the receivership and its popular acceptance, the Hartford Superior Court made the receivership permanent. By keeping Ringling Brothers out of the bankruptcy court, the Rogin-Schatz-Weinstein plan had fashioned something quite unique: a means to protect tort *claimants* in the face of a tortfeasor's bankruptcy. Rather than face certain liquidation, which would yield little compensation to claimants, the otherwise profitable circus had found a successful way to meet its obligations to tort claimants and creditors, rebuild itself, and go on to future success. The arbitrated settlement scheme to provide compensation to individual claimants made the receivership even more unusual.

Nationally, the use of a state receivership to protect tort claimants was virtually unprecedented. Arthur Sachs noted only one other case in his 1951 note in the *Yale Law Journal*:[3] the Winecoff Hotel fire of 1946, in which a state court contemplated the appointment of a receiver.[4] Initially the state court followed the general rule that "in the absence of some broadening statutory provision, a receiver will not be appointed at the behest of one claiming to be a creditor unless he has some lien or judgment."[5] The *Irwin* court explained the rationale for this rule:

> It is the duty of the State government, through the instrumentality of the courts, to protect the property of a citizen and his right to possess

and control it. This duty is not performed when the court, through the agency of a receiver, deprives the citizen of the possession and control of his property where he had not forfeited such right under some provision of the law. One of the highest privileges of a citizen is the full enjoyment in conformity with the law of the possession and use of his property. The fact that he might be poor or even insolvent will never justify, without more, a court of equity, before trial and an adjudication of disputed issues in the manner provided by our law, in depriving him of this right and subjecting his property to unnecessary expense.[6]

Quoting another court, the *Irwin* court again rejected the concept of a receivership for tort claims as "one of the harshest remedies which the law provides for the enforcement of rights, . . . allowable only in extreme cases, and under circumstances where the interest of creditors is exposed to manifest peril."[7]

As it happened, a receivership for the Winecoff Hotel *was* granted one year later in *Geele v. Willis*, after the court found that "extraordinary circumstances" warranted it.[8] Unfortunately, the court reporter does not explain the precise nature of those circumstances.

One reason that equity receiverships were so rarely employed to help tort claimants was that such relief has traditionally been considered inappropriate for nonjudgment creditors — that is, plaintiffs whose cases have not come to judgment. As Arthur Sachs explained:

> This rule is based on the old division between law and equity and rooted in the idea that a non-judgment creditor has not yet pursued his remedy at law and therefore cannot seek equitable relief. Furthermore, courts have been reluctant to apply a remedy which deprives parties of jury trials in disputed claims. And an underlying fear exists that nuisance claimants will use the threat of receivership to coerce the defendant into making a favorable settlement.[9]

Courts have also looked askance at receiverships that do not result in reorganization or liquidation, writes Sachs, because they "cannot remedy the normally long-run financial imbalances which characterize most business difficulties."[10]

Apart from the judicial barriers, it is not surprising that few claimants in mass tort cases have sought equity receiverships. Before the 1978 reforms in bankruptcy law, mass disasters or toxic torts

were aberrations that hardly justified overriding the traditional doctrinal barriers. And after the 1978 reforms were enacted, the new
bankruptcy code provided a more functional substitute forum for
supervising mass tort litigation; an equity receivership for tort claimants today would seem gratuitous.

As more commentators become disenchanted with the treatment
of mass tort claims in Chapter 11 proceedings, efforts are underway
to find more efficient, equitable ways for courts to deal with mass
torts. Before examining those efforts, let us look first at how the
Bankruptcy Reform Act of 1978 made Chapter 11 a more attractive
tool—initially, at least—for dealing with the mass tort explosion
of the 1980s.

The Evolution of Bankruptcy Law

As a legal backwater that rarely provokes popular passions or major
policy debate, bankruptcy law has indeed been slow to evolve.
Significant changes in the law have occurred only every forty years,
from the Bankruptcy Act of 1898[11] to some minor amendments in
1938[12] to the major restructuring in 1978.[13] The philosophical foundations of bankruptcy law are not well-developed and its specific
mechanisms are conceived more in response to pragmatic happen-
stance than to overarching principle.[14]

Given the baroque nature of pre-1978 bankruptcy law, it is not
surprising that Ringling Brothers desperately wanted to avoid its
maw. At the time of the fire, there were three types of business
reorganizations—Chapter X, Chapter XI, and Chapter XII—but
the eligibility requirements and procedures for reorganization in
each chapter were often ill-suited to an insolvent company's needs.
Only corporations could file under Chapter X; both corporations
and individuals were eligible to file under Chapter XI; and only
individuals and partnerships could file under Chapter XII.[15]

Although Chapter X allowed businesses to restructure both their
debt and equity, it frequently required a trustee to take possession of
the company; conduct broad investigations into company finances
and operations; and supervise costly, cumbersome, and lengthy administrative procedures. Chapter XI did not have these disadvan-

tages and offered the possibility of a rapid reorganization, but it could be used only to restructure unsecured debts, offering no relief from hostile secured creditors. Because the two bankruptcy chapters for major companies could yield radically different results, prospective debtors faced a complex, risky decision when choosing between Chapters X and XI. The result, as one commentator writes, was that "all too frequently the patient died on the operating room table while the would-be doctors quarrelled over the form of the operation."[16]

These troublesome complications were swept aside with the Bankruptcy Reform Act of 1978, which sought to eliminate many of the artificial, impractical distinctions between Chapter X, Chapter XI, and Chapter XII. In their place, Congress created a single Chapter 11 proceeding, which is more flexible and inclusive than the previous code yet still faithful to the basic goals of bankruptcy law—to provide orderly, equitable financial reorganization or relief for insolvent debtors while protecting the interests of creditors. The 1978 law offered a far more useful vehicle for reorganizing unstable companies because it gave bankruptcy courts far more sweeping jurisdiction to adjudicate pending civil litigation affecting debtors.

Most notably, the new Chapter 11 expanded the definition of a "claim" against a debtor company to include a "right to payment, whether or not such right is reduced to judgment, liquidated, fixed, contingent, matured, unmatured, disputed, undisputed, legal, equitable, secured or unsecured."[17] Furthermore, the value of such claims could be *estimated* by the court, facilitating a more expeditious plan of reorganization or relief. As one scholar summarized the new provision, "The definition of 'claim' . . . was intended to encompass all legal obligations of a debtor seeking relief, no matter how remote or contingent; it was intended to provide the broadest possible relief."[18]

The new Chapter 11 generally gives debtors the chance to retain possession; there is usually no trustee appointed who might meddle with business operations. Filing under Chapter 11 also produces an automatic stay of all pending litigation against the debtor and blocks payment of all unsecured debts incurred before the filing, including interest payments and attorneys' fees. With such authority, the bankruptcy court could far more effectively give a crippled company a "fresh start," protect jobs, and provide a broader range of equitable relief to creditors.

In fact, precisely these factors led the nation's leading asbestos manufacturers to file for Chapter 11 — not because they were close to insolvency but because they were being overwhelmed by a flood of tort claimants. The apparent misuse of bankruptcy law to evade mass tort claimants was a novel, scandalous development that triggered a policy debate that continues to this day. Although the morality of such uses of Chapter 11 may be dubious, the legal and economic advantages are undeniable. "If tort liability alone, and not commercial failure, spurs the bankruptcy filing," writes one commentator, "the potential reduction of tort liability may even enhance the corporation's commercial value."[19] The diminished stigma and financial attractiveness of Chapter 11 is illustrated by the popularity of a 1989 symposium, "Investing in Bankrupt Securities." Its sponsor, the Leonard N. Stern School of Business of New York University, declared in a press release, "Bankruptcy is no longer the worst word on Wall Street. In fact, bankrupt companies are attracting investors as though Chapter 11 contained a formula for success instead of a description of failure."[20]

The Johns-Manville Corporation (since renamed Manville), Amatex Corporation, and UNR Industries filed under Chapter 11 in late July and August 1982. At the time there were over 16,500 suits pending against Manville and at least 35,000 more likely to be brought; Amatex and UNR also faced thousands of suits. The plaintiffs were mostly shipyard workers who alleged that Manville had failed to warn them of the dangers of asbestos and that this failure had led to their contracting a variety of serious, often fatal, lung diseases.[21]

Manville's apparent strategy was to have the bankruptcy court estimate their future tort liability, set aside enough money to deal with it, and emerge from Chapter 11 in eighteen months. This arrangement seemed to offer a relatively "clean" way to mop up a messy, costly problem. With the cost of settling each asbestos case estimated at approximately $40,000 and new suits pouring in at the rate of 400 a month, Manville was becoming inundated with a potentially gargantuan liability.[22] Merely the cost of attorneys' fees related to the asbestos lawsuits exceeded the company's payments for health benefits for its work force.[23] In 1977, the Federal Judicial Panel on Multidistrict Litigation had foreclosed any coordination of trials in a single district, ruling that there were too many diverse issues of fact (apart from the scientific arguments over the health effects of asbestos) to warrant such an order.[24]

Even though Manville was quite financially secure, enjoyed a positive cash flow, and ranked 181 on the Fortune 500, its officials claimed that an accounting rule required it to establish a $1.9 billion cash reserve for future liabilities, which would give the company a negative net worth. And so, with a somewhat brazen attitude unbecoming to a company seeking refuge in bankruptcy court, Manville filed for Chapter 11.[25]

The result proved to be far more tumultuous than the company anticipated. It took more than six years for the company to thrash its way through Chapter 11, negotiating with commercial creditors, shareholders, about twenty plaintiffs' representatives, another dozen representatives of co-defendants and a representative for future claimants. (Future claimants are unknown individuals who had been exposed to asbestos prior to 1982 but who had not yet evidenced symptoms of any asbestos-related disease.) A turning point in a complex legal odyssey came when the bankruptcy court named attorney Leon Silverman to represent future asbestos claimants. At the bargaining table, Silverman threatened to seek the replacement of management with a court-appointed trustee, a move that dramatically changed Manville's attitude. "That's what did it," says a lawyer involved in the negotiations. Manville "went from . . . arrogance to complete capitulation."[26]

In bare outline, the plan for reorganizing Manville created a $2.5 billion trust fund to compensate some thirty thousand asbestos claimants and tens of thousands of anticipated future claimants. The plan also created a second trust to pay for property damage to schools, hospitals, and businesses that must remove asbestos. The trust funds control a majority of Manville's stock; will receive $75 million a year for twenty-four years beginning in 1991; and, if necessary, will receive up to 20 percent of the company's net earnings each year to cover claims. As a quid pro quo for establishing the trust, Manville won the right to pay compensation only, not punitive damages, to settle the claims. The company also insisted upon mandatory settlement procedures before future litigation could be waged and has no obligation to pay all claims that may eventually materialize in full.[27]

Although the settlement plan may eventually provide meaningful compensation to claimants, many of them did not fare too well during the lengthy reorganization. Between 1982 and 1988, 2,000 of the original plaintiffs died, and none of the original 16,500 claimants had received a cent by 1988. Meanwhile, the court approved fees totalling $102 million for lawyers, accountants, and investment bankers involved in the bankruptcy proceeding. The total fee for Leon Silverman, the representative for future claimants, was $4.5 million.[28]

As it emerged from Chapter 11 in November 1988, Manville had divested itself of all asbestos products and diversified into forest products, fiberglass, and specialty products. With a $164 million profit on $2.06 billion sales in 1987, one bankruptcy analyst called the restructured Manville "a terrific company for the regular investor who wants to invest in a strong American industrial company."[29]

The claimants' trust, however, was floundering by July 1990. Trust officials anticipated finishing 1990 with a cash deficit of nearly $20 million, with no new payments from Manville expected until 1991. More claimants than anticipated were stepping forward (150,000 instead of 100,000), and the average settlements were higher than anticipated (an average of more than $43,500 each instead of $25,000). New claimants will not receive payment for at least fifteen more years, according to the trust. With no clear plan for paying some $6 billion in outstanding claims with only $2.5 billion in assets, the trust is not likely to be the claims innovation of the future.[30]

Should Bankruptcy Courts Handle Mass Torts?

However robust the new company, the Manville experience dealt a serious blow to bankruptcy law. The settlement plan eventually negotiated showed that it was indeed possible, if cumbersome and complicated, to use Chapter 11 as a vehicle for resolving an unprecedented crush of tort litigation. But at what cost to the principles and operational norms of Chapter 11? "Congress simply did not contemplate that a corporation facing massive tort liability might seek refuge in bankruptcy in order to bring thousands of claims arising under different states' laws and subject to highly individual questions of fact within the control of one judge," writes one commentator.[31] The asbestos experience and its imitation by A. H. Robins in its Dalkon Shield litigation[32] have prompted a spirited debate over whether, and with what qualifications, Chapter 11 should be used to resolve mass torts.

One of the first objections generally raised is that Chapter 11 is designed for those with a contractual relationship—a debtor and his creditors—not tort claimants. As a result, claimants are usually deemed to be involuntary, unsecured "creditors" with a lesser claim to the debtor's assets than secured creditors. Not surprisingly, transplanting tort law into the context of bankruptcy law has resulted in ongoing controversy over the larger philosophical goals that should prevail—the deterrence of tortfeasors and compensation to victims favored by the tort system or the "fresh start," equitable liquidation, and sound financial restructuring of bankruptcy law?

As if to prevent such clashes in the first place, many commentators focus on the question of whether an otherwise solvent tortfeasor commits fraud by filing for Chapter 11 status. Under current bankruptcy statutes, there are no provisions restricting a "solvent debtor" from entering Chapter 11. A *Harvard Law Review*[33] note argues persuasively, however, that creditors might successfully challenge the insolvency claims of tortfeasor companies by demonstrating either a "bad faith" filing or fraud. "If the creditors [including asbestos claimants] succeed in showing that Manville is more likely than not to remain solvent for the foreseeable future, the reorganization petition should be dismissed as an attempted misuse of the bankruptcy power," the note urges.[34] But if financial ruin seems likely, then the bankruptcy proceedings should continue.

Although "good faith" standards in filing for Chapter 11 may be fully warranted and help preserve the integrity of the bankruptcy process, they do little to help resolve a tangled knot of mass tort litigation. The overriding motive for Manville's entry into bankruptcy, after all, was to secure some form of consolidation and control over a far-flung, expensive, duplicative litigation process. Chapter 11 may not have been the ideal "solution" for either the tortfeasor company or plaintiffs, but it did provide a valuable consolidation of cases, a more orderly adjudication process, and a single forum for settlement negotiations.

A significant shortcoming of the bankruptcy "solution" is its inability to coordinate multiple co-defendants. In the circus fire litigation, the city of Hartford and officers of the Ringling Brothers were targets of suits, along with the circus itself. But plaintiffs did not ultimately pursue them because the arbitration proved successful. In today's more litigious climate, however, Chapter 11 would not likely provide a "global" solution because it insulates only one defendant, temporarily, from liability. Other co-defendants may not be bound by the bankruptcy court, and they may have conflicting strategies for responding to claimants; some want to settle quickly before their insurance is exhausted, others with greater resources may be determined to fight a pitched battle to the end. The problem of coordinating legal defense and settlement strategies among co-defendants has plagued both the asbestos and Dalkon Shield litigation.[35]

Perhaps the more vexing difficulty in using Chapter 11 to settle mass tort claims is the dilemma of "future claimants," the people exposed to a hazardous substance whose disease symptoms have not yet appeared. Despite the rather expansive notion of Chapter 11 "claims" set forth in the 1978 law,[36] bankruptcy traditionalists argue that "claims" should be limited to those "obligations incurred prior to the culmination of bankruptcy proceedings"[37]—obligations triggered not by the initial exposure to a harmful substance but by palpable symptoms. To force future claimants to participate in a reorganization could deprive them of their right to be heard and to a jury trial, such traditionalists argue.

Yet more broad-minded observers point out that the Bankruptcy Code requires any reorganization plan to be "feasible,"[38] and that "any plan that failed to accommodate future claimants would not be feasible" because those claimants would simply emerge at a later date to force another financial crisis and possible bankruptcy.[39] In the three asbestos settlement plans already established—for the Manville, UNR, and Amatex bankruptcies—future claimants were seen as interested parties to the proceedings, entitled to have a say in the development of the trust fund.

This "solution" is not without problems of its own. On the one hand, it would seem terribly unfair for the bankruptcy court to simply ignore future claimants. On the other hand, providing a trust fund to make payments over time to future claimants may cause as much hardship for the tortfeasor corporation as being without the protection of the bankruptcy court. Indeed, one smaller company involved in the asbestos litigation simply decided to liquidate its assets; it could not afford to satisfy all the pending claims, let alone create a trust fund to serve future claimants.[40]

Still another option for dealing with future claimants, class action certification, has rarely been embraced by the courts because it would abrogate the traditional right of individuals to pursue their own cases and would consolidate hundreds or thousands cases that often have very different factual circumstances.[41]

New Approaches to Mass Torts?

If Chapter 11 is a feasible yet flawed approach for dealing with mass torts, could an analogous system—a special "mass tort" forum—be devised to deal with the specific problems posed by such litigation? That question may become more urgent as more mass litigation arises, forcing the courts to muddle through with creative adjudication and controversial innovations.[42] Clearly the toxic tort poses more obtuse legal dilemmas than mass disasters because it can be more difficult to assign blame, prove causality, and identify and compensate future victims.

As of 1991, the American Law Institute was vigorously exploring procedural reforms that would permit more efficient handling of complex litigation.[43] The American Bar Association, too, convened a special inquiry into mass tort litigation and issued a major report on the topic in 1989 that favored federal legislation to consolidate mass torts into one court.[44] The report disapproved of judges compelling the litigants in a mass tort to engage in ADR except in instances where plaintiffs had different issues in dispute. These efforts affirm the gnawing sense among many observers that "there's got to be a better way." However necessary and ingenious the court's ad hoc experiments, few observers dispute that a more deliberative approach tailored to the special needs of mass tort adjudication is needed.

As for mass disasters, whose disposition can be less complex than toxic torts, Chapter 11 may just provide an adequate framework for coping with their special problems. Margaret Lyle, writing in the *Texas Law Review*, outlines a typical scenario of a tortfeasor company using Chapter 11 to deal with a mass disaster:

> As a *quid pro quo* for establishing the trust, Manville won the right to pay compensation only, not punitive damages, in settlement of claims. The company also insisted upon mandatory settlement procedures before future litigation could be waged, and has no obligation to pay all claims that may eventually materialize in full. Suppose, for example, (1) that a corporation whose creditors consist only of tort claimants with liquidated judgments files for Chapter 11 reorganization and (2) that few, if any, future tort claims will arise, since the tort claims result from a single incident, and the cause of the tortious injury produces only immediate, not latent, effects. If some form of bankruptcy is not available to the debtor, the tort claimants will race to levy on their judgments and dismantle the debtor's assets piecemeal. Those who levy first will be compensated fully and will satisfy any judgments for punitive damages. Those who are slow to levy, perhaps because of the absence of the debtor's assets in the jurisdiction, will receive nothing.
>
> The basic premise of reorganization is that unsecured creditors will be able to obtain a greater proportion of their claims if the debtor continues as an ongoing business capable of generating a stream of payments in the future than if the debtor liquidates immediately. That is, the value of the debtor as an ongoing enterprise is greater than the value of its assets sold piecemeal. If this premise is correct with respect to the tortfeasor, then a Chapter 11 reorganization plan may create an equitable compensation system superior to the "race-to-the-courthouse system," at least in this limited example.[45]

The equity receivership for the circus fire clearly fits within this framework. Indeed, it prefigures the modern Chapter 11 proceeding. Although the circus claimants' judgments were not liquidated—no plaintiff had won a civil suit in court—there were few future tort claims expected; there was a "race to levy" the assets; and there was a need to keep the debtor in business in order to create a "stream of payments" to compensate claimants. Finally, there was a need to create a plan for equitable treatment among creditors and claimants. By its very success, the equity receivership for the circus cast a harsh light on contemporaneous bankruptcy law and illustrated the need for a more flexible authority for reorganization—a need eventually fulfilled in 1978.

There are, to be sure, some remaining problems with resolving mass disasters through bankruptcy court. Claimants who have already obtained judgments for punitive damages might clash with claimants who have only received compensatory damages. Current claimants may quarrel with representatives of future, anticipated claimants who have not yet stepped forward. Which party ought to have priority to the debtor's assets? There may be similar conflicts between commercial creditors and tort claimants over who should have priority in claiming assets. If the victims of a mass disaster come from numerous jurisdictions, efficiency and justice might well be served by consolidating otherwise duplicative trials into a single court, a solution being contemplated by the American Law Institute.

It may well be that Chapter 11 is the most feasible means available, all things considered, for dealing with the serious issues raised by mass torts. It is one solution, however, not a panacea; it will never please doctrinal purists.

With respect to mass disasters, however, there may be at least one further solution worth exploring—an approach that can in special circumstances yield more bountiful results, at less cost, more rapidly, and with arguably greater compassion and justice for victims. That approach, of course, is alternative dispute resolution. Its impressive results in two major cases—the Hartford circus fire of 1944 and the L'Ambiance Plaza collapse of 1987—give us glimpses into a neglected realm of mass tort law that surely deserves further inquiry and emulation.

Chapter 9

WHY ARBITRATION
SAVED THE CIRCUS

It is tempting to dismiss the extraordinary resolution of the circus fire tort claims as a fluke of history, an aberration with limited contemporary relevance. And truly, many circumstances surrounding the equity receivership and arbitration plan were unique to the tragedy, its principals, and the 1940s. Still, the circus fire settlement is more than a quaint historical oddity.

Seen through the prism of time, the success of the arbitration offers an actual, not hypothetical, counterpoint to the process by which mass torts are resolved today. The episode provides a commentary on contemporary legal and cultural norms for dispute resolution. Scholars of mass tort litigation might understandably wonder, for example, how is it that the crush of lawsuits could be resolved without the massive costs, delays, inequities, and uncertainties that would most certainly result today. What factors enabled such a creative innovation in the law to succeed in the first place? Are there principles or "techniques" used in the settlement that might be put to good use today?

One clear lesson from the circus fire arbitration is that the process of dispute resolution is organically related to its social and cultural context. However much our judicial system encourages the fiction that legal principles are neutral abstractions existing in a realm beyond place and time, dispute resolution is, in actuality, a product of culture. Sally Engle Merry, an anthropology professor at Wellesley College, explains:

> Disputing . . . is cultural behavior, informed by participants' moral views about how to fight, the meaning participants attach to going to court, social practices that indicate when and how to escalate disputes to a public forum, and participants' notions of rights and entitlement. Parties to a dispute operate within systems of meaning; they seek ways of doing things that seem right, normal, or fair, often acting out of habit or moral conviction. The normative framework shapes the way people conceptualize problems, the ways they pursue them, and the kinds of solutions they look for.[1]

From this perspective, the circus fire settlement must be seen as an artifact of a more stable, community-minded society engaged in an unparalleled war effort. After nearly four years of war, Americans had developed a keen sense of national unity. Patriotic voluntarism and cooperation were normative social virtues. When the fire hit, citizens accustomed to wartime sacrifice, victory gardens, and civic involvement sprang into action. The State War Council alerted its network of emergency action groups and supervised hundreds of volunteers who directed traffic, assisted in medical treatment, located lost family members, and transported victims and their kin. Various companies in the Hartford area released their employees from work to assist in the effort, earning them awards from the federal office of civil defense at a ceremony on September 8, 1944.

In his radio address a week after the fire, Governor Baldwin expressed the widely held sentiment that the fire was a home front war casualty: "[We] were organized for protection against enemy attack—a bombing raid which has never come. But a bomb attack could not have struck more swiftly, with less warning, or more cruel force than this circus fire. The injuries, indeed, were much the same as could have been expected in any enemy raid with incendiary bombs —many severe burns and a smaller number of fracture cases."[2]

The governor's wartime references were not rhetorical flourishes. Given the wartime scarcity of gasoline, railroad cars, and other supplies, the circus would not have been touring the country had it not been granted special government permission to do so. Federal officials saw the circus as a useful way to boost morale among a war-weary population, as well as a means for selling war bonds. The fire was literally war-related to the extent that vital flame-retardant, waterproofing chemicals were reserved for the war effort—for soldiers' tents—forcing the circus workers to rely on more flammable waterproofing agents.

In Hartford as elsewhere in the country, the war had intensified the sense of community and civic-connectedness that, even discounting the war's effect, was far more common in the 1940s than it is today. Americans of that time were not as mobile or transient. Extended families commonly lived in the same towns. Communities were more self-reliant, frequently to the extent of being isolated and parochial. Postwar innovations that we take for granted—television, universal telephone service, the interstate highway system, a more integrated national economy—had not yet emerged. American culture lacked the homogeneity and sense of national focus prevalent today. The very scale of daily experience was smaller, more personal and human. Moral norms were more consensual and accepted. Dissenting political and cultural movements that would splinter community norms over the next twenty years—beatnik culture, civil rights agitation, consumerism, environmentalism, feminism, youth culture, and antiwar activism—were scarcely imaginable in 1940s culture. And understandably so. Enmeshed in a titanic struggle against clear and powerful enemies, Americans could hardly admit of moral complexities or dissent. The war created an urgent, shared imperative of national purpose.[3]

Given these special circumstances, it is easier to understand how hundreds of fire victims and their attorneys could unanimously consent to an arbitration scheme to settle their damage claims. Professor Merry writes, "In general, anthropological studies indicate that when disputants are bound together by multi-stranded social relationships, they will seek to compromise their differences, but when they have only single-stranded social ties, they will seek victory in adversarial contests rather than attempt to reach compromise."[4] In the wartime climate, a pitched battle of litigation over a war-related disaster would have been perceived as distinctly mean-spirited and antisocial. For attorneys, the idea of exploiting a terrible community tragedy for personal gain would be seen as repugnant. Chastened by peer pressure and public sentiment, plaintiffs' attorneys were willing to accept a modest fee schedule under the arbitration plan, and Edward Rogin offered to serve as receiver for free until every last claimant was paid in full.

Wartime patriotism and the cultural climate of the 1940s helped make the arbitration work, yet these were not the only influential factors. Much of the arbitration's success stemmed from the personal initiative and courage of several public-spirited attorneys and humane circus officials. Two major circus stockholders—Edith Ringling and her niece by marriage, Aubrey Haley—were especially distraught at the human suffering caused by the fire. The two women had recently wrested control of the circus from John Ringling North and placed Edith's son, Robert Ringling, at the helm. Robert was billed to the nation as a "true Ringling," not like the "upstart" without the Ringling last name.[5] With the family name on the line, Edith was fierce in her desire to see the circus succeed. In the face of the tragedy, Edith and her niece were eager to take whatever action would help them keep the circus solvent and the Ringlings in control—while also making amends to the fire victims. The arbitration agreement promised to accomplish all these ends. Edith's support for the settlement plan was critical to its initial acceptance and eventual success, according to the late U.S. District Judge M. Joseph Blumenfeld, an attorney for the plaintiffs at the time.[6]

The very fact that stockholders can feel personally responsible for a tragedy caused by their business is something of an anachronism today, when most significant businesses are no longer owned and operated by identifiable families but by anonymous investors and transient managers. One need only consider the distinct lack of remorse among holders of Manville stock for the asbestos tragedy[7] to realize how the nature of corporate ownership and control affect the sense of corporate responsibility. Without a stinging sense of personal moral obligation, today's corporate owners, managers, and attorneys are more inclined to pursue tenaciously every available legal defense, no matter how costly or morally obtuse, than to promote fair-minded settlements.[8] And to favor a compromise is viewed as a cowardly form of surrender.

Of course, the circus's attorney, Dan Gordon Judge, also played an important role in encouraging the "gallant ladies" (as the press called Edith and Aubrey) to agree to the settlement plan. Judge, an expert in receivership law, realized at once that prolonged litigation would sound the death knell for the circus. He saw that the settlement scheme held the most promise for helping the circus survive with its finances and honor intact.

If Edith Ringling, Aubrey Haley, and Dan Judge were at least receptive to the receivership and arbitration, the original impetus for the plan came from three Jewish attorneys for the plaintiffs who enjoyed only modest standing in their WASP-dominated profession, despite their keen legal minds and personal daring. To appreciate the magnitude of Rogin, Schatz, and Weinstein's achievement, one must understand the stratifications of class and ethnicity in the legal profession at the time.

In his 1966 history of legal ethics, Jerome Carlin notes that elite law schools in the mid-1930s and 1940s did not accept ethnic groups, including Jews.[9] Many "mixed" law schools, which did accept ethnic minorities (if only to make money from them), closed down during the Depression, further limiting the supply of ethnic attorneys. The top 20 percent of the bar worked in elite firms, primarily serving corporate clients. The lower strata of the bar served clients from the middle class, and those of Jewish, African-American, and Puerto Rican backgrounds. These lower-prestige attorneys were also more likely to take on plaintiffs' personal injury cases, accept criminal cases, and spend more time in court. Jewish attorneys in particular often suffered from discrimination and found it harder to earn an income from "blue chip" clients or ascend to high-status positions in the bar.[10] Julius Schatz was one of the first Jewish lawyers in Hartford to storm the Yankee-dominated bar to obtain insurance company referrals—a breakthrough that engendered more than a little resentment in the inner circles of the establishment bar.

In responding to a massive tragedy that galvanized the most elite circles of the Hartford bar, it was something of a coup for three Jewish plaintiffs' attorneys to rally their colleagues behind an inventive settlement scheme with scant legal precedent. It is perhaps significant that a creative plan to secure *real* justice rather than a formulaic equivalent originated with men who realized they were underdogs in the aristocratic legal profession. Whatever anti-Semitic sensibilities lurked among the bar's leading lights, the urgency of dealing with the circus fire tragedy helped neutralize the religious discrimination that assuredly existed at the time. By giving their backing to the plan, such pillars of the Hartford bar as U.S. Attorney Robert Butler, State's Attorney Meade Alcorn, and circus attorney Cyril Coleman also helped ensure its success.

Lawyers' integrity and reputation proved indispensable to making the arbitration work, recalls Olcott Smith, a former president of Aetna Life and Casualty and now the oldest partner at Day Berry & Howard, the old-line Hartford law firm. Smith knew Cyril Coleman, a fellow partner at the law firm, quite well. Because Coleman was a modest, popular man seen as fair-minded and straight-shooting by his colleagues in the bar, plaintiffs' attorneys were willing to trust him in the settlement process. They did not fear wily tactics or backstabbing; his word meant a great deal. The same spirit of trust and goodwill applied to Daniel Campion, one of the arbitrators. Smith, who once served as a part-time prosecutor in West Hartford while Campion was the municipal judge, said that Campion's reputation as a fair and reasonable man gave everyone added faith in the arbitration process. For some lawyers, the circus arbitration gave them the visibility and stature to transform their small firms into the mainline Hartford law firms of today.[11]

Judge King deserved great credit for giving his judicial imprimatur to a venturesome, necessary legal experiment. At a time when more conventional legal minds might easily have balked, King astutely saw that there was greater peril in not stretching legal precedent than in rigidly following the black letter of the law. Once the popularity of the temporary receivership became evident, it became fairly easy for Superior Judge O'Sullivan to ratify King's decision two months later and make the receivership permanent.

Fortunately, the Hartford insurance establishment was also quite eager to see this unconventional scheme succeed. For an industry that sells peace of mind in the face of risk, the fire was profoundly unsettling. Insurers make it their business to prevent catastrophe, to the extent possible, and here was one of the worst imaginable tragedies occurring in their own backyard. To give added piquancy to the disaster, the instantaneous death and disfiguring injury came in the context of the circus, one of the most escapist, happy forms of mass entertainment. Even insurers, it turned out, could do little to prevent such a disaster or console survivors. Rather than acquiesce to a circus bankruptcy in which everyone would lose, financially and emotionally, Hartford insurers lent their strong moral support to the arbitration plan.

If Hartford in the 1940s offered a hospitable social, cultural context for settlement, there were also some cold, hard legal reasons for seeking an arbitrated resolution. As discussed in chapter 8, bankruptcy law at the time was just too impractical and unpalatable an option. If forced into bankruptcy, the circus would probably have been forced to liquidate its assets before any equitable or substantial payments could be made to all plaintiffs. And even if the circus had remained solvent, enabling fire claimants to go to court, Julius Schatz estimated the litigation would have clogged the courts for ten years, enriching attorneys while yielding modest, perhaps minuscule, damage awards to claimants.

Another reason that the hard-nosed plaintiffs' bar was ready to dispense with litigation and move to arbitration was the legal limit of $15,000 in damages for wrongful death cases. Weinstein and other members of the bar indicated that family members could not achieve a higher recovery by pursuing a court case instead of arbitration. And the arbitration process, as we have seen, was speedier and less expensive than the court system. Moreover, the $15,000 figure was not inconsistent with the expectations of surviving family members; it was considered a generous sum of money in 1944.[12] By contrast, the $3,000 cap for wrongful death awards contained in the current state workers' compensation law (for workers with no dependents) is obviously unacceptable to the surviving spouses of contemporary work-related mass disasters. Families are understandably motivated to find ways to *avoid* the workers' compensation (arbitration) approach in favor of mass tort litigation.

The success of arbitration in resolving the circus fire may be closely related to its factual circumstances as a mass disaster. A toxic tort, which has more ambiguous causality and blame, may be less amenable to arbitrated settlement. Professor Richard Epstein notes that the fire settlement "involved harms to separate individuals that arose out of a single act by the defendant. The time between the defendant's wrongful conduct and the occurrence of the injury was relatively short, and the causal chains . . . did not give rise to any colorable claim of remoteness of damages, contributory negligence or assumption of risk."[13] For these reasons, the Hyatt Regency skywalk disaster of 1986 and the L'Ambiance Plaza collapse of 1987 are more susceptible to alternative dispute resolution than the Agent Orange incidents or the Bhopal tragedy. The latter two disasters involved latent harms, which typically make it very difficult to define the pool of claimants, let alone bargain or litigate a just award for them in a procedurally acceptable manner.

As seen by this analysis, the success of the circus fire arbitration must be attributed to many complex, interconnected factors. It is tempting to seize upon the unique factors that made the settlement "one of the most civilized arbitration agreements in modern history," as one commentator put it.[14] After all, the settlement drew upon the spirit of wartime patriotism and voluntarism; the sense of community made possible by a smaller, more human scale of society; the sense of personal responsibility that came with family ownership of the circus; the more stable, consensual moral norms of the time; and a more staid legal culture less prone to cutthroat litigiousness. These social and cultural factors are far less prevalent today.

Were the claimants better off under the receivership and arbitration than had they pursued their own lawsuits in court? Unquestionably so. Under the plan, the amount of damages was speedily established for each claimant and the full amount due was soon paid out. By contrast, a court suit would have prolonged the assessment of damages and may well have been fatal to the circus's recovery — to everyone's detriment.

Of course, an equally important concern was the fairness of the damage awards themselves. At the time, some claimants grumbled that their awards were too low. One granddaughter of a fire victim recalls that her family received only a negligible sum for the death of her grandfather, a very healthy man of seventy. And the last holdout, William Derby, found $100,000 grossly inadequate for the harm

done to his family. Leaving aside the merits of these and other particular objections to the size of awards, it bears remembering that
all the victims and their lawyers did consent to accept the arbitration agreement, even though they had a clear right not to do so.
Traditionalists who argue that the pressure to settle itself constituted a form of coercion must concede that mass tort litigation has
its own elements of coercion as well. Given the many delays, costs,
and other complications of mass torts that overwhelm the interests
of individual claimants, the conceit that individual rights are better
protected through traditional litigation can be illusory.

Ultimately, the real question is whether the outcome of the circus
arbitration was "just." Donald Weckstein contends that in the resolution of legal disputes one must not only aim for "truth" but also
for "justice."[15] And the values of justice, he notes, "may be political,
religious, social, psychological or simply pragmatic." Here, in the
context of the social, legal, and pragmatic realities of the 1944, it
must be said that the circus receivership and arbitration yielded far
greater justice than would have been possible via traditional litigation. The rights and protections of the American system of justice
are an admirable achievement that no reasonable person would want
to erode. Yet it is a Procrustean notion of justice to believe that only
traditional litigation procedures can adequately serve the complex,
multifarious ends of "justice."

Despite its blemishes, the success of the receivership and arbitration generated a distinct sense of triumph. The amicable, civilized, and ingenious manner in which the awful tragedy was resolved
left a moral glow among the Hartford bar and the community. In
the hearts and minds of the participants, the sense of justice done in
an honorable manner more than compensated for the imponderable
shortfalls in damage awards and attorneys' fees. There was general
gratitude that the legal aftermath of the fire did not compound the
initial tragedy.

Although American society and its attitudes toward dispute resolution have changed dramatically over the past five decades, it would
be a mistake to conclude that the circus fire and ADR more generally have little relevance to contemporary mass disasters. If anything,
the disincentives to traditional mass tort litigation have grown, as

chapter 7 illustrates, even as (or because) a spirit of litigiousness has intensified. Arbitration may seem a less promising option today, given the normative framework for conceptualizing legal problems and solutions. But even in today's more aggressive legal culture and atomized society, it is possible for enterprising attorneys and judges with a keen sense of community and decency to tap into a latent spirit of "wanting to do the right thing," sidestepping the debilitating, often inconclusive dance of adversarial litigation. To be sure, the traditional process of litigation is an invaluable tool for generating clear policy judgments, fair determinations of fact, and the orderly resolution of disputes; it would be fatuous to propose any wholesale alterations to that framework. Yet ADR is not without its own considerable merits.

When creative litigants operating in a spirit of mutual respect and goodwill can overcome cultural norms that encourage rancorous, prolonged litigation, their behavior generates an uplifting sense of moral transcendence. Surely this is one reason that the circus fire settlement retains its fascination and why ADR is experiencing something of a ground swell today. The example of an honorable process yielding estimable results has a compelling moral attraction in a legal system that is too often nasty, brutish, and interminable.

The circus fire settlement as historical fluke? Skeptics can make a plausible case for that conclusion. Yet the creative resolution of the L'Ambiance Plaza collapse litigation suggests that ADR in mass disasters, although still relatively rare, is not as impractical or visionary as traditionalists might argue. Its chief defect may be that it is simply not tried often enough to prove its promise.

Chapter 10

ALTERNATIVE
DISPUTE RESOLUTION
AND MASS TORTS

It is significant that virtually every group of mass tort cases that begins with litigation eventually results in settlement; a final judgment rendered by the courts is rare. Sooner or later the litigation-weary participants realize that there has got to be a better way to resolve the bewildering crush of complex, multifaceted disputes. Even the chief attorney defending the Union Carbide Corporation against lawsuits arising from the Bhopal disaster—a man who could more easily and profitably endure a litigation ordeal than his poverty- and disease-stricken adversaries—conceded at the end, "The regret I have is that it was not settled earlier."[1] Although the American Law Institute does not necessarily endorse settlement as the best way to resolve complex litigation, it does agree that "the time has come to replace ad hoc innovation with procedures developed specifically for complex cases. This is especially true because the essential features of complex litigation are predictable, and the number of cases is bound to increase."[2]

However strong the consensus that reform is needed for handling mass torts, it is difficult to move away from the principles that have historically governed tort litigation. Who is eager to stray from the principle that individuals ought to be allowed to pursue their particular grievances against defendants, under the aegis of due process, as a means to establish blame and force full compensation for harm? The basic model of tort litigation, writes Professor Peter Schuck, is "deeply embedded in American legal traditions and individualistic liberal values that sanctify certain doctrines and institutions—the fault standard, private control of litigation, trial by jury, the dominance of "reasonableness" criteria, the preponderance-of-the-evidence rule for proof of causation, and a relatively passive judicial role in tort cases."[3] To embrace alternative dispute resolution (ADR) as a substitute means to depart from many of these values. This understandably troubles some commentators. One of the more adamant critics of settlement, Professor Owen M. Fiss, explains his revulsion: "Settlement is for me the civil analogue of plea bargaining: Consent is often coerced; the bargain may be struck by someone without authority; the absence of a trial and judgment renders subsequent judicial involvement troublesome; and although dockets are trimmed, justice may not be done. Like plea bargaining, settlement is a capitulation to the conditions of mass society and should be neither encouraged nor praised."[4]

It is difficult to quarrel with Professor Fiss's defense of the values embodied in traditional adjudication: its legitimacy, its protections of individual rights, its value in clarifying legal rights and responsibilities, its counterbalance to inequitable distributions of power. Yet such a defense, at least with respect to mass torts, fails to grapple with the sheer impracticalities that attend mass litigation—and *their* accompanying injustices, as described in chapter 7. Indeed, it is only because the impracticalities have become so grotesquely overwhelming that creative jurists and attorneys have sought out more attractive, and arguably more just, alternatives.

Almost by definition, none of the novel settlement alternatives concocted in recent years (such as the Asbestos Claims Facility or Dalkon Shield Claimants' Trust) has been achieved through a process having the same moral stature of traditional adjudication. Yet they usually have the inestimable advantage of yielding crudely equivalent results more quickly and efficiently, at less expense and in a less searing manner than litigation. Indeed, settlement can offer a more responsive, flexible, and satisfying remedy to plaintiff grievances and defendant concerns than adjudication.[5]

Identifying and implementing large-scale reforms requires many years, much study, and bold choices that depart from traditional norms.[6] That inquiry is beyond the scope of our analysis here, which is both more modest and action-oriented. Until larger policy or procedural solutions can be forged, the parties embroiled in litigation naturally want to explore solutions that lie more within their own control. For this reason, settlement innovations have flourished as mass tort litigation has become more onerous, perplexing, and commonplace in the 1980s. Necessity has become the mother of invention. The new claims resolution models—from Agent Orange to the Dalkon Shield to asbestos—implicitly challenge the moral foundations of traditional litigation. By April 1989, the breadth of innovation had reached a sufficient critical mass to warrant a special conference, "Mass Settlements of Mass Torts," at which participants in some of the major claims resolutions efforts traded notes on the new extrajudicial settlement mechanisms and institutions.[7]

Given the fitful, ad hoc trend toward exploring efficient yet fair settlement solutions, it makes sense to ask what could be achieved if settlement negotiations were initiated, instead, at an earlier stage of the process. Under what circumstances would an early, more structured settlement process be feasible and desirable? What techniques might facilitate such a process? What protections ought to be built into any such talks? In short, what might an ADR approach toward resolving a mass tort look like and how might it be replicated?

For those who find the circus fire receivership and arbitration too antiquated a model for today's mass torts, a more contemporary version exists that merits consideration: the remarkable settlement of litigation triggered by the collapse of the L'Ambiance Plaza, a thirteen-story apartment building under construction in Bridgeport, Connecticut, in 1987.[8] Its applicability to massive toxic torts may be limited. Even for mass disasters, it need not be construed as a universal settlement model. Yet it does dramatically illustrate the promise and potentialities of ADR in mass tort situations.

The L'Ambiance Plaza Settlement

At 1:30 P.M., April 23, 1987, the concrete slabs for the partially completed L'Ambiance Plaza building suddenly and without warning gave way. Within ten to fifteen seconds, the entire structure, then six stories, came crashing down, killing twenty-eight workers and seriously injuring another sixteen. The death toll made it one of the worst accidents in the history of construction in the United States. The legal aftermath of the tragedy promised to be "among the most complicated, lengthy and expensive to hit a state court in recent years," reported the *Hartford Courant*.[9] One month after the disaster, Superior Court Judge Sidney Landau complained that the voluminous court file that had already materialized was "a foreign animal that I have not seen before."[10] A leading plaintiffs' attorney estimated the case would generate as many as 500,000 documents.

Plaintiffs' attorneys quickly filed initial suits called "bills of discovery" in the Bridgeport Superior Court to gain information needed to help frame complaints, such as the names of subcontractors and suppliers working at the site and their working relationships. The looming tidal wave of pretrial discovery prompted Judge Landau to call nearly forty attorneys into court and ask them to "step out of the box we're very comfortable in and look at something that's been done in other jurisdictions," namely, to rationalize the process. Attorneys were asked to divide into three groups—plaintiffs, defendants, and insurance companies—in order to arrange for a site inspection, organize a system for preserving evidence along with a means of cost sharing, organize a master filing system, and propose a court schedule for filing motions. Although most defendants approved of Landau's modest attempt to streamline the process, others felt that they could not work with other defendants. One attorney complained about the court's departure from traditional principles of procedure.[11]

One of the chief problems of the impending litigation was the potentially large number of defendants. Anyone who had contact with the site—government bodies, suppliers, architects, engineers, subcontractors, financiers, insurers, and others—was a potential defendant. By early 1988, it was expected that over two hundred state and federal lawsuits and over one thousand cross-claims, counter-claims, and others causes of action would be instituted by more than eighty different parties.[12] In actual fact, however, fewer than ten lawsuits had been filed within six months after the accident because most lawyers were awaiting the completion of investigations by the Occupational Safety and Health Administration (OSHA), the National Bureau of Standards, and the Connecticut State Police.

At this early stage, Senior Judge Robert C. Zampano of the United States District Court in New Haven, at the suggestion of Judge Eginton in whose court the federal litigation resided, suggested a bold attempt to avert a nasty sinkhole of litigation. Zampano, the youngest federal judge when appointed in 1964 and a long-time advocate of ADR, later recalled what impelled him to take on the case and seek out an early settlement:

> It was evident that these lawsuits would involve numerous difficult factual and legal issues, millions of dollars in litigation expenses, additional emotional stress and economic strain upon the plaintiffs and defendants alike, and judicial and administrative forums in several states. Attorneys and parties predicted that there would be at least five to eight years of pretrial, trial and appellate proceedings before litigation was completed, causing a tremendous burden upon the state and federal court dockets.[13]

Recognizing that he would need to coordinate with the state court, in which most of the lawsuits would be filed, Zampano asked Superior Court Judge Frank S. Meadow to sit on a mediation panel with him to seek out an amicable settlement.

In January 1988, Zampano and Meadow joined together to convene the L'Ambiance Plaza Mediation Panel. Its purpose, they stressed, would be to mediate the disputes, not to decide or rule on factual and legal questions. The sessions were to be regarded as confidential and informal and would have no implications for possible future litigation. Any settlement proposals advanced by the panel would be nonbinding. No information shared in the mediation would be disclosed to outsiders.

Zampano's decision to convene a mediation effort so early in the process, before most cases had even been filed, struck many observers as grossly premature. After all, it was not even clear which parties would be sued, what allegations the complaints would make, what conclusions the pending investigations would make, or what evidence would emerge through discovery. Nonetheless, the mediation panel contacted all the likely parties to the litigation and urged them to participate in a mediation process "with an open mind, candidly appraising the strengths and weaknesses of their positions *as they now perceive them*, and to refrain from all pretrial procedures, except those necessary to avoid time limitations" (emphasis in original).[14] The mediation panel's request was granted, and all pending state and federal lawsuits were stayed and transferred to the mediation panel "for settlement purposes only." No additional suits were filed, and OSHA even temporarily suspended its administrative inquiry into the accident.

The judges' early intervention in the litigation proved crucial. It arrested the forward momentum of the adversarial process, preventing the future litigants from getting locked into intractable rhetorical postures and personal animosities. And it brought all parties to the same table to make some frank assessments of the legal realities awaiting everyone. As in the circus fire arbitration, the L'Ambiance mediation aspired to prevent a grim Dickensian *Jarndyce v. Jarndyce* scenario, in which the defendant's huge resources would be slowly consumed in their entirety by legal expenses. As Zampano later wrote:

> [T]he Mediation Panel had to come to grips with the unfortunate and stark reality of the lack of large liability insurance coverage, the financial instability of the majority of the defendants, and the likelihood of bankruptcy if these companies were pushed beyond their limits. The availability of resources to compensate the plaintiffs would not increase with the passage of time; rather, they would surely diminish as the economic benefits to settle are reduced and as opposing positions become "cast in concrete."[15]

Zampano and Meadow entered the mediation process thinking that they could focus solely on the forty-four personal injury and death cases. It soon became clear, however, that settlement of those cases would also require settlement of at least six other complex issues: (1) subcontractors' claims against the contractor and mechanics' liens; (2) numerous cross-suits, indemnification actions, and counterclaims among defendants; (3) liability coverage disputes involving several insurance companies; (4) claims being advanced under the builder's risk policy and the performance bonds; (5) OSHA administrative litigation; and (6) reconstruction of the collapsed building.[16]

A further complication on the proceedings was the Connecticut Tort Reform Act of 1986, which went into effect in 1987. The new law limits the doctrine of "joint and several liability" so that defendants are liable only for the proportional share of their liability. The common law doctrine that previously prevailed held that *any* defendant of multiple defendants could be held liable for the *entire* jury verdict. Also, the law eliminated the "collateral source rule" that previously allowed tort claimants to retain out-of-court settlements without deducting them from any final court awards. Because of this change, plaintiffs' counsel feel compelled to name as many defendants as possible in order to ensure an adequate recovery—a practice that also complicates the litigation and makes settlement more difficult.

In short, the "global settlement" that the mediators hoped to achieve for the death and personal injury cases ended up becoming a much larger, more complex process than anticipated. The two judges nonetheless adopted an ambitious one-year schedule for the mediation, with four primary stages: preliminary "get-acquainted" sessions with all the parties, negotiations to settle the death and personal injury cases, the writing of forty-four separate settlement opinions for those cases, and resolution of all remaining disputes. If "irreconcilable differences" arose at any stage of the process, the mediation would terminate and formal judicial proceedings would begin. Since all defendants and potential defendants knew that they could present plausible and sometimes compelling legal defenses in an adversarial setting, the challenge of the mediation was to help participants recognize the practical merits of settling.

Zampano and Meadow's first step was to spend three months consulting with construction experts, federal investigators, and state police, in an effort to understand how the collapse might have occurred. Much attention centered on the "lift-slab" methods of construction, in which concrete floor slabs are poured and hardened at ground level before being hoisted by hydraulic jacks to their correct height. But it also became clear that there was plenty of blame to go around. Zampano became "absolutely convinced that everybody on that job was negligent. Different degrees, but there is no way that one little jack slipping on one floor could cause a building of that magnitude to collapse in ten seconds. I checked this out. An implosion expert couldn't bring that building down faster with 200 pounds of dynamite, with three days of strategically placing the dynamite!"[17] Although allocating liability among the defendants might prove difficult, Zampano was convinced that the proof of ultimate liability would be easy.

Armed with a detailed understanding of the construction process and its likely shortcomings, Zampano met privately with each of the defendants to get their views on what caused the accident and what their legal defenses would likely be. "When I called each party in," Zampano later explained, "I knew where their vulnerability was. I'm not saying they didn't have a defense or maybe they could not win {at trial}. But at least I knew where they were vulnerable. And once they knew that *I* knew where they were vulnerable, they were ready to talk."

How does one begin to estimate the value of the lives and personal injuries sustained in the tragedy? Typically, the plaintiffs' or defendants' counsel would make their respective offers, and negotiations would begin from those points. But the mediation panel instead decided to issue its own proposal of fair and reasonable awards—for settlement purposes only—by reviewing each plaintiff's case individually.

In June 1988, the month he called the saddest month of his life, Zampano invited friends, families, coworkers, former employees, and fiances of the victims into his chambers to talk to the mediation panel. "We asked them to tell us about the person that was killed, tell us about their dreams and ambitions, what you'd like to have, what you could have looked forward to had they lived."[18] They brought photo albums, bowling trophies, videotapes, and other personal mementos. In one video, Zampano and Meadow watched a young child talking about his father, the vacations they took and how he found out he had died. One plaintiff's attorney recalls that an ironworker broke down crying in the judge's chambers as he talked about digging at the rubble of the collapsed building, trying to find his friend, until his fingers bled.[19] The panel also consulted witnesses to the tragedy, economists' reports, exhibits, medical reports, and briefs submitted by counsel. Researching the death cases, said Zampano, "was like going to 28 funerals and 28 wakes."[20]

Like Rogin in the circus fire arbitration, Zampano believed that an important sense of moral dignity and decency were served by keeping the personal dimensions of the tragedy uppermost; he did not allow the profound loss of human life to be lost in a blizzard of legal abstractions. "When individual negotiation sessions became particularly heated," the *Hartford Courant* reported, "the judge would refer to the men who died and the photos of their lives he kept in portfolios on his bookshelf. 'That was used in a very demonstrative way,' one lawyer said. 'It was a very effective tool.'"[21]

At the end of each session with victims' friends and family, Zampano and Meadow determined the "absolute minimum settlement figure" and a second figure that represented "a very good settlement figure."[22] When all the cases had been reviewed, the judges put them on a big chart to see if people in similar circumstances had been treated in roughly commensurate ways; they usually had. The total of the minimum settlement figures came to $24 million with a guaranteed payoff—or maximum to be paid over time—of about $45 million; the more generous sum came to $30 million with a guaranteed payoff of over $60 million. If negotiations did not yield at least $24 million, the mediation panel would disband and formal litigation would ensue. But there was at least one sign of optimism: the mediation panel estimated that "jury verdicts" required to equal the value of these awards would have to total 30 to 35 percent more than the awards proposed by the panel.[23] On the other hand, insurance coverage for the potential defendants amounted to only $20 million.

Before approaching the defendants to try to obtain the $24 million sum, the mediation panel wrote forty-four separate opinions (based on the minimum settlement awards) to obtain plaintiffs' agreement to the specific dollar amounts. The plaintiffs agreed to the proposed awards within the allotted time, clearing the way for a more difficult challenge—persuading the many defendants (and potential defendants) to settle with a joint contribution of at least $24 million rather than litigate scores of cases to an uncertain, perhaps more costly result.

In approaching defendants and likely defendants, the mediation panel suggested contributions to the settlement fund based on several criteria: "1) the degree of responsibility in terms of potential liability; 2) the insurance policy limits; 3) the financial condition of the defendant; 4) the potential 'costs of defense'; and 5) the existence of special factors which, in particular situations, would increase or decrease the amount contributed to the fund."[24] Based on the perceived potential liability, the panel asked those companies with "primary" liability to assign their total insurance policy coverage to the plaintiffs, without deductions. Companies with "questionable" liability were asked to give varying percentages of their policy limits, and those with "no responsibility" were asked to contribute certain estimated costs of legal defense. Before the complex allocations could be resolved, however, the panel had to resolve the contractual claims submitted by thirty-nine L'Ambiance subcontractors totalling $3 million, and another $11 million in claims against the builder's risk policy and the performance bonds on the project.

In orchestrating the settlement process, Zampano was described by defense attorneys as a man with an "iron fist inside a velvet glove."[25] Widely admired and sometimes feared, Zampano gave attorneys his assessment of the facts and the likely legal implications, based on his extensive investigation of the accident and his judicial experience. "I said [to the defendants]," Zampano recalled, "'If any one of you think you're going to walk out of this courthouse without some degree of negligence being found, you have another guess. Now, are you ready to talk or aren't you?'" A key part of his meetings with defendants, Zampano explained, was to remind them of the cold legal realities and likely costs of litigation: "I had parties come in and say, 'Judge, we really don't think we're liable for more than 1 percent.' And I said, 'OK, with 28 deaths and 16 seriously injured, what's 1 percent of $200 million?'"[26] Zampano, more headstrong and explosive than his colleague, Judge Meadow, a soft-spoken man, claims he had no special, planned techniques for dealing with the defendants. He simply engaged in informal conversation, punctuated by occasional outbursts and periods of poker-faced calm. One company's attorney later confessed, "It was an unpleasant experience going through [*sic*] but the result was the work of genius."[27]

"Credibility was extremely important here, particularly among defendants," Zampano explained.[28] The mediation panel had to ensure the strictest secrecy of its discussions, a policy impressed on all participants. The judges had to demonstrate their extensive knowledge of the facts, the law, the likely course of the expected litigation —and point out each party's points of legal vulnerability. Yet they also had to build bonds of trust and explain to each party how the ultimate settlement would indeed be advantageous and equitable. In the end, said Zampano,

> We didn't have any credibility problems at all. We knew that four defendants had to put in full [insurance] policy. We had ten defendants put in full policy. I haven't had one formal or informal complaint. In fact, it's just the opposite. The lawyers come up to us and say, 'Judge, I know why I threw in my full policy but how the hell did you get "Bill Smith" to throw in his full policy?' . . . We knew there was no defendant with egg on his face.[29]

Zampano and Meadow eventually managed to untangle the knotty ball of related litigation problems. The subcontractors accepted $8 million to settle their contractual claims. Workers compensation insurers agreed to waive their rule requiring repayment of benefits from any worker who received a court award. The city of Bridgeport, another defendant, was persuaded to contribute $2 million in deferred funds to the settlement. The owner/developer of the L'Ambiance Plaza agreed to quitclaim the site and cede all rights and title to the plaintiffs, creating another source of funding for the settlement fund. And OSHA, which had levied $5 million in fines, consented to scale back its penalties by 90 percent so that defendants and insurers would not balk at making contributions to the settlement fund. For their part, plaintiffs' attorneys agreed to reduce their traditional one-third contingency fees by $2.5 million, yielding a more modest yet adequate fee of slightly less than 20 percent of the final awards.[30]

Eleven months after the mediation began, Judges Zampano and Meadow had secured $30 million in settlement commitments—$6 million more than needed—which would yield an eventual payout of $41 million. Individual settlements ranged from $50,000 to $1.3 million, with various schemes for immediate and structured payouts. In a remarkable gathering on December 1, 1988, the U.S. District Court, Connecticut Superior Court, Probate Court, State Workers' Compensation Commission, and an OSHA administrative court all convened simultaneously in New Haven to give final approval to the settlement.

With well-deserved pride, Judge Zampano later summarized the significance of the historic negotiations: "We proved that 92 lawyers *could* agree to a settlement, and that 90 percent of the potential defendants would be willing to settle before they would be sued. We proved that we could settle a mass tort case before discovery. We proved that you could settle negligence cases along with contract claims and along with government involvement [OSHA, the city of Bridgeport]. So I'm hoping that L'Ambiance will serve as a model for saying *it can be done*, because they did it in Connecticut."[31]

But can the art of settlement be replicated in cases of different character and circumstances? Much depends upon the commitment and creativity of the judge and litigants, but many valuable insights and mechanisms enhance the likelihood of settlement.

The Art of Achieving Settlement

Because the process of settlement is based on trust, accommodation, and mutual consent—attributes not notably present in adversarial litigation—there is a common perception that ADR is one of "the gentler arts."[32] It is not. Success in forging settlements for disputes —especially those entailing high stakes, as mass torts do—requires the same fierce determination and creative lawyering that scorched-earth litigation does. What differs is that ADR grapples more fully with the human, psychological complexities of disputes and offers a more flexible framework for meeting each party's respective needs.

One insight that Edward Rogin and Judge Zampano both exploited was that most people *want* to find some expeditious, fair way to resolve major disputes without prolonged personal hardships and nasty public spectacles that accompany litigation. "We as human beings are basically congenial, sociable and conciliatory," Zampano contends. "Almost all aspects of the litigation process are painful and it is natural to seek to avoid them. We abhor verbal assaults as well as physical assaults. We resent attacks on our credibility and we are offended when our assertions and our version of an occurrence are not accepted as truth." In Zampano's experience, "the most significant factor bringing parties to amicable resolution is their *personal*, intense desire to avoid the rigors of a trial" (emphasis in original)[33] —which is one reason why Zampano prefers to deal directly with the litigants instead of through their attorneys.

Traditional litigation does not take into account how the litigants may *feel* about the process and what they want from it. Subjective sensibilities, to be sure, should not prevail against objective law, yet it is also true that litigants' psychological attitudes can affect the manner in which disputes are resolved. Aside from obtaining a just award, plaintiffs put a certain premium on having their stories told and their grievances understood. Mary Stone, a Dalkon Shield plaintiff, is pursuing her litigation even though she does not especially care about the money. "I can't put a money value on my pain or the child I couldn't have. All I want is this pain gone away." What would really please her, she said, would be "to get [A. H. Robins officials] across the table and get them to apologize to me. That would be worth millions."[34] Participants in ADR, such as a woman who steadfastly refused to settle her food poisoning lawsuit, often agree to settle after having a chance to tell their story of victimization.[35] A plaintiff's attorney agrees: "The most important factor is having the client tell his/her story to the mediator and [insurance] carrier. This provides a catharsis for the client and gives the carrier a chance to see and hear the client directly, not through intermediaries."[36] Aggrieved victims often want the simple satisfaction of "their day in court" and a vehicle for achieving an emotional denouement to a painful episode.

For their part, defendants often have their own reasons for wanting to reach a quick, fair resolution. Judge Zampano finds that corporate presidents are among the quickest to realize the merits of

settlement: "You know why? Because corporate presidents are negotiating all day long, with unions, to buy buildings, and so on. But
when it comes to law, they're not part of it. They have inhouse
counsel. Bring [the CEO] in and you'll see how fast they negotiate."
There are, of course, circumstances in which multiple defendants
have such divergent interests that it is difficult for them to unite for
negotiations with plaintiffs—the chief problem plaguing the now-
defunct Asbestos Claims Facility set up with the help of former Yale
Law School Dean Harry Wellington.[37] The asbestos claims resolution experiment illustrated, also, that defendants who enter into the
settlement process with closed minds and mendacious attitudes are
not likely to achieve settlements.[38]

One frequent problem in achieving settlement is that talks often
commence long after litigation has begun. By that time, adversarial
postures have been assumed and shifts of psychological attitude
and legal polemics become more difficult. "It is in those [early]
stages that patterns and expectations are set and thus it is in
those stages where an infusion of intellectual discipline, common sense, and more direct communication might have the most
beneficial effects," writes Wayne Brazil.[39] Notably both the circus
fire and L'Ambiance Plaza negotiations were initiated at the very
outset; as a result, each side had room to change positions, develop
bonds of trust, and candidly confront the problems at hand. As
shown by the Early Neutral Evaluation (ENE) process pioneered
by the Federal Court for the Northern District of California, ADR
can:

> encourage each party, at the outset, to confront and analyze its own
> situation in the suit; provide each litigant and lawyer with an opportu-
> nity to hear the other side present its case; help the parties isolate the
> center of their dispute and identify the factual and legal matters which
> will not be seriously contested; help parties develop an approach to
> discovery that focuses immediately on the key issues and that would
> disclose promptly the key evidence; offer all counsel and litigants a
> confidential, frank, thoughtful assessment of the relative strengths of
> the parties' positions, provide the parties with an early opportunity to
> try to negotiate settlement.[40]

What makes ADR attractive to many litigants and particularly useful in mass tort cases is its usefulness in providing an early, informed appraisal of each side's case. When nearly nineteen hundred attorneys were queried concerning what makes a settlement negotiator effective, the factor mentioned twice as often as any other was the negotiator's "willingness to express an opinion, to comment specifically on the strengths or weaknesses of evidence or arguments, or to offer a valuation of the case."[41]

The discovery process cannot provide an adequate substitute for this sort of early, impartial assessment of a case. Although discovery certainly swells the evidentiary record and sometimes reveals important facts, the findings are rarely unequivocal. "I have had very, very few civil cases where there hasn't been two sides," Zampano said. "Even baloney has two sides. Discovery only gives an attorney an opportunity to show the judge strengths. But it also gives the opponent an opportunity to show the weaknesses. Now, there may be some weight on one side or another. All I'm saying is that in very few cases will discovery have the lawyers come in and say, 'My goodness, we are 100 percent liable.'"[42]

In the aftermath of a mass tort, what is often missing is an early catalyst for activating people's natural inclinations for settlement and a framework for productively harnessing those sentiments toward agreement. A classic example of missed opportunity is the litigation imbroglio that resulted from the 1986 San Juan Dupont Plaza Hotel fire. Settlement was achieved only after more than one million pages of court papers, including two thousand depositions, had been generated over the course of three years. Many of the pretrial expenses and delays could have been avoided had settlement options been explored early on.

As the circus fire arbitration and L'Ambiance Plaza settlement demonstrate, a tough, creative judge or attorney can serve as the catalyst; a variety of ADR models can provide the framework; and with luck, propitious circumstantial factors such as community goodwill or existing bonds of trust among parties can foster settlement. Although litigants or private ADR groups sometimes instigate ADR efforts on their own, such initiatives generally require greater reservoirs of goodwill to succeed than those instigated by judges. Trial judges, and particularly senior judges like Zampano who have special stature and experience, can use the prestige of their positions to help get talks underway and prod them along. U.S. District Judge Robert R. Merhige, Jr., of Richmond, Virginia, who forged the Dalkon Shield settlement, notes that "there are certain cases that cry for settlement" yet "each side, psychologically, seems to be reluctant to make the first move, so to speak. And I try to get them to make a move, that's all. If the judge tells them to make a move, it makes it easier."[43] Most attorneys approve of this sort of intervention. According to the survey of attorneys mentioned above, 85 percent feel that involvement by federal judges is likely to improve significantly the prospects for achieving settlement; 70 percent believe that federal judges should try to facilitate settlement even in cases where no one has asked them to.[44]

The manner in which judges choose to foster settlement can take many forms. Arbitration, a process by which disputants submit their case to an impartial third party in order to obtain a binding decision, is probably the oldest and most respected ADR method. Unlike litigation, arbitration is quicker, less formal and less technical. Because arbitration does not require public hearings or disclosures, it is a process that preserves the privacy of the parties involved. Parties can also maintain greater control over the process by selecting their own arbitrators, who may have specialized knowledge that bears on the dispute. Because of the narrow grounds for appeal, the arbitrators' decision is nearly always final, giving the outcome more certainty than many jury verdicts.[45]

Arbitration also has its drawbacks, especially when one or both parties are not fully committed to the process. A recalcitrant party can indulge in procedural challenges, delaying resolution of the dispute. The flexibility of traditional rules of evidence, civil procedure, and relevant law may expedite the process but can also diminish its rigor and fairness. The lack of pretrial discovery can permit cunning parties to surprise the other party during negotiations to gain an advantage. For skeptics, arbitration is merely a disguised version of the adversarial process.

Another ADR variant, mediation, is more popular with many attorneys because it is not binding. The third party seeks not to impose a settlement but only to move the parties in that direction. Plaintiffs especially like this option because it allows them to hear the defendants' claims and evidence and, if no settlement results, still proceed to court. Most tort cases heard by the Hartford office of the American Arbitration Association are mediated; only about 10 percent involve pure arbitration.

Apart from arbitration and mediation, there are less formal versions of traditional adjudication such as the mini-trial and summary jury trial.[46] Whatever the ADR model used, special care must be taken to choose a process suitable for the situation at hand. "Every case has its own unique facts," Zampano points out, adding:

> Each party's attitude, wealth and personality differ, and the attorneys have varying degrees of skill and experience. No particular process or format works in every case. Flexibility, a combination of techniques and procedures, and innovative approaches to unusual situations are required. Hardly any case settles, of course, by recommending the acceptance of one of the parties' positions, nor by splitting the parties' perceptions of the value of a case down the middle.[47]

The judges who have had success in fostering settlement in mass torts—Judge Robert Merhige (Dalkon Shield), Judge Jack Weinstein (Agent Orange), Judge Robert Zampano (L'Ambiance Plaza), among others—are usually strong-willed, creative jurists. They show a willingness to take risks and improvise, and they have an intuitive, personal flair for moving the parties toward common ground and keeping them talking. Professor Harry H. Wellington, who helped organize the now-disbanded Asbestos Claims Facility, agrees that settlement depends a great deal on "keeping the parties talking, stopping when they threaten to explode, and persuading one side or another of the realities of the situation."[48] Wellington recalls the course of the asbestos talks:

> In those early days little substantive progress was made; there was too much friction. Yet the time was well spent, for it was necessary for the parties to let off steam and for all of us to feel our way toward an approach that would help the parties learn to trust each other and, indeed, the neutrals. Progress depended on everyone's belief in the oth-

ers' good faith. Each participant had to prove that he wanted the enterprise to succeed, that he was willing to give up something important to
make it succeed, and that he was not using our group merely as a way of
advancing his own or his company's special interests.[49]

As a private mediator, Wellington did not enjoy the same prestige,
moral influence, and legal authority that a federal judge might bring
to settlement talks. There were also many centrifugal forces working
against cooperation among asbestos manufacturers.[50]

In keeping the parties talking, there can be a paradoxical advantage to there being a large number of complex issues to be addressed, notes Professor Carrie Menkel-Meadow: "[T]he greater the
number of issues, the greater the likelihood of achieving a greater
number of solutions as a result of complementary, and not conflicting,
values parties place on different items."[51] Ironically, reducing the
array of contestable issues is more likely to generate an impasse.
Judge Zampano discovered the truth of this dynamic in trying to
fashion a global settlement among the L'Ambiance Plaza litigants;
the range of possible revenue sources and players helped make settlement easier, relatively speaking.

There is not likely to be a "magic bullet" reform for mass tort
litigation, whether the focus is adjudication or settlement. The solutions, like the problems, will be complex. But it has become clear
that certain preconditions must be met for whatever alternative frame-
works for dispute resolution are adopted. Judge Jack Weinstein,
who oversaw the Agent Orange settlement, identifies seven key pre-
requisites for improved management of mass torts:[52]

1. The decision making of the parties is concentrated.
2. The litigation is in a single forum before a single judge.
3. A single set of substantive legal principles is applicable.
4. The tribunal has adequate support to perform its function.
5. Flexible methods of fact-finding are authorized.
6. Total maximum liability for a single disaster is limited, a method for
   allotting costs among the defendants is devised, and there is a sure
   source of funds.
7. A single distribution plan, which eliminates punitive damages and
   extreme claims for pain and suffering, is adopted.

These conditions more or less prevailed in both the circus fire and L'Ambiance Plaza settlements. (Item 3 — "a single set of substantive legal principles" — is not truly applicable if settlement talks preempt litigation.)

However promising we find ADR for mass disasters and, perhaps eventually, toxic torts, ADR entails distinct risks that must be kept in mind. Dangers arise when judges subtly use their judicial authority to coerce settlements in some fashion. Can a judge be both a neutral and disinterested jurist on the one hand yet an interventionist mediator personally invested in settlement on the other hand? The solution to this conundrum in the L'Ambiance Plaza case was to use a senior judge, with no potential role in subsequent adjudication, to mediate. The danger of activist, managerial judging requires that ADR be a truly voluntary process in which settling judges are conscientious about the persuasive techniques used to achieve settlement.

Another risk of settlement is the possible suppression of important facts of a public character as part of the settlement bargain. Manufacturers of Agent Orange sought to prevent disclosures about how the chemical was manufactured and used, a matter of no small import to Congress and the Veterans Administration. Critics eventually convinced Judge Weinstein to order release of certain documents because of their potential public benefit but other judges may not be as obliging.[53] Although the L'Ambiance Plaza settlement entailed no sealed records, some critics charged that the settlement preempted the search for the actual causes of the accident and made reforms of construction practices less likely.[54]

For all the criticism of ADR, it retains its appeal largely because it offers many pragmatic advantages over the process of formal adjudication. "[A]fter all is said that can be said about process," writes Professor Wellington with respect to the Asbestos Claims Facility, "it probably in the end is the case that our group reached agreement because the alternative — the present formal justice system — is too costly and is seen by almost everyone as no more than a second best way of dealing with the asbestos problem."[55] If ADR is not a fully acceptable substitute for traditional litigation, it does serve as an eloquent witness to the limitations of litigation.

If there are good reasons to avoid the use of ADR, there are even better reasons to develop innovations to make litigation more affordable, accessible to the average person, expeditious, and fair. Unfortunately, writes U.S. Circuit Judge Alvin Rubin,

> The reforms essential to speedy and inexpensive determination of mass torts . . . have been blocked by a lack of consensus concerning the substance of reforms and the opposition of those who are so close to the present system that they cannot perceive its defects. As Dean Richard Pierce has said, "No consensus is likely to develop because neither potential accident victims nor society at large has an effective voice in the lawmaking process."[56]

The lack of a consensus is one reason why attempts to *prevent* the occurrence of mass torts in the first place so often fail; it is difficult to organize the diffused, future beneficiaries of regulatory programs into an effective political force. The very frequency of mass torts in recent years testifies to the inadequacy of relevant regulations and enforcement, information disclosures to those at risk, and legal remedies by which consumers and workers can effectively deter would-be tortfeasors. Such preventive measures are far cheaper, more effective, and humane than virtually any procedural or ADR reform that can be imagined.

Once litigious harm on a mass scale occurs, however, the legal profession has a duty to provide a dignified, practical, and fair means of compensating victims while protecting the defendants' rights. This sometimes requires departures from received legal practices and good faith risk taking, which is to say a profession steeped in conservative traditions must periodically learn to embrace bold innovations to meet new social and legal needs. The aftermath of the Ringling Brothers circus fire of 1944 is breathtaking for this very reason: it achieved a breakthrough in the legal disposition of a mass tort and potential bankruptcy while illuminating facets of moral character and legal imagination that rarely achieve such glorious display.

Translating the lessons of one incident of history into something enduring and institutional is, of course, not easily accomplished. Yet the dilemmas raised by contemporary mass torts suggest that the challenges faced by the Hartford bar of 1944 are not really so remotely historical after all. Many canons of law have changed; the moral urgency for more humane legal solutions has not.

NOTES

Chapter 1: Fire at the Circus

1. Raymond Baldwin, "Address before the Junior Bar Luncheon," 30 *Connecticut Bar Journal* 253 (1956).

2. The appendix of the *1951 Route Book: Route, Personnel and Statistics for the Season of 1951* (Sarasota, Fla.: Ringling Bros. and Barnum & Bailey Circus, 1951), gives the yearly schedule of the circus from 1919 through 1951.

3. *Hartford Courant*, July 8, 1944, 1.

4. Administrative details regarding the circus's appearance in Hartford are set forth in *Report of the Municipal Board of Inquiry on the Circus Disaster* (November 1944), 9.

5. "$1,642,967,146 for Connecticut," *Hartford Courant Magazine*, November 19, 1944. Other details about the Connecticut wartime economy can be found in Herbert F. Janick, Jr., *A Diverse People: Connecticut, 1914 to the Present* (Chester, Conn.: Pequot, 1975), 58–66. The per capita war production sum of $3,000 is from the memoirs of Governor Baldwin's associate, Curtis Johnson, *Raymond E. Baldwin: Connecticut Statesman* (Chester, Conn.: Pequot, 1982).

6. Bruce Fraser, *The Land of Steady Habits: A Brief History of Connecticut* (Hartford, Conn.: Connecticut Historical Society, 1988), 57–58. Additional background on Connecticut in the 1940s can be found in Janick, *A Diverse People*, 58–66. Also, Harold J. Bingham, "The Home Front in World War II," *A History of Connecticut* (New York: Lewis Historical Publishing Co., 1962), esp. chapter 33.

7. George Chindahl, *A History of the Circus in America* (Caldwell, Idaho: Caxton Printers, 1959), 60.

8. *Transcript of Police Investigation*, on file at the Connecticut State Library [hereinafter CSL], RG [Record Group] 161, Box 66, Statement of Segee.

9. *Police Investigation*, RG 161, Box 63. For a detailed discussion of the War Production Board's role in allocating use of flame-proofing chemicals, see *Supporting Statement and Data on Motion for Suspension of Sentences and for Leave to*

Withdraw Pleas of Nolo Contendere, filed by attorneys for Ringling Bros. in *State of Connecticut v. Ringling Bros. and Barnum & Bailey Combined Shows, Inc. et al.* on March 29, 1945, as a supplement to a motion filed on March 27, 1945, 21–23 (courtesy of Arthur Weinstein).

10. *Police Investigation*, RG 161, Box 61, Statement of Blanchfield.

11. Official circus program of July 6, 1944.

12. Peter Mobilia, WPOP/Newsradio 14, Radio news show on the fortieth anniversary of the circus fire [hereinafter WPOP Radio news show], broadcast on or about July 6, 1984. Transcript on file with the Jewish Historical Society of Greater Hartford.

13. T. E. Murphy, "The Day the Clowns Cried," *Readers Digest*, June 1953, 59–62.

14. *Police Investigation*, RG 161, Box 61, Statement of Blanchfield.

15. Mobilia, WPOP Radio news show.

16. Ibid.

17. Interview with Kenneth Wynne, January 18, 1989.

18. "Strange Case of Circus Fire Arsonist" [drawings of circus fire arsonist], *Life*, July 17, 1950, 51–52.

19. "Hartford Circus Fire," American National Red Cross, Report No. 1525 (January 1946), 2.

20. Mobilia, WPOP Radio news show.

21. "Hundreds Saved as Crippled Lad Cuts Holes in Tent with Jackknife," *Hartford Courant*, July 9, 1944, 1.

22. Mobilia, WPOP Radio news show.

23. John Cleary, *Accent, The Hartford Times Sunday Magazine*, June 30, 1974.

24. Interview with Edward Rogin, December 12, 1986. Other people place Robert Ringling in Chicago or Evanston, Illinois. *Hartford Courant* July 6, 1945, 12.

25. Interview with Marianne Z. Lorenzo of West Hartford, April 1987.

26. Interview with Joseph Hurwitz of West Hartford, April 1987.

27. Interview with Dr. Milton Fleisch, July 21, 1987.

28. "Hartford Circus Fire," 5. The breadth of assistance rendered to fire victims is detailed in the circus fire archives at CSL, RG 161, Box 63.

29. Cleary, *Accent, The Hartford Times Sunday Magazine*, 11.

30. Ibid.

31. Johnson, *Raymond E. Baldwin*, 148–49.

32. "Hartford Circus Fire," 14.

33. P. T. Barnum's two autobiographies were published in 1855 and 1869, with later additions made to subsequent editions. A 1927 selection from earlier autobiographies, edited by Waldo R. Browne, appeared in 1927. The most recent edition, a paperback reprint, is Waldo R. Browne, ed., *Barnum's Own Story* (New York: Dover Publications, 1961). On 1943 Ringling fire, see *Hartford Courant*, July 7, 1944.

34. *Hartford Courant*, July 24, 1987.

35. Attribution of this theory to Tom Barber came from his daughter, Gloria Vieth, in 1984 (Mobilia, WPOP Radio news show). See also Linda Shilling, "The Circus Fire," *Hartford Times*, July 6, 1969.

36. Joseph A. O'Brien, "Notes Renew Mystery of Hartford Circus Fire," *Hartford Courant*, July 24, 1987, and O'Brien, "Notes Claiming to Reveal Victims of Circus Fire Believed to Be Hoax," *Hartford Courant*, August 1, 1987.

37. *Hartford Courant*, March 9, 1991, 1.

38. CSL, RG 161, Box 63; RG 161, Box 64.

39. *Hartford Courant*, March 9, 1991, 1, 4.

40. Associated Press story, "Circus Fire Author Goes to Jail," *Hartford Times*, November 3, 1950. Segee was apprehended in Circleville, Ohio, on May 18, 1950, and underwent extensive psychiatric evaluation. Additional details on Segee can be found in *Police Investigation* at CSL, RG 161, Box 67, and in *Life*, July 17, 1950, 51–52.

41. Ibid.

42. *Hartford Courant*, March 9, 1991, 1, 4.

Chapter 2: The Rescue of a Circus

1. Dunn's account of his involvement with the fire's legal aftermath is detailed in the *Transcript of Receiver Compensation Hearing* [hereinafter *Receiver Transcript*], *Records and Briefs* in Supreme Court, State of Connecticut [hereinafter *Records and Briefs*], January 1954, 398.

2. *Receiver Transcript*, 398.

3. Ibid.

4. Ibid.

5. Interview with Olcott Smith, a partner of Coleman's at Day Berry & Howard, May 27, 1987; interview with Mary Coleman, daughter of Cyril Coleman, May 4, 1987; and obituary for Coleman, *Hartford Courant*, September 21, 1958.

6. *Receiver Transcript*, 398.

7. "Hartford Circus Fire," American National Red Cross, Report No. 1525 (January 1946), 12.

8. *Hartford Courant*, July 8, 1944, 1.

9. *Hartford Courant*, July 9, 1944, 1.

10. Cornelius Shea, an associate of Rogin's, later described how sheriffs even placed stickers on the poles of the big top to make the attachment. Interview with Shea, July 15, 1988.

11. *Hartford Courant*, July 9, 1944, 1.

12. Ibid.

13. Interview with Arthur Weinstein, November 6, 1986.

14. *Records and Briefs*, 81.

15. *Hartford Courant*, July 12, 1944, 1.

16. On Connecticut attachment law, see *Lynch v. Household Finance Corp.*, 405 U.S. 538 (1972).

17. At common law, an attachment in a state was effective only within the borders of that state. *Harris v. Balk*, 195 U.S. 215 (1905). Of course, the plaintiffs were free to obtain a judgment and under the Constitution's "full faith and credit" clause attempt to enforce that judgment in another state. But this would have entailed much expense and a knowledge of where the Ringling assets were deposited. As a practical matter, the items under Connecticut attachment were the only assets the plaintiffs could look to recover from if the case proceeded to trial.

18. *Jacobs v. Ringling Bros.*, 141 Conn. 84, 87 (1954).

19. [Arthur Sachs], "The Equity Receivership in Mass Tort," 60 *Yale Law Journal* 1417 (1951).

20. *Receiver Transcript*, 399.

21. Interview with Arthur Weinstein, November 6, 1986.

22. *Hartford Courant*, July 8, 1944, 1.

23. The balance sheet for the circus is not available, but the circus, as will be seen in chapter 4, had for years operated under the threat of insolvency. The balance sheet would probably have shown an extremely precarious enterprise. Even after surviving the economic devastation of the 1930s and a reorganization under John Ringling North (see chapter 4), the pinched wartime economy was barely able to support the circus. In the book *The Circus Kings: Our Ringling Family Story* (Garden City, N.Y.: Doubleday, 1960), Henry Ringling North (with Alden Hatch) states that the circus had its best year in 1942 when it grossed $900,000 before taxes (330). The claims from the fire totaled at least $15 million, an especially huge sum in its day, which the circus could never have met and remained in business. Although the circus did have insurance, which was entirely committed to the payment of fire victims, it totaled less than $1 million.

   According to a memorandum in the State Police files (CSL, RG 161, Box 61), the circus had a net worth of $1 million as of December 20, 1943. The memo reports that the circus had a successful year in 1943; that the circus owned properties and personalty in Connecticut (Bridgeport), New York, and Florida; and that a bank note in the amount of $800,000 had been reduced to $364,000.

   A more precise accounting of the circus's muddled finances in the 1940s is now impossible, not only because the enterprise was a privately held company but because John Ringling North engaged in many elaborate subterfuges to dispose of numerous (prefire) claims against the circus and the estate of John Ringling, as Henry Ringling North describes in *Circus Kings* (338).

24. There is no record today of the owners of the secured debt, but they probably included the Ringling family, several banks, and, under John Ringling's will, the state of Florida. The U.S. Government had a large tax lien arising from the John Ringling estate (North and Hatch, *Circus Kings*, 338).

25. Under the Chandler Act of 1938, there was a Chapter XI, but its provisions

at the time of the circus fire were significantly different than those that prevail today under Chapter 11. Although Chapter XI had a "debtor-in-possession" provision, the circus could not avail itself of Chapter XI because its chief debts were secured debts—and Chapter XI authorized reorganizations of *nonsecured* debt only. By the 1960s, however, clever attorneys discovered that by using federal restraining orders they could make use of Chapter XI to fend off the hostile actions of secured creditors.

In 1944, however, when the circus fire hit, the Ringlings were trapped. Chapter X was too complex and cumbersome to solve their plight, yet Chapter XI would only allow them to rid themselves of unsecured debt. Secured creditors would have been unaffected and would certainly have forced a complete liquidation of the company. These deficiencies in bankruptcy law were rectified by the Bankruptcy Act of 1978, which combined the former Chapters X, XI, and XII (Railroad Reorganization) into a new, more versatile Chapter 11 that allows general use of "debtor-in-possession" and does not include the rigid requirements of Chapter X. See discussion in Special Report of CCH Bankruptcy Law Reporter, No. 251, *Report of the Commission on Bankruptcy Laws* (July 30, 1973).

26. See, e.g., W. Homer Drake, Jr., *Bankruptcy Practice for the General Practitioner*, vol. 1 (Colorado Springs, Colo.: Shepard's/McGraw-Hill, 1986), 12-2–12-6. An example of the complexities of Chapter X is pointed out by Lawrence King, ed., *Collier on Bankruptcy* (New York: Matthew Bender, 1989), 1129.02[3][a]. Under the 1938 code, Chapter X explicitly required that the debtor seeking reorganization demonstrate from the outset as an element of "good faith" that the reorganization would probably succeed. This requirement did not exist for Chapter XI or XII. Today, after the 1978 bankruptcy reforms, the "good faith" requirement is implied in Chapter 11 proceedings but is not specifically set forth in the act. The bankruptcy court may thus choose not to disqualify the debtor and must take into account the findings of fact about the debtor's business. See also Senator DeConcini's reference in the Senate floor debate to the "stilted procedures" of Chapter X. 124 *Cong. Rec.* S17, 417–19 (daily ed., October 6, 1978).

27. Patrick A. Murphy, *Creditors' Rights in Bankruptcy* (Colorado Springs, Colo.: Shepard's/McGraw-Hill, 1985), 16–3.

28. Rogin biography in *Martindale-Hubbell Law Directory* (Summit, N.J.: Martindale-Hubbell, 1987). Also, interview with Edward Rogin, December 12, 1986.

29. Veteran political columnist Jack Zaiman rendered a hilarious and telling portrait of Schatz in his column in the *Hartford Courant* on April 16, 1962: "[Schatz] is a superb arm-waver when he is in routine conversation. He throws himself around in mock anguish, agony, and delight to lay emphasis on his words. He is a complete extrovert, a master of timing and a marvelous chooser of words. . . . Schatz, by himself, supports the country's cigar industry. What

he does to a cigar is beyond description. He attacks it like a tiger closing in on its prey. If a cigar were made for smoking, you certainly would be unable to prove it by Schatz. The only concession he makes to the protocol of smoking a cigar is to light it. After that, the cigar is on its own."

30. Schatz biography in *Martindale-Hubbell Law Directory* (1987). Also, interview with Arthur Weinstein, November 6, 1986, and Schatz obituary, *Hartford Courant*, December 4, 1986.

31. Weinstein biography in *Martindale-Hubbell Law Directory* (1987).

32. Interview with Arthur Weinstein, November 6, 1986.

33. *Records and Briefs*, 81. Also, interview with Arthur Weinstein, November 6, 1986.

34. *Hartford Times*, August 23, 1950, 22.

35. On Connecticut receivership law, see [Sachs], *Yale Law Journal* 1417.

36. Interview with Edward Rogin, December 12, 1986.

37. Butler biography in *Martindale-Hubbell Law Directory* (1945).

38. *Receiver Transcript*, 344.

39. Ibid.

40. King obituary tribute, 174 *Connecticut Reports* 811 (1979).

41. Gerald J. Demeusey, "King of the Judicial System," *Hartford Courant Magazine*, October 6, 1963.

42. *Records and Briefs*, 83.

43. Interview with Arthur Weinstein, November 6, 1986.

44. Rogin described the encounter with Judge King in the *Receiver Transcript*, 199, and in an interview on 12 December 1986.

45. *Records and Briefs*, 84.

46. Interview with Edward Rogin, December 12, 1986.

47. Ibid.

48. *Receiver Transcript*, 345.

49. Interview with Edward Rogin, December 12, 1986.

50. *Hartford Courant*, July 13, 1944.

51. See text at note 26.

52. *Receiver Transcript*, 400.

53. Interview with Edward Rogin, December 12, 1986; *Records and Briefs*, 94.

54. *Records and Briefs*, 94. Also, *Receiver Transcript*, 199.

55. An unidentified newspaper clipping from Julius Schatz's files, clearly written from the circus's viewpoint and perhaps by a circus publicist, describes how Edith Ringling reacted when told of the limited insurance coverage: "'And is that all those poor people would get?' Mrs. Ringling asked, suddenly. 'I'm afraid so,' one of the company counsel answered. The two women conferred briefly, then Mrs. Ringling spoke up again, 'We'll not sell! If the lawyers can find a way for us to operate free of harassment, we'll pay all those claims— 100 cents on the dollar!'"

56. *Records and Briefs*, 94. Testimony of Edward Rogin, *Receiver Transcript*, 199.

57. *Receiver Transcript*, 399–400.

58. Ibid., 201–2.

59. Ibid., 399–400.

60. Ibid., 400. Another account of this July 13, 1944, courtroom meeting was given in the *Hartford Times* that afternoon. Julius Schatz noted that the pending lawsuits could result in $5 million in damages. He therefore suggested that a $5 million bond be posted by the circus as a condition for its departure from Hartford. But Dan Gordon Judge objected to the amount of the bond and suggested that, given the circus's available assets, $300,000 would be a more appropriate sum. Although Judge pledged to "give all we have and what will be available to take care of approved claims," he did not guarantee that all claims would be approved. Citing the health problems at the fire site and the large number of unemployed men loitering there, Hadden urged a quick circus departure from Hartford.

Attorney Anson McCook demanded that the circus freeze its assets in other states. Robert Butler suggested that the matter might have to be removed to federal court, and three receivers appointed: one from Hartford, such as Rogin, who was now the state receiver; another receiver who had sufficient circus experience to run the show; and a third, auxiliary receiver in Florida. The meeting concluded with the decision, indicated in the text, to form a local bar committee and work with the state-appointed receiver. Lucius Robinson, as noted, appointed the committee from Chicago, by telephone (*Hartford Times*, July 13, 1944, 29).

61. *Receiver Transcript*, 400.

62. Ibid., 200.

63. Ibid., 202, 401.

64. Interview with Arthur Weinstein, November 6, 1986.

65. *Hartford Courant*, July 15, 1944, 1.

66. Ibid., 4.

67. *New Haven Register*, July 15, 1944, 1.

68. *Records and Briefs*, 95.

69. *Hartford Courant*, July 15, 1944, 4.

70. *Hartford Courant*, July 17, 1944, 1.

71. *Receiver Transcript*, 403.

72. Ibid.

73. Esse O'Brien, *Circus: Cinders to Sawdust* (San Antonio, Tex.: Naylor Co., 1959), 103.

74. *Receiver Transcript*, 403.

75. Fred Bradna, *The Big Top: Forty Years with the Greatest Show on Earth* (New York: Simon & Schuster, 1952).

Chapter 3: Anatomy of an Arbitration

1. *Hartford Courant*, September 16, 1944, 1.

2. *Receiver Transcript*, 402.

3. Interview with Arthur Weinstein, November 6, 1986.

4. A clear inspiration for the arbitration agreement was an adaptation of Sections 5840–56 of the Connecticut Statutes of 1930. This statutory scheme, permitting agreements to arbitrate and controlling the step-by-step process of arbitration, was seen as a judicial reform measure when enacted in 1929.

   In an article, "Arbitration—A Vital Tool for Lawyers," 21 *Connecticut Bar Journal* 455 (1947), Frances L. Roth declared that "Connecticut legislators have been leaders in the adoption of modern arbitration laws." In 1947 the use of arbitration by attorneys had just caught on, as Roth explains: "Lawyers have become the architects and practitioners of the new practice of arbitration. As an indication of how materially the times have changed, in 1926, when the national system known as the American Arbitration Association was founded, only 37 percent of all matters submitted to the tribunals of the Association either came from law offices or had parties represented by lawyers; in 1946, in this widely distributed system, covering 1,537 cities in the United States, this percentage rose to 82, in the hundreds of matters settled each year. Lawyers now appear before arbitral tribunals in 80% of all of the hearings" (at p. 463).

   As the reasons that attorneys were opting for arbitration Roth lists (1) the "saving of time" in resolving disputes outside of the crowded court system; (2) the reliability of recovery from the debtor before his assets dissipate; (3) the freedom to choose a "technically competent tribunal"; and (4) the "friendly atmosphere" for the settlement of disputes.

5. *Hartford Courant*, November 18, 1944, 1.

6. Ibid.

7. The text of the arbitration agreement is contained in *Records and Briefs*, 86.

8. The agreement here refers to the circus's "lavish spectacles" as a normal overhead expense.

9. On the obtaining of 100 signatures by wrongful death claimants, see [Arthur Sachs], "The Equity Receivership in Mass Tort," 60 *Yale Law Journal* 1417 (1951), which states in note 12, "Public opinion in Hartford and the fear that the Connecticut court, which strongly favored the arbitration device, would look with disfavor upon non-agreement claimants strongly influenced acceptance of the arbitration by most claimants." Also, interview with Edward Rogin, December 12, 1986.

10. *Receiver Transcript*, 250–54.

11. In 1988, Rogin recalled how he had obtained approval for the agreement in seven "death cases" by reassuring one attorney that he would be taking no fees as a receiver until all claimants had been paid in full.

12. Abraham S. Bordon obituary, "Services Today for Justice Known as 'Settling Judge,'" *Hartford Courant*, August 9, 1981, B10. In this article, Abraham

Ribicoff, a former associate, states, "He taught me there can be integrity in compromise, and this I believe."

13. Daniel Campion obituary, *Hartford Courant*, April 18, 1967. Also, interview with Olcott Smith, senior partner, Day Berry & Howard, May 27, 1987.

14. Alfred C. Baldwin obituary tribute, 144 *Connecticut Reports* 749 (1958). Baldwin was described as a cautious judge who worked long into the night to understand the facts of a case and the legal arguments.

15. [Sachs], *Yale Law Journal* 1417, note 13.

16. *Hartford Times*, February 6, 1945.

17. Interview with Arthur Weinstein, November 6, 1986. Cornelius Shea recalled in 1988 that he went to a prearbitration meeting at Day Berry & Howard with a young child in tow who had a claim against the circus. The child had bought a balloon just before the conference began and the winsome portrait made an excellent impression on the defense attorneys, Shea noted.

18. John Cleary, *Accent, The Hartford Times Sunday Magazine*, June 30, 1974, 13.

19. These examples are culled from arbitration records on file at CSL, RG 3. Also, *Hartford Times*, February 2, 1946.

20. Interview with Arthur Weinstein, November 6, 1986.

21. CSL, RG 3. Also, *Hartford Times*, February 2, 1946.

22. *Receiver Transcript*, 214.

23. Ibid., 350.

24. Ibid., 402.

25. Ibid., 219.

Chapter 4: The Fight for Control of Big Bertha

1. Testimony of Cornelius Shea, *Receiver Transcript*, 304, 305, 307.

2. *Records and Briefs*, Exhibit A, 94.

3. *Receiver Transcript*, 204.

4. Ibid., 267.

5. Ibid., 212.

6. Ibid., 222.

7. Ibid., 221.

8. Ibid., 207.

9. Ibid., 214.

10. Ibid., 249.

11. Ibid., 258.

12. George Chindahl, *A History of the Circus in America* (Caldwell, Idaho: Caxton Printers, 1959), 175.

13. Memorandum to Police Commissioner Hickey, Circus Fire Archives, CSL, RG 161, Box 63.

14. *1951 Route Book: Route, Personnel and Statistics for the Season of 195[1]* (Sarasota, Fla.: Ringling Bros. and Barnum & Bailey Circus, 1951).

15. Chindahl, *A History of the Circus in America*, 176.

16. Governor Raymond Baldwin's radio address is on file in the circus fire files at CSL, RG 5, Box 451.

17. "Ringling Wrangling," *Fortune*, July 1947, 167. See also *New York Times*, February 22, 1945, 29.

18. *Coroner's Report*, circus files at CSL, RG 161, Box 63. See also *Report of the Commissioner of State Police as Fire Marshal to the State's Attorney* in RG 161, Box 63.

19. *Hartford Courant*, July 6, 1945, 12. See also *New York Times*, February 22, 1945, 29.

20. Files of Arthur Weinstein. See also "Bradenton [Fla.] Hits Sentencing of Circus Group," *Tampa Morning Tribune*, March 1, 1946. The city council of Bradenton formally adopted a resolution "to be transmitted to the clerk of the superior court at Hartford County, Conn.," protesting the "unnecessarily harsh" prison sentences for the six Ringling officers. The resolution complained that the prison sentences "will make it impossible for the show to carry on, thus depriving the youth of the nation [of] the benefits that their parents enjoyed on account of this unique American circus."

21. *Hartford Courant*, July 6, 1945, 12. *Fortune*, July 1947, 164.

22. *Receiver Transcript*, 230.

23. *1951 Route Book*, esp. 78.

24. *Fortune*, July 1947, 114.

25. Testimony of Dan Judge, *Receiver Transcript*, 411.

26. Larry Ribstein, *Business Associations* (New York: Matthew Bender, 1983), 3-29–3-43. See also *Fortune*, July 1947, 161.

27. Ribstein, *Business Associations*, 3-30.

28. Ibid.

29. Henry Ringling North and Alden Hatch, *The Circus Kings: Our Ringling Family Story* (Garden City, N.Y.: Doubleday, 1960), 321. See also Ribstein, *Business Associations*, 3-30.

30. Ribstein, *Business Associations*, 3-30.

31. North and Hatch, *Circus Kings*, 316. See also Ribstein, *Business Associations*, 3-30.

32. Ribstein, *Business Associations*, 3-30. See also, *Fortune*, July 1947, 163–64.

33. North and Hatch, *Circus Kings*, 322. See also testimony of John Ringling North in circus files at CSL, RG 161, Box 63.

34. North and Hatch, *Circus Kings*, 324.

35. See also testimony of John Ringling North in circus files at CSL, RG 161, Box 61.

36. *Receiver Transcript*, 206.

37. Ibid., 202.

38. *Fortune*, July 1947, 164. See also *Hartford Courant*, July 6, 1945, 12.

39. Ribstein, *Business Associations*, 3-31.

40. Ibid.

41. Ibid., 3–33.
42. Ibid., 3-32–3-33. There may well have been one last fight between Edith
    Ringling and the Haleys that would also account for James Haley's breaking
    with the Ladies' Agreement. Delaware Supreme Court Judge Pearson, in his
    review of the shareholders meeting, referred to "something Mrs. Ringling
    had done" on the morning of the vote, which led to Haley's refusal to post-
    pone settling the dispute. Professor Abram Chayes, in his article, "Madam
    Wagner and the Close Corporation," 73 *Harvard Law Review* 1532, 1540
    (1960), mocks Haley for failing to continue the Ladies' Agreement and, when
    elected to the board, for failing to join with North to defeat Edith Ringling.
    Perhaps there were reasons other than a quest for the presidency that prompted
    Haley to break with Mrs. Ringling.
43. 29 Del. Ch. 318, 49 A.2d 603 (1946).
44. Ribstein, *Business Associations*, 3-38.
45. 29 Del. Ch. 610, 53 A.2d 441 (1947).
46. Ribstein, *Business Associations*, 3-42.
47. Testimony of Dan Judge, *Receiver Transcript*, 405.
48. Testimony of Cornelius Shea, *Receiver Transcript*, 307.
49. *Receiver Transcript*, 299.
50. Ibid., 285.
51. Ibid., 204.
52. Ibid., 214, 232.
53. Ibid.
54. Circus files at CSL, RG 161, Box 63.
55. *Records and Briefs*, 133.
56. *Receiver Transcript*, 281.
57. Ibid., 282.
58. Ibid., 211.
59. Files of Arthur Weinstein, which contain the original Pinkerton report. Also,
    Receiver Transcript, 211.
60. *Hartford Times*, August 23, 1950, 1.
61. *Receiver Transcript*, 260.
62. *Hartford Times*, August 23, 1950, 1.
63. *New York Times*, December 10, 1950.
64. *Receiver Transcript*, 260.
65. Ibid.
66. Ibid.
67. Ibid., 407.
68. John Cleary, *Accent, The Hartford Times Sunday Magazine*, June 30, 1974, 13.

Chapter 5: The Receiver's Just Rewards
 1. Raymond Baldwin, "Address before the Junior Bar Luncheon," 30 *Connecticut
    Bar Journal* 253, 259 (1956).

2. *Records and Briefs*, 84.

3. *Receiver Transcript*, 264. Time-keeping in parts of an hour by the legal profession was not introduced on a regular basis until the 1950s in any event. See Howard J. Mudrick, "Billing Is Serious Business," *ABA Journal*, December 1990, 43.

4. Ibid., 353.

5. Mike Burke, *Outrageous Good Fortune* (Boston: Little, Brown & Co., 1984).

6. *Records and Briefs*, 120. Interview with Arthur Weinstein, November 6, 1986.

7. *Records and Briefs*, 93.

8. Ibid., 94.

9. Cullinan biography in *Martindale-Hubbell Law Directory*, (Summit, N.J.: Martindale-Hubbell, 1950). See also *Bridgeport Post*, January 13, 1953, and January 15, 1955, and *Bridgeport Journal Courier*, January 8, 1955. In 1952 Judge Cullinan was at the pinnacle of his career. Newspapers routinely carried articles about his cases, including one where a group presented him with a miniature model of their church. Tragically by 1955 he was no longer a superior court judge. In August 1954 he took a voluntary leave of absence to spend ten days in Bridgeport Hospital for undisclosed health problems (*Bridgeport Journal Courier*, January 8, 1955). On November 1, 1954, only shortly after his service as judge in the receiver dispute terminated, he asked for a four-month leave of absence for an "acute glandular disorder" (*Hartford Courant*, November 25, 1954). He resigned on January 28, 1955 (*Bridgeport Post*, January 28, 1955). He was to be afflicted with health problems throughout the remainder of his life. An undated *Bridgeport Post* article of 1957 (on file at the newspaper's morgue) reported that Cullinan had left the city for "rest, a change and medical treatment." The degree to which the judge was, in fact, incapacitated in 1952 when he took evidence and wrote his decision in the receivership controversy will, of course, never be fully known. Judge Cullinan died in January 1985.

10. Alcorn's case is found in *Receiver Transcript*, 198–302 (Rogin testimony).

11. Ibid.

12. Other witnesses, *Receiver Transcript*, 303–343.

13. Shea, *Receiver Transcript*, 303.

14. 18 *American Bankruptcy Reports* 96 (1931).

15. *Receiver Transcript*, 309, 314, 327.

16. Coleman's case is found in *Receiver Transcript*, 343–433. Judge's comments on receivership are at 401.

17. *Receiver Transcript*, 343–383.

18. *Jacobs, Adm'r v. Ringling Bros.*, 18 Conn. Supp. 134 (1952).

19. 18 Conn. Supp. 134, 137.

20. 18 Conn. Supp. 134, 139.

21. Ibid.

22. *Records and Briefs*, 110. Also, 18 Conn. Supp. 134, 140.

23. 18 Conn. Supp. 134, 140.

24. Coleman's brief is found in *Records and Briefs*, 157–189 and 190–195.

25. Alcorn's brief is found in *Records and Briefs*, 141–156.

26. *Jacobs, Adm'r v. Ringling Bros.*, 141 Conn. 84 (1954).

27. Joseph I. Lieberman, *The Legacy: Connecticut Politics, 1930–1980 (Hartford, Conn.: Spoonwood Press, 1981)*, 39.

28. This account is told in Curtis Johnson, *Raymond E. Baldwin: Connecticut Statesman* (Chester, Conn.: Pequot, 1982), 148–49.

29. *Jacobs, Adm'r v. Ringling Bros.*, 141 Conn. 84 (1954).

30. 141 Conn. 84, 95 (1954).

31. *Hartford Courant*, June 6, 1954, 1.

32. *New York Times*, July 7, 1954, 35.

Chapter 6: Fire Safety Reforms

1. Charles Perrow, *Normal Accidents: Living with High-Risk Technologies* (New York: Basic Books, 1984).

2. *Hartford Courant*, November 18, 1944, 1.

3. *Report of the Municipal Board of Inquiry on the Circus Disaster* [hereinafter *Board of Inquiry*], Hartford, Conn., 1944.

4. *Report of the Commissioner of State Police as State Fire Marshal to State's Attorney for Hartford County concerning the Fire in Hartford on July 6, 1944 at the Ringling Bros. and Barnum & Bailey Combined Shows, Inc.* [hereinafter *Hickey Report*]. Filed by Edward Hickey in Hartford, Connecticut, January 11, 1945.

   Fire marshal Hickey lost no time in curbing other circus fire risks. One day after the Ringling Brothers fire, on July 7, 1944, Hickey ordered that the World of Mirth Shows exhibiting in Waterford at Davis Field close down at once. He found that the same type of material was used on the three canvas tops as used in Hartford. He would permit the show to open only when fireproof tenting was put in place and proper fire fighting equipment was deployed (*Hartford Times*, July 7, 1944, 3).

5. *Board of Inquiry*, 6.

6. Ibid., 9.

7. Ibid.

8. Ibid., 13–14.

9. Ibid.

10. Ibid., 15.

11. Ibid., 11.

12. Ibid., 20.

13. Ibid., 15–16.

14. *Hickey Report*, 5.

15. *Board of Inquiry*, 21.

16. Ibid., 25. See also, *Hickey Report*, 3–4.

17. *Hickey Report*, 6–7, 12.

18. Ibid.
19. Ibid., 5.
20. *Board of Inquiry*, 28.
21. *Hartford Times*, July 12, 1944.
22. *Board of Inquiry*, 32.
23. Ibid., 41.
24. Hartford City Charter, Section 5 (1988).
25. *Hartford Courant*, November 18, 1944.
26. Charles Burton, "Circus Regulation by Municipalities," National Institute for Municipal Law Officers, Report No. 110 (Washington, D.C., 1944).
27. "Fire Hazards Report," in *Report of the Legislative Council*, State of Connecticut, November 16, 1944, 39.
28. Hearing Transcript, Public Health and Safety Committee, February 27, 1945, 17.
29. Record on Senate Bill 87, *Connecticut House Proceedings*, June 6, 1945, 984.
30. John Cleary, *Accent, The Hartford Times Sunday Magazine*, June 30, 1974, 13.
31. *Hartford Courant*, December 22, 1986, A1.
32. *Hartford Courant*, April 30, 1987, C4.
33. Schneller's recommendations are embodied in state law in *New Public Acts*, P.A. 88-256, P.A. 88-359.

Part II: Mass Torts and the Art of Creative Settlement
1. In its Complex Litigation Project, the American Law Institute provides a thorough overview of mass tort litigation with numerous references to noteworthy cases, yet no mention of the circus fire case is made (American Law Institute, Complex Litigation Project, *Council Draft No. 1* [November 23, 1988]). It is also worth consulting *Tentative Draft No. 1* (1989) and *Tentative Draft No. 2* (1990), both of which reflect the official approval of the American Law Institute, pending further discussion.
2. The only available text in the legal literature devoted to the circus fire receivership and arbitration is [Arthur Sachs], "The Equity Receivership in Mass Tort," 60 *Yale Law Journal* 1417 (1951). The Hartford arbitration agreement was cited by early atomic energy analysts as a proposed means to resolve negligence claims resulting from nuclear accidents. See *Atoms and the Law* (Ann Arbor: Michigan University Press, 1959), and D. F. Cavers, "Improving Financial Protection of the Public against Hazards of Nuclear Power," 77 *Harvard Law Review*, 644, 674 (1964). In the decade following the completion of the circus settlement, the Hartford arbitration agreement served as a model for liability claims arising from the sinking of the *Andrea Doria* on July 25, 1956; a disastrous fire at the Hartford Hospital in 1961; and a flood that occurred in Norwich, Connecticut.
3. Professor Richard A. Epstein of the University of Chicago Law School, for example, is one of the few legal commentators who have made reference to the circus fire settlement. See Epstein, "The Legal and Insurance Dynamics

of Mass Tort Litigation," 13 *Journal of Legal Studies* 475 (1984). But Epstein erroneously states that resolving "the Ringling Brothers litigation [sic]" was "a task much simplified when the defendant stipulated both to its own negligence and to the plaintiffs' freedom from contributory negligence." Neither stipulation was actually made, and other factors played a far more influential role in resolving the "litigation," as chapter 9 explains.

4. American Law Institute, Complex Litigation Project, *Council Draft No. 1*, 17. The authors of the report regard the voluntary cooperation among litigants in the MER/29 case (a harmful drug that elicited 1,500 lawsuits in the mid-1960s) as an anomaly with no likely applicability to contemporary mass torts.

5. A typical example of the glorification of epic litigation with large damage awards can be seen in "The Ten Largest Jury Verdicts of 1988," *ABA Journal*, March 1989, 45. The special prestige and money that attaches to litigation can also be seen in John A. Jenkins, *The Litigators: Inside the Powerful World of America's High-Stakes Trial Lawyers* (New York: Doubleday, 1989).

Chapter 7: The Mass Tort Mess

1. Alvin B. Rubin, "Mass Torts and Litigation Disasters," 20 *Georgia Law Review* 429, 450 (1986).

2. Harry H. Wellington, "Asbestos: The Private Management of a Public Problem," 33 *Cleveland State Law Review* 375 (1984–85). This assessment of the asbestos personal-injury cases was echoed by a committee of federal judges appointed by Chief Justice William H. Rehnquist to study the role of the courts in asbestos cases. In March 1991, the panel predicted that the number of asbestos cases would grow by 50% within the next three years and that the federal judiciary would be "unable to cope" with the glut. The report urged Congress to devise a "national solution" (Stephen Labaton, "Judges See a Crisis in Heavy Backlog of Asbestos Cases," *New York Times*, March 6, 1991, 1).

3. Mark Diamond, "Anatomy of a Disaster," *ABA Journal*, August 1987, 100.

4. Martha Brannigan, "Lawsuits in Suit over 1986 Hotel Fire in Puerto Rico Hold Talks on Settlement," *Wall Street Journal*, March 15, 1989.

5. In 1947 a government ship carrying nitrite fertilizer bound for Europe under the Marshall plan exploded in the harbor of Texas City, Texas, killing about 560 people. Plaintiffs filed claims amounting to over $200 million but were unable to recover because the defendant, the United States Government, successfully claimed immunity. The course of the litigation can be seen in *In re Texas City Disaster Litigation*, 197 F.2d 771 (5th Cir. 1952), *aff'd sub nom. Dalehite v. United States*, 346 U.S. 15 (1953).

   Plaintiffs faced similar difficulties in the famous Cocoanut Grove fire of 1942 because the defendant was a corporation without substantial assets, owned by a sole shareholder (*Welansky v. Commissioner*, 5 *Tax Commissioners' Memoranda* 663). The families of victims tried to recover on life insurance policies, with claims exceeding $1.5 million, and were generally successful but not always (*Ober v. National Casualty Co.*, 318 Mass. 27, 60 N.E.2d 90 [1945]). (Because "New Cocoanut Grove" was a restaurant or night club, and not a theater, recovery was barred under state law.) For further information on this disaster, see Paul Benzaquin, *The Shocking Story of the Boston Cocoanut Grove Fire* (New York: Henry Holt, 1959)., esp. 196–98 and 230.

Often the victims of mass torts look to the criminal process for vindication. The owner of Cocoanut Grove was prosecuted for manslaughter (*Commonwealth v. Welansky*, 316 Mass. 383, 55 N.E.2d 902 [1944]) as were the owners of the Triangle Shirt Company for their part in the notorious 1911 factory fire that killed nearly 150 people, mostly women and children (*People v. Harris*, 74 Misc. 353, 134 N.Y.S. 409 [1911]).

One exceptional resolution to a mass tort occurred in the case of MER/29, an anticholesterol drug developed and sold by Richardson-Merrell despite serious questions about the drug's safety. The story of the creative resolution of some 1,500 cases is told by Paul Rheingold in "The MER/29 Story—An Instance of Successful Mass Disaster Litigation," 56 *California Law Review* 116 (1968).

6. A California trial that consolidated six cases took two years to argue, generated three hundred thousand pages of transcripts in just the first of three phases of the trial, and required a special courtroom to accommodate the many parties involved (Andrew Pollack, "Judge Broadens Liability of Asbestos Insurers," *New York Times*, May 30, 1987). Litigation arising from the Dupont Plaza Hotel fire in San Juan, Puerto Rico, required a special depository and system for managing more than one million court documents, including over two thousand depositions. See *In re San Juan Dupont Plaza Hotel Fire Litigation*, CA 1, No. 88–1436, September 29, 1988.

7. Professor Peter H. Schuck notes a major risk of "managerial judging" in mass tort cases: "Judges, like other people, do not like to invest a great deal in a project without receiving the anticipated return. The Agent Orange experience suggests that fashioning a settlement in that kind of case requires an enormous judicial investment, and that a judge who makes such an investment is unlikely to remain indifferent to the outcome of the negotiations. The risk is that the judge's commitment may become excessive, compromising the appearance or reality of the judge's fairness as to whether the case will be litigated or settled, and possibly even with regard to the merits" (Peter Schuck, "The Role of the Judge in Settlement: The Agent Orange Example," 53 *University of Chicago Law Review* 337, 361 [1986]).

8. For example, the litigation resulting from the Dupont Plaza Hotel fire presented a novel issue about the privileged nature of attorneys' work product. See *In re San Juan Dupont Plaza Hotel Fire Litigation*, CA 1, No. 88–1436, September 29, 1988.

9. Charles Perrow, *Normal Accidents: Living with High-Risk Technologies* (New York: Basic Books, 1984).

10. Stanford University Law School Professor Robert L. Rabin, in analyzing the shifting sociolegal climate affecting tort litigation, notes that Ralph Nader and the consumer movement did not just bring consumer safety issues to the fore, they help contribute to "the removal of intangible barriers to claims consciousness—not unlike the erosion of the professional mystique of physicians. . . . In tandem, the demand for regulation and compensation expanded, and the characterization and valuation of personal harms took on a more expansive aspect" (Robert L. Rabin, "Tort Law in Transition: Tracing the Patterns of Sociolegal Change," 23 *Valparaiso University Law Review* 1, 14 [Fall 1988]). Businesses have responded to this new climate accordingly. See, e.g., Joann S. Lublin, "Occupational Diseases Receive More Scrutiny since the Manville Case," *Wall Street Journal*, December 20, 1982, 1.

11. The suppression of damning evidence has been a salient factor in the Dalkon Shield case, as shown by Morton Mintz, *At Any Cost: Corporate Greed, Women and the Dalkon Shield* (New York: Pantheon Books, 1985), 149–246, and in the asbestos exposure cases, as shown by Paul Brodeur, *Outrageous Misconduct* (New York: Pantheon Books, 1985). Indeed, the suppression of evidence is one reason why many juries have been particularly hostile to many mass tort defendants. The cases have set clear legal standards for an otherwise uncodified moral standard, as the new president of the Manville Company (formerly Johns-Manville), W. Thomas Stephens, acknowledged in 1988: "Society has sent a very clear message: 'We want producers of products to fully inform us about the risks we take when we consume a product, and we have the right to assume it is safe, unless we've been warned'" (Mark Clayton, "As It Leaves Bankruptcy, Manville Must Overcome Past," *Hartford Courant*, November 30, 1988).

12. Spencer Williams, "Mass Tort Class Actions, Going, Going, Gone?" 98 *Federal Rules Decisions* 323 (1983).

13. Williams, *Federal Rules Decisions*, 324.

14. Rubin, *Georgia Law Review*, 429.

15. American Law Institute, Complex Litigation Project, *Council Draft No. 1 (November 23, 1988)*, 21. See also *Tentative Draft No. 1 (1989) and Tentative Draft No. 2 (1990)*.

16. Much of the following description of "typical" mass tort litigation is derived from the *Manual for Complex Litigation* (2d ed. 1985), and from Rubin, *Georgia Law Review*, 429.

17. Rubin, *Georgia Law Review*, 438–39.

18. See Peter H. Schuck, *Agent Orange on Trial: Mass Toxic Disasters in the Courts* (Cambridge, Mass.: Belknap Press, 1986), 151–52. See also Sonja Steptoe, "Women Challenge Right of Robins to Drop Claims," *Wall Street Journal*, February 15, 1986.

19. See, e.g., Cynthia F. Mitchell and Paul M. Barrett, "Novel Effort to Settle Asbestos Claims Fails as Lawsuits Multiply," *Wall Street Journal*, June 7, 1988, 1.

20. A discussion of the problems posed by "choice of law" can be found in Paul S. Bird, "Mass Tort Litigation: A Statutory Solution to the Choice of Law Impasse," 96 *Yale Law Journal* 1077 (April 1987).

21. Variations in insurance coverage among codefendants, and disputes between the insured and insurers, were one primary reason that the Asbestos Claims Facility, voluntarily set up by leading asbestos defendants, did not succeed (Interview with Harry H. Wellington, March 20, 1989). For more, see Wellington, *Cleveland State Law Review* 375.

22. Notes of Advisory Committee, 39 *Federal Rules Decisions* 69, 103 (1966). See also ''Class Certification in Mass Accident Cases under Rule 23 (b)(1), 96 *Harvard Law Review* 1143 (1983).

23. See, e.g., *In re Bendectin Products Liability Litigation*, 749 F.2d 300 (6th Cir. 1984); *In re Northern District of California, Dalkon Shield IUD Product Liability Litigation*, 693 F.2d 847 (9th Cir. 1982), *cert. denied*, 459 U.S. 1171 (1983); *In re Federal Skywalk Cases* 680 F.2d 1175 (8th Cir.), *cert. denied*, 459 U.S. 988 (1982).

24. See, e.g., *In re Agent Orange Product Liability Litigation*, 100 *Federal Rules Decisions* 715 (E.D.N.Y. 1983), *partition for mandamus denied sub nom.*; *In re Diamond Shamrock Chemical Co.*, 725 F.2d 858 (2d Cir.), *cert. denied sub nom.*; and *In re Diamond Shamrock Chemical Co. v. Ryan*, 104 *Supreme Court Reporter* 1417 (1984).

25. Rubin, *Georgia Law Review*, 439.

26. Diamond, *ABA Journal*, 100.

27. Ibid.

28. Brannigan, *Wall Street Journal*.

29. Interview with John Filer, April 3, 1989. The first of the five scheduled trials addressed the liability of the Dupont Plaza Hotel and its prior owner and builder, Sheraton. It also examined the liability of sister corporations and pondered whether to "pierce the corporate veil" to hold individual investors liable. The second trial was to have featured representative plaintiffs litigating the liability of product suppliers (manufacturers of chairs, walls ceilings, etc.). In the third trial, representative plaintiffs were to have litigated the liability of service providers (companies that maintain elevators, alarm systems, air conditioners, etc.). The fourth trial was to have tried any additional damages. And the final trial was to apportion damages owed by defendants, as allowed under Puerto Rican law, and other third-party claims.

30. Diamond, *ABA Journal*, 100.

31. Brannigan, *Wall Street Journal*.

32. Michael J. McCarthy, "Parties Settle Suits in '86 Hotel Fire in Puerto Rico," *Wall Street Journal*, May 11, 1989, B9.

33. Interview with John Filer, April 3, 1989.
34. An excellent critique of the limitations inherent in the traditional system of handling toxic torts and a presentation of possible alternatives can be found in E. Donald Elliott, "The Future of Toxic Torts: Of Chemophobia, Risk as a Compensable Injury and Hybrid Compensation Systems," 25 *Houston Law Review* 781 (1988).
35. Schuck, *Agent Orange on Trial*.
36. Brodeur, *Outrageous Misconduct*.
37. Mintz, *At Any Cost*.
38. Edwin Chen, "Asbestos Litigation Is a Growth Industry," *Atlantic*, July 1984, 32.
39. "Mass latent injury torts are the most volatile world of tort litigation," concludes a 1987 Rand Corporation report. "Costs, dynamic legal environment, and the uncomfortable fit between these cases and the tort system conspire to make the number, outcome, and future costs of these suits highly uncertain" (Deborah R. Hensler et al., *Trends in Tort Litigation: The Story behind the Statistics* [Santa Monica, Calif.: Rand Institute for Civil Justice, 1987], 34). Plaintiffs in the earlier asbestos and Dalkon Shield lawsuits often won less remunerative settlements than later ones that relied upon evidence of suppression of damning defendant documents.
40. Even had Rogin received his requested $175,000 fee for six years of work— worth the equivalent of $875,000 in today's inflation-adjusted dollars—his bounty would have been modest. Likewise, plaintiffs' attorneys in the circus fire made respectable yet not enormous sums: 10 percent of the awards in death cases, 15 percent of the first $5,000 in injury cases, 10 percent of the next $15,000 in injury cases, and no fees on awards larger than $20,000.
41. See, e.g, the profile of mass disaster attorney John Coale in John A. Jenkins, *The Litigators: Inside the Powerful World of America's High-Stakes Trial Lawyers* (New York: Doubleday, 1989), 67–120.
42. Hensler et al., *Trends in Tort Litigation*, 28.
43. American Law Institute, Complex Litigation Project, *Council Draft No. 1*, 18.
44. J. Kakalik, P. Ebener, W. Felstiner, and M. Shanley, *Costs of Asbestos Litigation* (Santa Monica, Calif.: Rand Institute of Civil Justice, 1983), viii.
45. Ibid.
46. Interview with Harry H. Wellington, March 20, 1989.
47. Thomas E. Willging, *Trends in Asbestos Litigation* (Washington, D.C.: Federal Judicial Center, 1987), 12.
48. Wellington, " Toxic Torts: Managing the Asbestos Problem," *Yale Law Report* (Spring 1985), 20.
49. Mintz, *At Any Cost*, 7.
50. Schuck, *Agent Orange on Trial*, 259.
51. Robert L. Rabin, "Tort System on Trial: The Burden of Mass Toxics Litigation," 98 *Yale Law Journal* 813, 829 (1989).

52. Diamond, *ABA Journal*, 106

53. 57 *U.S. Law Week* 2234 (October 25, 1988).

54. American Law Institute, Complex Litigation Project, *Council Draft No. 1*, 20. For more, see Schuck, *Agent Orange on Trial*.

55. Mintz, *At Any Cost*, 15.

56. "Managerial judging," Professor Schuck points out, is "designed to resolve cases in an expeditious fashion rather than leave them to the vagaries and pace of a lawyer-centered adversary process" (Schuck, *Agent Orange on Trial*, 265–66). The controversy that can result from managerial judging was notably evident in Judge Miles Lord's handling of the Dalkon Shield litigation. See Mary Williams Walsh, "Jurist's Tactics Hasten the Pace of Litigation in Dalkon Shield Cases," *Wall Street Journal*, September 14, 1984, 1.

57. *Almanac of the Federal Judiciary* (Chicago: LawLetters, Winter 1984), 57.

58. Schuck, *Agent Orange on Trial*, 150.

59. Mitchell and Barrett, *Wall Street Journal*, 1.

60. Thomas Rowe and Kenneth Sibley, "Beyond Diversity: Federal Multiparty, Multiforum Jurisdiction," 135 *University of Pennsylvania Law Review* 7, 15 (1986).

61. Kurt Eichenwald, "Lead Lawyer for Carbide Relieved by End of Case," *New York Times*, February 15, 1989, D3.

Chapter 8: The Bankruptcy "Solution"

1. [Arthur Sachs], "The Equity Receivership in Mass Tort," 60 *Yale Law Journal* 1417 (1951).

2. *Cogswell v. Second National Bank*, 76 Conn. 252 (1903).

3. [Sachs], *Yale Law Journal* 1417.

4. *Irwin v. Willis*, 202 Ga. 463, 43 S.E.2d 691 (1947).

5. *American Law Reports* Anno., "Receivership in Tort Action," 4 A.L.R.2d at 1281, commenting on *Irwin v. Willis*.

6. *Irwin v. Willis*, 202 Ga. 463, 43 S.E.2d 691 (1947), 4 A.L.R.2d 1274, 1277.

7. Ibid.

8. *Geele v. Willis*, 203 Ga. 267, 46 S.E.2d 126 (1948).

9. [Sachs], *Yale Law Journal* 1417, 1421.

10. Ibid., 1417, 1422.

11. Bankruptcy Act of 1898, Ch. 541, 30 Stat. 544.

12. Chandler Act of 1938, Ch. 574, 52 Stat. 840.

13. Bankruptcy Reform Act of 1978, Pub. L. No. 95-598, 92 Stat. 2549 (codified at 11 U.S.C. and scattered sections of 28 U.S.C. [1982]), as amended by the Bankruptcy Amendments and Federal Judgeship Act of 1984, Pub. L. No. 98-353, 98 Stat. 333.

14. See, e.g., Philip Shuchman, "At Attempt at a 'Philosophy of Bankruptcy,'" 21 *UCLA Law Review* 2 (December 1973).

15. For further discussion of the complexities of pre-1978 bankruptcy law, see W.

Homer Drake, Jr., *Bankruptcy Practice for the General Practitioners*, vol. 1 (Colorado Springs, Colo.: Shepard's/McGraw-Hill, 1986), 12-2–12-6. See also Patrick A. Murphy, *Creditors' Rights in Bankruptcy* (Colorado Springs, Colo.: Shepard's/McGraw-Hill, 1985), 16-2–16-4.

16. Murphy, *Creditors' Rights in Bankruptcy*, 16-3.

17. 11 U.S.C. S 101(4).

18. H.R. Rep. No. 595, 95th Cong., 1st Sess. 309 (1977), S. Rep. No. 989, 95th Cong., 2d Sess. 21 (1978), cited in Arthur S. Olick, "Chapter 11—A Dubious Solution to Massive Toxic Tort Liability," 18 *Forum* 361, 363 (1983).

19. Margaret I. Lyle, "Mass Tort Claims and the Corporate Tortfeasor: Bankruptcy Reorganization and Legislative Compensation versus the Common-Law Tort System," 61 *Texas Law Review* 1297, 1315 (April 1983).

20. Lawrence J. DeMaria, "An Overemphasis on Bankruptcies," *New York Times*, April 13, 1989, D2. A half-serious joke by the managing director of a firm specializing in the securities of troubled companies reflects a new moral acceptance of bankruptcy: "If Wall Street is really on its toes, we'll soon have initial public offerings of bankrupt stocks and bonds."

21. Lyle, *Texas Law Review* 1297, 1300, note 11.

22. William Glaberson, "High Court Move Aids Manville," *New York Times*, October 4, 1988, D1.

23. Dean Rotbart, "Manville Filing Expected to Have a Wide Effect," *Wall Street Journal*, August 30, 1982, 3.

24. *In re Asbestos and Asbestos Insulation Material Products Liability Litigation* 431 F. Supp. 906 (Jud. Panel on Multi-District Litigation, 1977).

25. A succinct overview of the Manville experience can be found in Cynthia F. Mitchell, "Manville's Bid to Evade Valance of Lawsuits Proves Disappointing," *Wall Street Journal*, July 15, 1986, 1. A book-length treatment of the history of the asbestos tragedy can be found in Paul Brodeur, *Outrageous Misconduct* (New York: Pantheon Books, 1985).

26. This account relies upon Mitchell, *Wall Street Journal*, 1.

27. Brodeur, *Outrageous Misconduct*, 346, and Mark Clayton, "As It Leaves Bankruptcy, Manville Must Overcome Past," *Hartford Courant*, November 30, 1988. For detailed treatments of the asbestos settlement and claims resolution scheme, see Marianna S. Smith, "Resolving Asbestos Claims: The Manville Personal Injury Settlement Trust, with Appendix A," and Lawrence Fitzpatrick, "The Center for Claims Resolution," papers presented at the conference on Mass Settlements of Mass Torts: Dealing with Claims Resolution in Asbestos, Dalkon Shield, Agent Orange and Others," Duke University School of Law, 28–29 April 1989.

28. Mitchell, *Wall Street Journal*, 1.

29. Glaberson, *New York Times*, D1. For the future directions of asbestos litigation, see Barnaby J. Feder, "Asbestos: The Saga Drags On," *New York Times*, April 2, 1989, F1.

30. See, e.g., William Gifford (AM-LAW News Service), "Manville Trust's Cash Dwindles as Torts Mount," *Connecticut Law Tribune*, August 6, 1990.

31. Gregory A. Bibler, "The Status of Unaccrued Tort Claims in Chapter 11 Bankruptcy Proceedings," 61 *American Bankruptcy Law Journal* 145, 148 (1987).

32. Morton Mintz, *At Any Cost: Corporate Greed, Women and the Dalkon Shield* (New York: Pantheon Books, 1985).

33. "The Manville Bankruptcy: Treating Mass Tort Claims in Chapter 11 Proceedings," 96 *Harvard Law Review* 1121 (1983).

34. 96 *Harvard Law Review* 1121, 1127–28 (1983).

35. The problem of schisms among co-defendants are portrayed in Cynthia F. Mitchell and Paul M. Barrett, "Novel Effort to Settle Claims Fails as Lawsuits Multiply," *Wall Street Journal*, June 7, 1988, 1. See also Harry H. Wellington, "Asbestos: The Private Management of a Public Problem," 33 *Cleveland State Law Review* 375 (1984–85), and Mintz, *At Any Cost*.

36. 11 U.S.C. S 101(4).

37. Bibler, *American Bankruptcy Law Journal* 145, 160.

38. 11 U.S.C. S 1129(a)(Supp. V 1981).

39. "The Manville Bankruptcy: Treating Mass Tort Claims in Chapter 11 Proceedings," 96 *Harvard Law Review* 1121, 1131, note 52 (1983). The unnamed author notes further, "After asserting that the future claimants are its justification for invoking the bankruptcy power, Manville cannot in good faith use that power to exclude those claimants from recovery."

40. The choice of liquidation by Forty-Eight Insulations, Inc., of East Aurora, Illinois, is detailed in Feder, *New York Times*, F1.

41. The problems posed by future claimants and class action certification for mass torts are discussed in Olick, *Forum* 361, 363. See also "Class Certification in Mass Accident Cases under Rule 23(b)(1)," 96 *Harvard Law Review* 1143 (1983), and Lyle, *Texas Law Review* 1297, 1325–36.

42. In 1988, a major legal publication alerted investors to beware of the potential financial impact of several emerging mass torts involving cigarettes, the Copper-7 intrauterine device, and the methyl isocyanide gas explosion in Bhopal, India (200 *New York Law Journal*, August 11, 1988, 5). Judge Burton R. Liflind, bankruptcy judge of the United States Court for the Southern District in New York, predicts that "more companies infected by product-liability disease, like the Manville Corporation, would eventually file for bankruptcy protection" (DeMaria, *New York Times*, D2).

43. American Law Institute, Complex Litigation Project, *Council Draft No. 1 (November 23, 1988)*.

44. American Bar Association, Commission on Mass Torts, "Report and Recommendations" (1989).

45. Lyle, *Texas Law Review* 1297, 1321–22.

Chapter 9: Why Arbitration Saved the Circus

1. Sally Engle Merry, "Disputing without Culture," 100 *Harvard Law Review* 2057, 2063 (1987).

2. Governor Raymond Baldwin, July 5, 1944, radio address, in archives at CSL.

3. For more on 1940s culture, see *Home Front: An Anthology of Personal Experiences, 1938–1945 (London: Chatto & Windsor, 1981)*.

4. Merry, *Harvard Law Review* 2057, 2061, note 17.

5. The 1944 circus program made a point of noting who was really running the show now: "Created by Ringlings, run by Ringlings and personally staged by the circus' president, Robert Ringling, this year's show sweeps into a still more 'circusy' groove, to the delight of the millions who prefer their tanbark tonic straight."

6. Interview with M. Joseph Blumenfeld, April 1988.

7. Calvert Crary, a litigation analyst with Martin Simpson & Co., complained to a reporter, "What Manville did was highly unethical to its shareholders. Management and the asbestos victims teamed up and took the equity for themselves—and basically wiped out common-stock holders" (Quoted in Mark Clayton, "As It Leaves Bankruptcy, Manville Must Overcome Past," *Hartford Courant*, November 30, 1988).

8. U.S. Judge Miles W. Lord issued an extraordinary fourteen-page denunciation of A. H. Robins executives for their failure to own up to their responsibilities to their victims: "It is not enough to say, 'I did not know—It was not me, look elsewhere,'" said Lord. "Time and again, each of you have used this kind of argument in refusing to acknowledge your responsibility and pretending to the world that the chief officers and directors of your gigantic, multinational corporation have no responsibility for the company's acts and omissions. . . . Your company in the face of overwhelming evidence denies its guilt and continues its monstrous mischief" (Barry Siegel, "Judge Seeking Product Accountability Faces Misconduct Charge," *Washington Post*, July 7, 1984, A2).

9. Jerome Carlin, *Lawyers Ethics* (New York: Russell Sage Foundation, 1966), 31–32. See also "The Jewish Law Student and New York Jobs—Discriminatory Effects in Law Firm Hiring Practices," 73 *Yale Law Journal* 635 (March 1964).

10. Carlin, *Lawyers' Ethics*, 21–22.

11. Many of the small firms represented by leading players in the circus fire have grown into the major Hartford law firms of today. Edward Rogin's firm became Rogin Nassau Caplan Lassman Hirtle; Robert Butler's firm became Butler Volpe Sacco (now defunct); Julius Schatz's firm became Weinstein Swirsky Needleman Connolly & Williams; Riscassi's became Riscassi & Davis; and Cyril Coleman's firm Day Berry & Howard now employs two hundred attorneys.

12. Even if a higher award would have been more just, either by contemporane-

ous or current standards, the generosity and "justice" of the arbitration must be measured against the only other alternative, traditional litigation. In the 1940s most states had statutory caps on wrongful death awards that were largely comparable to Connecticut's $15,000 cap.

The issue of what constitutes a "just" cap — or whether *any* cap ought to be imposed — remains a controversial issue today. Some state legislatures have imposed caps of $100,000 on specified tort damages, for example. If adjusted by the U.S. Bureau of Labor Statistics' Consumer Price Index, a $100,000 award in 1988 would have roughly the same purchasing power as $20,000 in 1950, which is modestly higher than Connecticut's $15,000 wrongful death cap of the time. (The $4 million paid out to all circus fire claimants by 1950 was equivalent to $19.6 million in 1988 dollars, the latest year for which figures are available.) See Table 756, "Purchasing Power of the Dollar: 1950 to 1988," U.S. Bureau of Labor Statistics, *Abstract of the United States, 1990,* 110th ed. (Washington, D.C., 1990).

13. Richard Epstein, "The Legal and Insurance Dynamics of Mass Tort Litigation," 13 *Journal of Legal Studies* 475 (1984).
14. T. E. Murphy, "The Day the Clowns Cried," *Reader's Digest,* June 1953, 59–62.
15. Donald Weckstein, "The Purposes of Dispute Resolution: Contemporary Concepts of Justice," 26 *Business Law Journal* 605 (1988).

Chapter 10: Alternative Dispute Resolution and Mass Torts
1. Kurt Eichenwald, "Lead Lawyer for Carbide Relieved by End of Case," *New York Times,* February 15, 1989, D3.
2. American Law Institute, Complex Litigation Project, *Council Draft No. 1 (November 23, 1988),* 21.
3. Peter H. Schuck, *Agent Orange on Trial: Mass Toxic Disasters in the Courts* (Cambridge, Mass.: Belknap Press, 1986), 263.
4. Owen M. Fiss, "Against Settlement," 93 *Yale Law Journal* 1073, 1075 (1984).
5. Carrie Menkel-Meadow, professor of law at the University of California at Los Angeles, writes, "Settlement offers substantive justice that may be more responsive than adjudication to the needs of parties, avoiding win/lose results, providing richer remedies, and achieving greater legitimacy through consent. Settlement also offers parties, as well as lawyers, a chance to participate in a communication process that might be more direct and less stylized than adjudication, with greater flexibility of procedures and remedies" ("Judges and Settlement," 21 *Trial* [October 1985], 24, 27).
6. One of the more significant steps in this direction has come from a Brookings Institution report, *Justice for All: Reducing Costs and Delay in Civil Litigation,* which was prepared by the Task Force of Civil Justice Reform at the suggestion of Senate Judiciary Committee Chairman Joseph Biden. The report, released in October 1989, recommends greater experimentation with ADR strategies as well as numerous non-ADR reforms.

7. The conference, "Mass Settlements of Mass Torts," was sponsored by the Duke University School of Law, the Private Adjudication Center, the Torts and Insurance Practice Section of the American Bar Association, the Association of Trial Lawyers of America, and the Defense Research Institute. The conference took place on April 28–29, 1989, at Research Triangle Park, North Carolina.

8. An excellent overview of the L'Ambiance Plaza mediation and behavioral theories of negotiation and dispute resolution can be found in Lucy V. Katz, "The L'Ambiance Plaza Mediation: A Case Study in Judicial Settlement of Mass Torts," 5:2 *Ohio State Journal on Dispute Resolution* 277 (1990). The L'Ambiance Plaza settlement is one example of the rapid expansion of dispute resolution techniques now taking place in our nation's court system. The newsletter "Alternatives to the High Cost of Litigation" reports in its January 1991 issue that thirty-six of ninety-three federal district courts and six of thirteen circuits have enacted a local ADR rule (9:1 *Alternatives*, 6). The U.S. Congress, in enacting P.L. 101-650 (signed December 1, 1990), the Civil Justice Reform Act, required all federal courts to devise ADR plans. See also "Your ABA—Attacking Court Costs and Delays," *ABA Journal*, March 1991, 98. The remaining federal courts without plans are now expected to develop them without delay.

9. Deborah Duffy, "Lawyers Build Collapse Cases," *Hartford Courant*, June 22, 1987.

10. Linda Stowell, "Bridgeport Judge Asks Lawyers to Organize Massive Proceedings," *New Britain Herald*, May 19, 1987, 24.

11. Elaine McArdle, "Early Discovery in L'Ambiance Case," *Connecticut Law Tribune*, August 21, 1987, 3.

12. L'Ambiance Plaza Mediation Panel, *Interim Report*, November 15, 1988, 5.

13. Ibid.

14. Ibid., 7.

15. Ibid., 10.

16. Ibid., 7.

17. Interview with Judge Robert C. Zampano, March 3, 1989.

18. Ibid.

19. Deborah Duffy, "L'Ambiance Settlement Satisfies Many, But Leaves Questions," *Hartford Courant*, December 3, 1988, 1.

20. Deborah Duffy, "Panel Proposes L'Ambiance Settlement," *Hartford Courant*, September 10, 1988, B1.

21. Deborah Duffy, "L'Ambiance Settlement Satisfies Many, But Leaves Questions," *Hartford Courant*, December 4, 1988, 36.

22. The settlement figures represented numerous factors, including the age and health of the decedent or injured plaintiff; past wage history; earning capacity; age of heirs; income and financial condition of heirs; severity of personal injuries; degree of permanent injuries; workers' compensation factors; life

expectancy; advantages, if any, to a structured award; particularized needs; and reasonable attorneys' fees (*Interim Report*, 11).

23. Ibid., 11.
24. Ibid., 12.
25. Duffy, *Hartford Courant*, December 4, 1988, 1, 36.
26. Interview with Judge Robert C. Zampano, March 3, 1989.
27. Duffy, *Hartford Courant*, 36.
28. Interview with Judge Robert C. Zampano, March 3, 1989.
29. Ibid.
30. A detailed account of the settlement process can be found in "Successful Mediation in Conn. Apt. Collapse Showcases Aptness of ADR in Larger Cases," 7:3 *Alternatives to the High Cost of Litigation* (March 1989), 41.
31. Interview with Judge Robert C. Zampano, March 3, 1989.
32. Derek Bok, "A Flawed System," *Harvard Magazine*, May–June 1983, 38.
33. Senior Judge Robert C. Zampano, "Supplement: Judicially Supervised Settlement Conference," in Philip J. Harter, ed., *Alternative Dispute Resolution: A Handbook for Judges*, Dispute Resolution Monograph No. 3 (American Bar Association, Standing Committee on Dispute Resolution, October 1987), 13.
34. Paul M. Barrett, "For Many Dalkon Shield Claimants Settlement Won't End the Trauma," *Wall Street Journal*, March 9, 1988.
35. *Final Report of the Connecticut ADR Project, Inc.* (Hartford, Conn., 1988), 21.
36. Ibid., 19.
37. Cynthia F. Mitchell and Paul M. Barrett, "Novel Effort to Settle Asbestos Claims Fails as Lawsuits Multiply," *Wall Street Journal*, June 7, 1988, 1.
38. "In retrospect," conceded Lawrence Fitzpatrick, acting chief executive of the Asbestos Claims Facility, "the facility's tough stance on settling cases undermined its mission to move the asbestos fray out of the courts. 'It's a philosophy that shoots you in the foot in the long term,' he said" (Mitchell and Barrett, *Wall Street Journal*, 1).
39. Wayne D. Brazil et al., "Early Neutral Evaluation: An Experimental Effort to Expedite Dispute Resolution," 69 *Judicature* 279 (1986).
40. Ibid., 280.
41. Wayne D. Brazil, "What Lawyers Want from Judges in the Settlement Arena," 106 *Federal Rules Decisions* 85, 86 (1985).
42. Interview with Judge Robert C. Zampano, March 3, 1989.
43. Larry Lempert, "Judge Shows Knack for 'Just Getting Parties Talking,'" *Legal Times*, August 10, 1981, 6.
44. Brazil, *Federal Rules Decisions* 85.
45. This discussion of advantages and disadvantages of arbitration draws upon Lowell Noteboom, "Arbitration: Understanding It Better, Utilizing It More Effectively," *Hennepin Lawyer*, May–June 1984, 10.
46. A good overview of the diverse ADR models available to judges can be found

in Harter, ed., *Alternative Dispute Resolution*. As summarized by the handbook, the most common ADR models over which a judge actively presides or supervises include:

Conditional summary trial. An abbreviated trial before the trial judge and representatives of the parties who have authority to settle. If the parties are unable to negotiate a settlement, the judge selects from the prepared dispositions submitted by the parties. A party who declines to accept the outcome of the abbreviated proceeding and who does not obtain a more favorable outcome in full trial must pay the adversary's litigation costs.

Summary jury trial. An abbreviated mock jury trial, presided over by a judge or magistrate, designed to help litigants determine how a jury might evaluate their case. Useful where informal settlement methods have failed and for civil disputes where evaluation of factual evidence is key.

Judicially supervised settlement conference. A settlement discussion held with the presence and active participation of the trial judge. Useful for civil litigation where settlement options have not yet been fully explored.

Special masters. An individual or individuals employed by the court to assist in resolving disputes or managing litigation. Useful for complex and/or multiparty civil litigation.

Settlement conference. A conference among parties, counsel and a neutral attorney or magistrate aimed at exploring options for settling the dispute.

Early neutral evaluation. A pretrial evaluation session attended by all counsel and parties and hosted by a neutral, experienced lawyer-mediator who appraises the case and discusses its merits with the parties.

Mini-trial. A private, consensual proceeding where a negotiated resolution is sought following an expedited summary presentation of the best case for each party in a dispute, made in the presence of those parties. A neutral advisor may make advisory opinions to assist the negotiations. Useful in larger inter-corporate disputes involving mixed questions of law and fact.

47. Interview with Judge Robert C. Zampano, March 3, 1989.
48. Interview with Harry H. Wellington, March 20, 1989.
49. Harry H. Wellington, "Asbestos: The Private Management of a Public Problem," 33 *Cleveland State Law Review*, 375, 386 (1984–85).
50. Mitchell and Barrett, *Wall Street Journal*, 1.
51. Carrie Menkel-Meadow, "Judges and Settlement: What Part Should Judges Play?" 21 *Trial* 24, 27 (October 1985). See also Menkel-Meadow, "Toward Another View of Legal Negotiation: The Structure of Problem Solving," 31 *UCLA Law Review* 754 (1984), and Aaron J. Broder, "Judicial Techniques in Settlement," *New York Law Journal*, December 11, 1986, 1.
52. Jack Weinstein, "The Role of the Court in Toxic Tort Litigation," 73 *Georgetown Law Review* 1389, 1390–92 (1985).
53. Con Hitchcock, "Finding Out the Full Story about Agent Orange," *Public Citizen Magazine*, Spring 1985, 10.

54. Brant Houston, "Investigators Should Continue to Seek Answers," *Hartford Courant*, December 4, 1988, 1.

55. Harry H. Wellington, "Toxic Torts: Managing the Asbestos Problem," *Yale Law Report*, Spring 1985, 20, 23.

56. Alvin B. Rubin, "Mass Torts and Litigation Disasters," 20 *Georgia Law Review* 429, 441 (1986).

SOURCE MATERIALS ABOUT
THE CIRCUS AND
THE CIRCUS FIRE

Identifying source materials concerning the circus fire and its legal repercussions was something of a scavenger hunt. Useful scraps of information kept turning up at unlikely—and opportune—times. Luckily for history buffs, the Connecticut Supreme Court still required in 1952 that an appellant print a copy of the transcript in the record. Thus there exists in the appeal of the receivership fee dispute to the Supreme Court a 481-page transcript that sheds a great deal of light on the nature of the receivership and actions taken. It may be found in the Connecticut Supreme Court Records and Briefs for January 1954. The remainder of the record is also helpful. It contains the original writ in the *Jacobs v. Ringling Bros.—Barnum & Bailey Combined Shows, Inc.*, the application for the receivership, Rogin's notes on his activities, the proposed findings of the parties and Judge Cullinan's findings. The briefs of the parties are, of course, also bound in this volume.

One of the most helpful legal sources on the circus fire is an unsigned law review note concerning the use of the equity receivership, which appeared in the *Yale Law Journal* in 1951 (vol. 60, p. 1417). The article provides an excellent summary of the law of receiverships that is of great historical value. Written by prominent New Haven attorney Arthur Sachs while a student at Yale Law School, the article includes numerous references to newspaper accounts of the fire, reports of communications with Julius Schatz, and footnotes that provide clues to a wealth of additional source material.

The archives on the circus fire at the Connecticut State Library are by far the richest single source of primary material about the tragedy. Among the most important documents in these files are an extensive collection of eyewitness reports and reports by police and fire personnel. Because these materials were gathered for use in a possible criminal trial, they include statements and interviews taken under oath from various circus personnel, including John Ringling North. The archives also include a radio speech given by Governor Baldwin on July 15, 1944, records of volunteers, and statements by city and state war council officials given in connection with a national civil defense award. A pamphlet published by the National Fire Protection Association, "Hartford Circus Holocaust," contains a diagram of the layout of the main tent just after the fire. (This diagram is reprinted in chapter 1.)

The specific archival boxes that we consulted include:

RG 1   Investigation files of the Department of Public Safety, Division of State Police.

Box 60   Niles St. Hospital Fire: Report of Commissioner of State Police as Fire Marshal to State's Attorney for Hartford County concerning the fire in Hartford on December 24, 1945, at the Niles St. Hospital, 60 Niles Street.

Box 61   Hartford circus fire: Documents relating to the Ringling Bros. and Barnum & Bailey circus fire (H-25-Z). Copies of death certificates; bleacher occupant lists; casualty lists; circus employees' statements; circus history and program; fire department personnel; Hartford Detective statements (A-Z); Hartford Police assignments; Hartford Police statements (A-Z).

Box 62   Hartford circus fire (cont.): missing person information (A-Z); out city police personnel; side wall witnesses (A-Z); State Police reports (A-Z); top tent witnesses (A-Z).

Box 63   Hartford circus fire (cont.): Fire Marshal hearing; miscellaneous; weather report; War Council reports; newspapers; miscellaneous statements (duplicate); Coroner's reports.

Box 64   Hartford circus fire (cont.): Pamphlet, "The Circus Fire," by the National Fire Protection Association; bound statements.

Box 65   Statements; police photos of individuals; correspondence; miscellaneous aftermath.

Box 66   Correspondence regarding criminal suspects; "Cox" a.k.a. Emmet
         Welch; James Segee materials; miscellaneous aftermath.
Box 67   Segee, including photos of Segee drawings.

Other boxes with material relevant to the fire include Boxes 473 and
474, Box RG 50, and Boxes 10, 95, and 115. Various files of newspaper clippings concerning the fire can also be found in the main
library area.

Several official documents and reports are particularly useful in
exploring the history of the fire. These include a pamphlet published by the American Red Cross, "Hartford Circus Fire," which
provides an excellent general summary of the fire and its aftermath
by an unknown writer who seems to have had contacts in the Hartford area; the official investigation by the city of Hartford, "Report
of the Municipal Board of Inquiry," which led to local ordinance
changes and national fire code reforms; and the "Report of the Commissioner of State Police as Fire Marshal," which was used by State's
Attorney Alcorn in his prosecution of the circus executives.

Several Connecticut legislative materials are also worth consulting. These include "Report of the Legislative Council"; the legislative history in the Public Health and Safety Committee and in the
House of Representatives, for June 6, 1945, at page 984; public act
427 (1945); chapter 532 (1987 statutes); and Hartford Code, article
III.

Surprisingly, there are very few informative works on the Ringling
Brothers circus itself. One, by Earl Chapin May, *The Circus from
Rome to Ringling* (New York: Duffield & Green, 1932), was published twelve years before the Hartford fire and misses the developments of the circus fire period. Another book with a similar title,
Circus: From Rome to Ringling (New York: Appleton-Century, 1956),
by Marian Murray, is not a serious effort and contains few facts about
the circus fire. This may have something to do with the fact that the
author, a former reporter for the *Hartford Courant* and the *Hartford
Times*, wrote the book while employed at the Ringling Museum in
Sarasota, Florida. Another book, by George Chindahl, *The History of
the Circus in America* (Caldwell, Idaho: Caxton Printers, 1959), is
complete but flawed; it degenerates into a list of events rather than
providing a useful narrative with interpretation or perspective. It

has about two pages on the circus fire and some additional information on circus programs from the 1920s to the 1950s.

Henry Ringling North, the brother of John Ringling North, has written (with Alden Hatch) an engaging history of the Ringling family, *The Circus Kings: Our Ringling Family Story* (Garden City, N.Y.: Doubleday, 1960). Henry North served in the Office of Strategic Services (OSS) during World War II and has no direct knowledge of the fire or its aftermath. He often engages in a juggling act —trying to defend his brother without offending "Aunt Edith" Ringling.

The American Circus (Boston: Twayne, 1984), a recent book by Professor Wilton Eckley of Drake University devotes a few pages to the fire and its aftermath, relying upon North's account. Another book with some material on the circus fire is Alvin F. Harlow's *Wizards of the Circus* (New York: Julian Messner, 1951), a biography of the Ringlings.

A more common genre of books about the circus is memoirs about circus life. Fred Bradhna's *The Big Top: Forty Years with the Greatest Show on Earth* (New York: Simon & Schuster, 1952) is a well-written account by the ringmaster and executive for Ringling Brothers. Various tales of circus days are told in Esse O'Brien's *Circus: Cinders to Sawdust* (San Antonio, Tex.: Naylor, 1959). Ten years after the fire, Mike Burke became the general manager of Ringling Brothers at the suggestion of his friend and fellow OSS officer, Henry North. In *Outrageous Good Fortune* (Boston: Little, Brown, 1984), Burke recounts the last days of the tented circus and his unpleasant parting of the ways with John Ringling North. Of course, the best of the circus memoirs is P. T. Barnum's autobiography, published at various times and in various forms during his career. A 1927 version, edited by Waldo Brown, has been reissued in paperback under the title, *Barnum's Own Story* (New York: Dover, 1961).

Fascinating insights into circus routines and schedules can be gleaned from an annual "Route Book" sold by the circus, which contains a complete profile of the corporate organization, a list of prior years' performance schedules and the current program.

Although the battle for corporate control of the circus may seem arcane to the general reader, it is standard fare in law schools today for what it illustrates about shareholder rights. Few accounts give as many details as the summary by Larry Ribstein in his casebook, *Business Associations* (New York: Matthew Bender, 1983). Additional, copious detail about the shareholders' dispute is supplied by an article in the July 1947 issue of *Fortune* magazine, and by Henry Ringling North's biography, *Circus Kings*.

Much of the information about the fire and later developments must be obtained from newspaper and magazine articles. William Clew, a close friend of Edward Rogin's, wrote many articles on the topic for the *Hartford Courant*. John Cleary of the now-defunct *Hartford Times*, also covered the subject fully. The *Times*'s "morgue" now resides at Southern Connecticut State University, with access granted by the department of journalism.

INDEX

Acosta, Raymond, judge, 110, 115, 119
Agent Orange, 116, 119, 120, 121
A. H. Robins Co. (Dalkon Shield), 116, 118, 120, 149, 163, 185n11
Alcorn, Hugh Meade, 11
Alcorn, Hugh Meade, Jr.: as prosecutor, xii, 11, 12, 52, 54; career, 72; as Rogin's attorney at fee dispute trial, 72, 80–83; arguing appeal, 87–88
Alternative dispute resolution (ADR): advantages over mass tort litigation, 4, 107–9, 152, 159–63, 167; judge as catalyst to, 120, 121, 163–64, 184n7; and social context, 140; objections to, 149, 166; psychological dimensions of, 160; types of, 163–64; 195n46; use in mass disasters, 182n2; in MER/29 case, 183n4, 184n5; Brookings Institution report, 192n6; congressional legislation in 1990, 193n8
Anderson, Donald, 10, 11
Arbitration agreement: statute of limitations for claims, 40, 43; drafting of, 41–44; and public opinion, 44, 176n9; arbitrators chosen, 45; hearings of arbitration panel, 45–47; attorneys' fee schedules, 47, 187n40; total awards made, 47–48; final payment of claims, 62–63; signatures of satisfaction of judgment, 66; publicity about payments, 79; influence of homefront culture on, 138–40; reasons for success of, 140–45; and insurance companies, 143–44
Asbestos, 116–18 passim, 122, 149, 164, 166, 183n2, 185n11, 186n21, 194n38
Aylesworth, Leonard, 52, 53, 54

Baldwin, Alfred C., 45
Baldwin, Raymond: speech to junior bar, 3, 69; as governor, 5; and circus fire, 12, 14, 139; as justice, 88–92
Bankruptcy law: Chapter 11, xi, xiii, xiv, 24, 125, 128–30 passim, 133–35; Chapters X, XI, and XII under 1938 Act, 24, 25, 128, 129; "race to levy" problem, 26–27, 136; history of, 128–29, 144; new definition

Bankruptcy law (*continued*)
of "claim" under 1978 Act, 129; as vehicle for resolving mass torts, 133; complexities of pre-1978 code, 172n25, 173n26
Bar Disaster Committee, 35, 47. *See also* Butler, Robert; Cooney, Joseph; and Schatz, Julius
Barber, Tom, 16
Barnum, P. T., 16
Bergman, Nathan, 21
Bhopal, India, disaster, 123
Bisco, Leonard, 58
Blanchfield, David, 42, 54
Blumenfeld, M. Joseph, 141
Bordon, Abraham S., 45, 176n12
Brazil, Wayne, 161
Brown, Warren, 63
Burgdorf, Dr. Alfred, 23–24, 35–36
Butler, Robert: and receivership, xii, 29, 32, 34; education and career, 28; as chairman of bar committee, 35; opposes Rogin, 78–79; interrogation by Alcorn, 80–83; assists Haley, 83

Caley, William, 52, 54
Campion, Daniel, 45, 143
Carlin, Jerome, 142
Carlson, Axel, 10
Circus fire: Barbour Street site, 5, 12, 24, 27; tent hazards, 7–10; and animal runways, 8, 94; suspected causes, 9, 17, 93; panic caused by, 9–14; investigation of, 11, 33, 94; outpouring of volunteers, 13; identification of dead at armory, 14; casualties, 14, 16; previous circus fires, 16; resulting civil litigation, 21, 22, 26; attachment of assets, 22, 23, 171n6, 172n17; criminal cases,

52–54; inadequate fire precautions, 99
Clarie, T. Emmet, 102
Cocoanut Grove fire, 13, 14, 99, 183n5
Cole, Morton, 40
Coleman, Cyril: as circus attorney, xii, 20, 40; at arbitration, 41, 46, 143; at fee dispute trial and appeal, 72, 73–79, 86–87
Connecticut Mutual Life Insurance Company, 63
Cook, Eleanor, as "Little Miss 1565," 17
Cooney, Joseph, 34, 35, 45, 75
Cullinan, John T., 72, 84–86, 180n9

Davey, Rick, 17, 18
Day Berry & Howard, 20, 42, 143
Dunn, William, 19, 56, 57
DuPont Plaza fire (San Juan, P.R., 1986), 14, 110, 114, 162, 184n6, 184n8, 186n29
DuVal, Herbert, 5

Ellery, Allen, insurance commissioner, 103
Elsner, Solomon, 95
Engel, Judge & Miller, 19
Epstein, Richard, 145, 182n3
Evans, Louis, 75, 77

Fire safety: fire preparedness, 5, 98, 99; inadequate safety rules and coordination, 99–100; smoking ban at outdoor shows, 100; recommendations of American Standards Association, 101; reforms nationwide, 102; city and state reform legislation, 102–4; tent safety reforms, 104; new insurance rules, 105

Fiss, Owen, 149
Fleisch, Dr. Milton, 12, 92
Flynn, Monsignor William, 94–95
Foster, George, 75

Goltra, William, 102
Groark, Eunice, 9

Hadden, William, 20, 28, 29, 32
Hager, Ralph A., 20–21
Haley, Aubrey (Ringling), 32, 55,
    57, 141, 176n4, 179n42
Haley, James: accused and sentenced,
    11, 52–54 passim, 58; as ally of
    North, 59–60; as congressman,
    61
Halloran, Robert, attorney, 44
Handler, Morris, 8, 9
Harris, Reese, Jr., 78
Hartford: public building commis-
    sion (site lease), 5, 95; police
    department, 5, 96–97; during
    war years, 5–6; health depart-
    ment, 23–24, 35–36, 97; build-
    ing commission (zoning), 98; fire
    department, 99–100
Haskin and Sells, accountants, 47
Healy, Frank, 52
Hickey, Edward J., fire marshal:
    investigation of fire, 11, 33,
    94; closes other tented shows,
    181n4
Howard, Arthur E., 40

Insurance industry, xi, xiii, 143–44

Jews in legal profession, xiii, 142–43
Johnson, Curtis, 14
Judge, Dan Gordon: as circus
    attorney, xii, 19, 23, 25, 32; and
    receivership, 33–35, 142; at fee
    dispute trial, 77–78

Kennedy, James, prosecutor, 11
King, John Hamilton, judge:
    approval of receivership, xii, xiii,
    29, 30, 126, 143; career, 29
Kosoff, Louis, 24

L'Ambiance Plaza building collapse:
    as promising candidate for ADR,
    4, 145; immediate aftermath,
    22, 151–53; mediation panel
    and settlement, 153–59, 193n8;
    and Schneller Committee, 105–6.
    See also Zampano, Robert C.
Landau, Sidney, judge, 151
Leikind, S. Burr, 11
Little Miss 1565, 16–17
Long, George, Jr., 95
Loos, Karl, 19, 20, 57
Lord, Miles W., judge, 188n56,
    191n8
Lowe, Ed, 16

Maltbie, William, chief justice, 45
Manufacturers Trust Company, 19,
    56
Marcus, Martin, 26
Marshall, George C., 39
Mass tort litigation: great difficulties
    of, 110–23; American Law Insti-
    tute report, 112, 117, 122, 133,
    148, 182n1; management of,
    112–14, 165; and the discovery
    process, 114, 151; Rand study of
    plaintiffs' recoveries, 117; legal
    costs, 117–20; risks of judicial
    intervention, 120–21, 184n7,
    188n56; suggested reforms of,
    122–23; ABA report on, 135–36
    problems of latent harm, 145,
    187n39, 190n42
McClain, W. Ross, 95
Meadow, Frank S., judge, 152
Menkel-Meadow, Carrie, 165, 192n5

Merhige, Robert R., Jr., judge, 163–64
Merry, Sally Engle, 139, 140
Mitchell, Harold, 33, 102
Mortenson, William, 23, 100
Murphy, James, 64
Murphy, Patrick, 25

North, Henry Ringling, 57
North, Ida, 55
North, John Ringling: showmanship of, 56; and Rogin, 56, 61–62, 64, 71–72; shareholder battle, 57–60 passim

O'Sullivan, P. B., judge, 40, 143

Paine, Walter S., 95
Perrow, Charles, 93

Rabin, Robert, 118
Receiver fee dispute: origins of litigation, 69–71; trial, 71–84; Cullinan ruling, 84–86; appeal, 86–88; state supreme court ruling, 89–91
Receivership: development of plan, 27–30; meeting with plaintiffs' bar, 28, 33, 34–35, 175n60; circus owners' reaction to, 32; option of federal receivership, 34, 79, 81; insurance payment to, 51; and Pinkerton incident, 63; final settlement meeting, 64; advantages of, 124, 126; arguments against, 127
Red Cross, 9, 10, 12, 13, 20
Reddy, John, Jr., 19, 38, 91
Ribicoff, Abraham, 45
Ringling, Alf T., 55
Ringling, Charles, 6
Ringling, Edith: and receivership, 33, 141–42, 174n55; as share-holder of circus, 54–57 passim, 141; litigation against Haleys, 59, 60, 179n42
Ringling, John, 55, 56
Ringling, Richard, 55
Ringling, Robert: as president of circus, 6, 51, 54, 58, 60; absence from Hartford performance, 11, 58, 170n24
Ringling Bros. and Barnum & Bailey Combined Shows: struggle for corporate control of, 4, 55–61, 179n42; arrival in Hartford, 5; and wartime, 6–7; animals, 8, 22, 23, 24, 57, 94; insurance coverage, 20; departure from Hartford, 36–37; itinerary, 52; criminal prosecution and sentencing, 53, 54, 58; North litigation against, 57, 58, 60; net worth, 172n23; secured debtors, 172n24
Riscassi, Leon, 102–3
Robins Co. *See* A. H. Robins Co.
Robinson, Lucius, president of bar, 35, 75
Rogin, Edward S.: as receiver, xii, xiii, 30, 31, 33, 49–51, 70; birth and education, 25; after fire, 26–28 passim; and death cases, 44, 176n11; and Ringling family, 50, 61; and John Ringling North, 56, 61–62, 64, 71–72; and James Haley, 61; and receiver fee dispute, 69–92, 117
Rosen, Sam, sheriff, 33
Roth, Frances, 176n4
Rubin, Alvin B., judge, 110–14 passim, 167

Sarasota, Florida, 38, 53
Schatz, Julius: role in obtaining receivership, xii, xiii, 29, 31;

education, 25; flamboyance, 25,
173n29; after fire, 26–28 pas-
sim; fee as attorney, 91
Schuck, Peter, 149
Segee, James Dale, 9, 17, 18,
171n40
Shea, Cornelius D., Sr., 25, 75,
171n10
Shea, William, judge, 53, 58
Shipman & Goodwin, attorneys,
21
Smith, George Washington, 11, 35,
52, 54
Smith, Olcott, 143
State Legislative Council, 94, 102
State Police, 13, 20, 104
State War Council, 12
Stewart, John, Jr., 10
Stiles, Walter, 102
Strong, Henry B., 33

Tent safety: hazards of Big Top,
7–10, 15–16; reform legislation,

104; tented circus today, 104–5
Thatcher, Raymond, 102

Versteeg, Edward, 52, 53, 54

Wallenda family, 8, 39
Weckstein, Donald, 145–46
Weinstein, Arthur: role in receiver-
ship and arbitration, xiii, 41, 71;
after fire, 26–28 passim
Weinstein, Jack, judge, 120–21,
164, 165
Wellington, Harry H., 110,
164–65, 166
Wish Elementary School, 5
Wynne, Kenneth, 9

Yale Law Journal, 1951 article by
Arthur Sachs, 23, 77, 126–27

Zampano, Robert C., judge, 152,
154–55, 157–62 passim, 164